D0948213

Understanding
CHRISTOPH HEIN

UNDERSTANDING MODERN EUROPEAN AND LATIN AMERICAN LITERATURE

JAMES HARDIN, *Series Editor*

Understanding Günter Grass
by Alan Frank Keele

Understanding Graciliano Ramos
by Celso Lemos de Oliveira

Understanding Gabriel García Márquez
by Kathleen McNerney

Understanding Claude Simon
by Ralph Sarkonak

Understanding Mario Vargas Llosa
by Sara Castro-Klarén

Understanding Samuel Beckett
by Alan Astro

Understanding Jean-Paul Sartre
by Philip R. Wood

Understanding Albert Camus
by David R. Ellison

Understanding Max Frisch
by Wulf Koepke

Understanding Erich Maria Remarque
by Hans Wagener

Understanding Elias Canetti
by Richard H. Lawson

Understanding Heinrich Böll
by Robert C. Conard

Understanding Céline
by Philip H. Solomon

Understanding Gerhart Hauptmann
by Warren R. Maurer

Understanding José Donoso
by Sharon Magnarelli

Understanding Milan Kundera
by Fred Misurella

Understanding Italo Calvino
by Beno Weiss

Understanding Franz Werfel
by Hans Wagener

Understanding Peter Weiss
by Robert Cohen

Understanding Eugène Ionesco
by Nancy Lane

Understanding Ingeborg Bachmann
by Karen R. Achberger

Understanding Christoph Hein
by Phillip McKnight

Understanding Thomas Bernhard
by Stephen D. Dowden

UNDERSTANDING

CHRISTOPH
HEIN

PHILLIP MCKNIGHT

UNIVERSITY OF SOUTH CAROLINA PRESS

Library of Congress Cataloging-in-Publication Data

McKnight, Phillip S.
    Understanding Christoph Hein / Phillip McKnight.
       p.   cm. — (Understanding modern European and Latin American
  literature)
    Includes bibliographical references and index.
    ISBN 1–57003–015–4
    1. Hein, Christoph, 1944– —Criticism and interpretation.
  I. Title. II Series.
  PT2668.E3747Z8 1995
  838'.91209—dc20   94–18721

CONTENTS

EDITOR'S PREFACE

*U*nderstanding *Modern European and Latin American Literature* has been planned as a series of guides for undergraduate and graduate students and non-academic readers. Like the volumes in its companion series *Understanding Contemporary American Literature,* these books provide introductions to the lives and writings of prominent modern authors and explicates their most important works.

Modern literature makes special demands, and this is particularly true of foreign literature, in which the reader must contend not only with unfamiliar, often arcane artistic conventions and philosophical concepts, but also with the handicap of reading the literature in translation. It is a truism that the nuances of one language can be rendered in another only imperfectly (and this problem is especially acute in fiction), but the fact that the works of European and Latin American writers are situated in a historical and cultural setting quite different from our own can be as great a hindrance to the understanding of these works as the linguistic barrier. For this reason the UMELL series emphasizes the sociological and historical background of the writers treated. The peculiar philosophical and cultural traditions of a given culture may be particularly important for an understanding of certain authors, and these are taken up in the introductory chapter and also in the discussion of those works to which this information is relevant. Beyond this, the books treat the specifically literary aspects of the author under discussion and attempt to explain the complexities of contemporary literature lucidly. The books are conceived as introductions to the authors covered, not as comprehensive analyses. They do not provide detailed summaries of plot because they are meant to be used in conjunction with the books they treat, not as a substitute for study of the original works. The purpose of the books is to provide information and judicious literary assessment of the major works in the most compact, readable form. It is our hope that the UMELL series will help increase knowledge and understanding of European and Latin American cultures and will serve to make the literature of those cultures more accessible.

J. H.

PREFACE

Christoph Hein considers himself to be primarily a playwright, but his international reputation was established by his narrative prose, especially with the appearance in 1982 in East Germany of his long novella *Der fremde Freund* (translated into English as *The Distant Lover*, 1989), widely known as *Drachenblut* (Dragon's Blood), the licensed West German title.

My presentation of Hein's works begins with an introductory biographical exposition and then treats his longer narrative-prose works (two of which have been translated into English), his dramatic oeuvre, several of his short stories, and, finally, a selection from his extensive body of essays. This approach does not follow strictly the chronological presentation of his writing. The long prose works are presented in the order in which they were published; the six major plays are treated in the order in which they were written—a sequence that differs from the order in which they were performed. Hein's talent and skill in each of these genres justifies this grouping. The dramas are of greater interest to a theater-oriented public and have a different impact when performed according to the individual interpretative concept of a specific director than when read. Outside of the theater, the general reading public is more likely to encounter Hein's prose works, which interact more directly with the individual reader, depending on his or her personal insight and interpretation. This approach should provide a more cohesive format for inquiry into and analysis of Hein's works. I have explicated relationships between works of different genres as necessary in order to clarify those issues associated with certain periods in Hein's life. In some cases, short stories and essays not treated in the chapters covering those genres are included in the discussion of prose or dramatic works, providing an additional base for intellectual and chronological continuity.

A new play by Hein, *Randow*, is being circulated to German theaters by Henschel Theater Publishers. The location for the premiere had not been determined by press time for this book and the text was not yet commercially available. Although deadlines do not permit a thorough analysis of this work, some points should be mentioned, inasmuch as the manuscript promises to be another extremely important and controversial contribution to the German stage. In the play, two anonymous foreigners are murdered in a field near the Polish border and a single woman, Anna Andress, living and working as a painter in a house nearby, is driven from her home by several factors: fear of violence, village elders who covet the property, a conspiracy on a part of the Western trust set up to re-privatize property in the east, and instances of neo-Nazi activity in the area. The play also treats issues of unemployment and alcoholism (Andress's ex-husband) in the eastern part of Germany, estrangement between older and younger generations (Anna, 36, and her daughter Susanne, 17), broken families, and the identity crisis experienced by the artist. Hein's mastery of authentic language captures a deeply rooted segment of German mentality within the context of uncomfortable current issues and this play, ironically designated in the subtitle as a comedy, will undoubtedly gain international recognition.

The biographical introduction in chapter 1, as well as some of my commentary on his works, is based on audiotapes I made of conversations with Hein and on many unrecorded conversations with him, his family members, and friends which took place during the seven summers I spent in East Germany before that country ceased to exist and during his four-week stay in Lexington, Kentucky, in April 1987.

The translations in the text are my own, not only of Hein's original works, but of quotes from secondary literature as well. In the case of the two prose works available in English, I have modified those translations to correspond more accurately to the original German. Page numbers refer to the most readily available text in German for all quotations from Hein's works, as listed in the table of abbreviations.

ABBREVIATIONS

B̲ook titles cited in the text have been abbreviated as shown below. Page numbers following these abbreviations refer to the original German editions. The West German *Drachenblut* is used instead of *Der fremde Freund,* as is the West German edition of *Horns Ende,* both of which were and are more readily available. Two of the play collections, *Schlötel, oder Was soll's* and *Die wahre Geschichte des Ah Q,* each contain additional plays and essays. *Cromwell* contains other plays as well.

AhQ	*Die wahre Geschichte des Ah Q*
Als Kind	*Als Kind habe ich Stalin gesehen*
Cr	*Cromwell*
Dr	*Drachenblut*
ELB	*Einladung zum Lever Bourgoise*
FF	*Der fremde Freund*
HE	*Horns Ende*
NS	*Das Napoleon-Spiel*
öa	*Öffentlich arbeiten*
Ohnmacht	*Und diese verdammte Ohnmacht*
Pa	*Passage*
Ri	*Die Ritter der Tafelrunde*
Sch	*Schlötel, oder Was soll's*
Ta	*Der Tangospieler*

CHRONOLOGY

1944 April 8: Hein born in Heinzendorf, Silesia (now in Poland), the third of six children of the protestant pastor Günter Hein and Lonny Hein, née Weber.

1945 Family flees advancing Red Army to Thüringen, then settles in Saxony, in the village of Bad Düben, near Leipzig.

1949 The German Democratic Republic is founded.

1958 As the son of a pastor, Hein is not permitted to attend high school. Attends the Evangelisches Gymnasium zum grauen Kloster (Evangelical Gymnasium at the Gray Cloister), a humanistic preparatory boarding school in West Berlin which took the sons of pastors, doctors, and intellectuals who were not members of the ruling Socialist Unity Party.

1960 Günter Hein moves family to East Berlin to lead his church's youth organization. Christoph moves home and commutes to the West Berlin school.

1961 Construction of the Berlin Wall forces a family decision. The elder Hein remains with his congregation and Christoph elects to stay with his family, foregoing the completion of a degree from the Gymnasium. Refused entry into preparatory schools, he attends the Vocational School for the German Book Trade, working as an apprentice in a bookstore on Alexander Square.

1964 Permitted to attend evening school.

1965 Director's assistent to Benno Besson without pay at the Deutsches Theater in Berlin. Writes short pieces for weeklies *Sonntag* and *Junge Welt.*

1966 Passes Abitur (comprehensive exams for high school) and marries Christiane Zauleck in May. Eldest son Georg is born October 20. Hein enrolls at the Cinema College in Babelsberg but the government invalidates his registration. He switches to the College of Theatrical Arts in Leipzig, but is denied entrance by the Ministry of Culture. Works as a waiter in Leipzig.

1967 In January Hein obtains work as an assembler in an adding machine factory and is finally admitted to the Karl-Marx University in Leipzig that September to study philosophy.

1970 Transfers to the Humboldt University in Berlin.

1971 Graduates in June with a diploma in logic. Second son, Jakob, born October 25. Employed as dramaturge at the Volksbühne (People's Stage) under Besson.

1973   Promoted to house author, a contract which runs six years, writing prose in addition to plays.

1974   Premiere of *Schlötel oder Was solls* (Schlötel or What's the Use), with approximately one third of its text cut by censors. One-act children's play *Vom hungrigen Hennecke* (Hungry Hennecke) premieres on the same day, outdoors.

1978   *Cromwell* printed in the theater journal *Theater der Zeit*.

1979   None of fifteen planned premieres of plays by Hein are allowed to take place. Besson and other directors at the Volksbühne leave because of constant harassment. Hein becomes a self-employed writer. Premiere of *Die Geschäfte des Herrn John D.* (The Deals of Mr. John D.) in Neustrelitz.

1980   April: premiere of *Cromwell* in Cottbus. November: premiere of *Lasalle fragt Herrn Herbert nach Sonja. Die Szene ein Salon.* (Lasalle Asks Mr. Herbert about Sonja. The Scene a Salon) in Düsseldorf, West Germany. First printing of short story collection *Einladung zum Lever Bourgeois* (Invitation to the Lever Bourgeois).

1981   Publication of *Cromwell und andere Stücke* (Cromwell and Other Plays).

1982   Becomes a member of the Writers Union. April: receives prestigious Heinrich Mann Prize from the Academy of Art; Peter Hacks delivers the laudatio. May: premiere of the comedy adapted from a play by J. M. R. Lenz, *Der Neue Menoza oder Geschichte des kumbanischen Prinzen Tandi* (The New Menoza, or History of the Kumban Prinz Tandi), in Schwerin. *Der fremde Freund* (The Distant Lover) appears and makes Hein internationally famous.

1983   December: premiere of *Die wahre Geschichte des Ah Q* (The True Story of Ah Q) at the Deutsches Theater, Hein's first and only premiere in Berlin.

1984   Receives the Literature Prize of the Association of German Critics, West Berlin. First printing of *Das Wildpferd unterm Kachelofen* (The Wild Pony under the Tiled Stove), a children's story written for his son Jakob. *Die wahre Geschichte des Ah Q. Stücke und Essays* (The True Story of Ah Q. Plays and Essays) printed in West Germany.

1985   *Horns Ende* (Horn's End) printed after lengthy delays by censors.

1986   *Schlötel oder Was solls. Stücke und Essays* (Schlötel or What's the Use. Plays and Essays) printed in West Germany. Literature Prize, "Der erste Roman" (The First Novel), bestowed by the New Literary Society of Hamburg. April: Hein's planned trip to the USA is cancelled due to interference by the Writers Union.

1987   March: two-month trip to the USA. Visits dramatists, workshops, and theaters in Virginia, New Orleans, San Francisco, and New York. Gives workshops, lectures, and readings at the University of Kentucky Foreign Language Conference; lectures at Amherst College, New York University, Vanderbilt University, the University of Texas, and UCLA. *Öffentlich arbeiten. Essais und Gespräche* (Working Publicly. Essays and Interviews) printed. November: delivers inflammatory anti-censorship speech in a workshop at the 10th Writers Convention of the GDR.

1988   Premiere and publication of *Passage* in West Germany. Publication of *Die wahre Geschichte des Ah Q. Passage* appears in East Germany.

1989   January: receives Lessing Prize, the highest recognition for playwrights in the GDR. April: premiere of *Die Ritter der Tafelrunde* (The Knights of the Round Table) in Dresden. Named Visiting Scholar at the Folkwang School in Essen, West Germany. *Der Tangospieler* (The Tango Player) printed. September: receives Stefan Andres Prize from the city of Schweich, West Germany. September: gives speech on *Die fünfte Grundrechenart* (The Fifth Math Function) at the Berlin faction of the Writers Union. November 4: delivers short speech at the massive demonstration at Alexander Square in front of 500,000 people. October: begins work with the commission for the investigation of police brutality at the October 7 and 8 demonstrations. Numerous political essays in the Western media and speeches in East Berlin. November 9: the Berlin Wall is opened. December: receives the Heinrich Heine Prize from the city of Düsseldorf.

1990   Publication of *Die Ritter der Tafelrunde und andere Stücke* (The Knights of the Round Table and Other Plays) and *Als Kind habe ich Stalin gesehen. Essais und Reden* (As a Child I Saw Stalin Once. Essays and Speeches). Recipient of first Erich Fried Prize in Vienna; laudatio by Hans Mayer. Elected to both the West and East Berlin Academy of Arts. October 3: unification of East and West Germany.

1991   February: Hein's essay *Kein Krieg ist heilig, kein Krieg ist gerecht* (No War Is Holy, No War Is Just) is read on virtually every stage in Berlin to protest the Gulf War. Honorary recipient of the German Cultural Prize in Munich. Elected member to the combined Academy of Arts. Speaks out against harassment of foreigners by rightist youths.

1992   Suffers stroke on stage at an event in Frankfurt. Rescued by a neurosurgeon from the audience. Two serious surgical procedures and a long period of recuperation leaves Hein weak, able to work only an hour a day for many months. Withdrawal from public and political life.

1993   His novel *Das Napoleon-Spiel* (The Napoleon Game) appears.

1994   Publication of *Exekution eines Kalbes* (Execution of a Calf), sixteen short stories written between 1977 and 1990. Completes *Randow. Eine Komödie;* distributed by Henschel Theater Publishers, Berlin. At the time this volume went to press, a premiere date for *Randow* had not yet been announced.

Understanding
CHRISTOPH HEIN

CHAPTER ONE

Introduction to a Contemporary Chronicler

Understanding Christoph Hein as a contemporary requires an understanding of the political, social, and literary environment in which he worked as a chronicler of the connections between the past and his own day. Without a sense of historical correlations in the present, ordinary citizens, regardless of the type of government they live under, are more likely to be swept along by events over which they have little control than to be able to determine or even to influence the future. The active attempt by an individual to reach an understanding about the junctures of history which affect his life can cause him to be "afflicted with his own time."[1] The ensuing impact on his personal awareness legitimizes for him the right to consider himself a contemporary, a participant. Christoph Hein often wrote about people who attempted to avoid being "afflicted with their own time" at all costs. The uneasy feeling thus experienced by the reader of Hein's works is the product of an unavoidable and disquieting contact with history and contemporary civilization and the relationships between the two.

Writing in East Germany

Hein undertook his task as a chronicler in the former German Democratic Republic, where he was forced to construct the kinds of implicit yet sharply critical linguistic barrages that were meticulously culled by readers East and West as they read between the lines of his prose and essays and viewed performances of his plays. Hein became known for the cool precision of language he employed to chronicle what had occurred, statements sometimes more devastating and insightful than the events themselves. The unstated content of his work is an additional, powerful force used to register events and lives, including poorly lived lives, in poetic form. Germans on both sides of the Wall were notorious for a collective tendency to forget the trauma of history—a circumstance that damaged society, as the German sociologist and cultural critic Norbert Elias wrote in his *Studien über die Deutschen* (Studies on the Germans), by preventing its members from experiencing a "cathartic cleansing and the liberation and alleviation which accompanies it."[2] Hein's "chronicles" are humorous, ironic, bitter, shocking, and carefully formulated. They dredge up trauma and require the reader's participation.

Reading between the lines was common practice in the GDR. And such readings invariably attested to the kind of moral and intellectual integrity Hein assiduously cultivated while living in a threatening but peculiarly absurd and self-contradictory climate—the principle feature of which was the repression of information and critical thinking in the face of the public's open access to every imaginable bit of news or opinion on West German television. That Hein remained an engaged thinker of enlightenment equipollence is underscored by his courageous leadership in publicly calling for an end to censorship in East Germany in 1987, an act that served as an important catalyst to events ultimately resulting in the fall of the Berlin Wall, the end of the Stalinist version of Socialism in that ill-fated country, and the eventual problematic union of the two German States.

With the end of the East German state in 1989, the economic structure, the cultural life and mentality, and the considerable literature of that country were all publicly debunked. At the same time, a new process of obscuring history was rapidly invalidating the East German experience even further. In West Germany, the East German writers were quickly categorized as "state" poets, blind utopians, closet dissidents, or self-censoring conformists. A number of presumably dissident and avant garde writers were revealed to have been informers for the State Security Police (*Stasi*). None of these charges had anything to do with the artistic quality of work produced or with the extent to which social conflicts and the dynamics of life in the GDR were brought into the public domain through the cultural pipeline.

Although a significant portion of that literature and its authors were unfairly treated, Christoph Hein remained an exception. Hein was recognized early on as a craftsman of the German language who plied his trade uncompromisingly over a range of genres seldom covered by one writer with such adeptness: drama, short story, novel, essay, and children's stories, all of which were widely read or performed in Eastern and Western Europe. Most of his major plays and prose were translated into numerous European languages, almost immediately after the first editions or premiere performances. Only *Der fremde Freund,* 1982 (*The Distant Lover*), which had earlier been translated into nineteen other languages, and *Der Tangospieler,* 1989 (*The Tango Player*) have been translated into English, with original plans for *Horns Ende,* 1985 (Horn's End) to appear in the future now in doubt. Two plays, *Die wahre Geschichte des Ah Q,* 1984 (The True Story of Ah Q) and *Die Ritter der Tafelrunde,* 1989 (The Knights of the Round Table) have been performed in English in Great Britain. The relatively mild interest in Hein's writings in the United States may be related to a general decline of interest in "serious" literature, but it is also attributable to the general lack of public interest in things East German (other than their athletic program) and to the protracted image of "enemy" firmly fixed to the tiny former German Democratic Republic, with its population of about 17 million. The quality of the translations, to be discussed briefly, may have had something to do with the unexpectedly weak reception as well. Reunification, of course, has drastically altered general perceptions of former East Germans and the area where they live. Their current struggle with extremely difficult economic and social conditions is not being covered in the American media, but it has certainly played a significant role in the declining emphasis on cultural production in that area of the world.

Few who are familiar with Hein's works, however, would argue that any other author, not even Christa Wolf or Volker Braun, provides a better insight into the struggle, hopes, and contradictions experienced in everyday life by people living in the former GDR before the opening of the Wall than Hein does. The connection between the past and the present necessary to understand the new, united Germany—the struggle, the hopes, and the contradictions now emanating from that country—is contained in the rapidly fading history and culture of the GDR.

America's political stance towards the GDR "enemy" as a hard-line member of the "evil empire" possibly limited interest in East German literature—other than that of Christa Wolf, whose cause was effectively and convincingly taken up by feminist Germanists in the United States—to academic circles here. GDR literature became a staple among course offerings in German academic programs in this country during the 1980s. Although this interest has been sustained somewhat, voices here have echoed criticism in Germany that questions the quality of all GDR literature. GDR literature may well take its place as one sub-category of "post 1945 literature." Although Christa Wolf, a friend and mentor to Hein, must be considered one of the principal international forces in the establishment of a strong core of feminist criticism and literature written by women, Hein was uncomfortable with how Wolf's fame inevitably forced her onto a pedestal and into the role of patron saint of women writers, thinkers, and other women oriented towards emancipation of their gender.

The remarkable outpouring of readers' responses after the appearance in 1982 of *The Distant Lover* (a more accurate English title would be "The Alienated Friend") and his sudden world-wide fame worried Hein. Accordingly, he became determined not to become an authoritative spokesperson for his readers as Christa Wolf was perceived to be—a writer on whose words they would hang and whose words could therefore usurp the formulation of their thoughts about their own lives. Perhaps relying on the strength of his background in European theater—which attempts to move its audiences to respond critically to current problems, both cultural and political—Hein was determined not to provide solutions and thus not to take away the reader's responsibility for his or her own critical thinking. In spite of his political activism, especially during the last two years of his country's existence, Hein was determined not to become the Vaclev Havel of his country and resisted the many overtures of his literary and political friends to consider running for political office.

The quality of Hein's writing—the effort he puts into creating literature devoid of what he refers to as "maculature" (a term he often uses in reference to the language typical of best-sellers as opposed to that of serious literature) and the integrity involved in putting his experience and thoughts into writing—remained and remains the guiding principle behind his work, not his political activism or the dissident aspect of his writing. Such integrity has a special meaning in a country where the conditions for earning a living as a writer promoted an "inward emigration," a silent self-censorship or, worse, a disingenuous acknowledgement of party ideology within the written text as a device or prerequisite to get the text printed.

Participation in the production of literature always is characterized by a struggle for a voice in the public domain, even if it is a voice (unlike Hein's) proclaiming that literature ought to exist in an aesthetic vacuum and has no right to be politically engaged. From the earliest stages of his career, Hein's writing is noteworthy for its relentless interaction with the public sphere, for its attempt to create "space" for public debate and simultaneously to disavow any function of literature as a mere substitute for the missing free news media. He accomplished this task in part by following the principles of Walter Benjamin's *Montage,* seeing history by means of the small moments, gleaned from the shards and fragments that reflect the larger picture.

When Hein's characters are politicians, leaders, or public figures, they are usually assigned common character traits and personalities. Many are *handlungsunfähig* (unable to take action) in the eighteenth-century sense of that word as it applied to intellectuals and the upwardly striving middle class as well. Hein's work most often presents the way in which history affects ordinary, otherwise unnoticed people attempting to cope with their lives in the face of changing historical events. Banal conversations between his characters have the capacity to mirror world politics. For Hein, these lives represent a substantive montage of history, or a microcosmic view of how history affects social reality on a scale ignored in higher places and in standard histories. Contemplation of the relationship between the past and the present becomes unavoidable in Hein's view, and for German readers especially, the past on both sides of the Wall was troubling.

For Hein, poesy cannot be *Sklavensprache* (slave language); it cannot reflect the enforced attitude of the political ruler, regardless of the historical period and its corresponding system of patronage—systems to which, for example, writers like Horace, Boileau, or Racine had to adapt. An author cannot afford to allow himself to be coerced or duped into the uncritical adoption of prevailing current political viewpoints, especially under threat of reprisal for failure to do so. Hein differentiates carefully among his characters, and the constellation of attitudes among them is inherent and evident in the distinction between those who do and do not use *Sklavensprache.* The term *Sklavensprache,* ascribed to Lenin in his earlier formulations of legality and illegality and used by Brecht, was commonly used in a broader sense, according to Hans Mayer, "whenever topics were discussed which contradicted official doctrine (and lies) . . . whenever various items could only be hinted at without naming them specifically. One counted on the understanding of readers who, also as slaves, availed themselves of the language of slaves among themselves."[3] Mayer distinguishes between *Verfremdungseffekt* (alienation effect, a dramatic technique employed by Brecht to prevent the audience from identifying emotionally or sympathizing with the characters so they could react critically to the issues) and the technique of *Sklavensprache* with the example of Uwe Johnson's unspoken references to names like Stalin or institutions like the State Security Police (*Verfremdung*) and Hermann Kant's reference to Russians as the "Friends" or to the secret police as "investigating organs" (*Sklavensprache*). For Hein, the use of "Sklavensprache defined the social status of its user as helpless, subjugated, deprived and dependent upon a code which only others with the same social experiences could solve. This, however, renders *Sklavensprache* into an unwitting accordance with the rulers, "an agreement of the repressed with the powerful through the power of language," allowing *Sklavensprache* to function as a "useful safety valve of the rulers over the slaves" (Ah Q 137). Hein's works contain ample usage of *Sklavensprache* but, unlike the case of Kant, it is not the author's use of *Sklavensprache* himself but the characters' use of it which Hein captures as part of his chronicles of existing phenomenon in the world of East Germany.

Toward the end of the 1980s, Hein was generally internationally recognized—along with Wolf, Heiner Müller, and Volker Braun—as one of the major figures of GDR literature and as a major author in German-speaking countries. The critical reception of Hein's works in the United States and Europe is dependent upon radically different circumstances prevalent on both sides of the Atlantic, some of which should be mentioned as an aid to understanding Hein's works. The factors influencing the different receptions within socialist countries and Western European democracies are quite different from those influencing the reception of foreign literature in the United States.

With the end of the GDR and the ensuing end of socialism in the Soviet Union and Eastern Europe, some American Germanists—and to some extent, their West German counterparts—with a Marxist orientation writing on socialist literature and writers in East Germany were seen to have been apologists for totalitarian regimes. Most Germanists interested in the GDR were, of course, not apologists for the regime. Inasmuch as the literature of each country reflects cultural, social, political, and intellectual viewpoints of that particular society and its history, it therefore deserves study and analysis by informed members of other societies.

Furthermore, the relatively short history of the GDR may tend to obscure the evolution of literary conventions. In the 1950s and most of the 1960s, GDR literature was "a literature of enlightenment with the exclusion of enlightenment's immanent dialectics,"[4] as Wolfgang Emmerich has stated. However, instead of advancing the goals of enlightenment by means of education and critical inquiry, public experience was falsified and, as David Bathrick has put it, the population became "objects whose legal incapacitation advanced."[5] If applied to literature, such criticism would be somewhat questionable in light of the fact that literature has clearly played a much greater role in East German life and politics than in any other country this century, with the possible exception of the former Soviet Union. It might be warranted in this context to consider if and how incapacitation was related to the methodology of socialist realism. At any rate, the 1970s and 1980s, the period in question for Hein's literary effort, saw an enormous paradigmatic change in thinking by critical intellectuals who rejected orthodox versions of Marxist belief that history would necessarily progress to the "triumph" of socialism and the final advent of communism. This didn't mean that utopian and humanitarian ideals were renounced as false; they just couldn't be force-fed to the population from above any more. Credibility was slipping rapidly.

The problem is compounded by the fact that the history of literature in East Germany was subject to specific state interventions that determined its course and limited its scope. The notion that writers and intellectuals should support the eradication of nazism and the creation of a socialist state—rather than being social outsiders, disinterested observers, or aesthetic islands to themselves—

was generally embraced by writers of the early and middle historical periods of the GDR, roughly from 1949 to about the mid-1970s. However, the mandate to adhere to "socialist realism," which became a focal point in the 1950s and 1960s, and which more or less required shallow heroization of socialist ideals, was often resented, resisted, and eventually disregarded by good writers.

The meaning which can be ascribed to literature based on whether or not it is subjected to state censorship cannot be reduced to the granting or the denial of permission to exercise public criticism—that is, on the issue of freedom of speech. In West Germany and in the United States, it has long been self-evident that one should doubt the ability of literature to wield any direct political effect. This fact is regrettable for many authors, especially those interested in social change, but for others, according to Andrea Jäger, it is regarded as a "special freedom of the literary sphere not to have to legitimatize themselves according to the criteria of functionality, utility and purposeful rationality."[6] This "special freedom" contains a special dialectical inversion: for authors with a social-aesthetic agenda, "freedom of speech" means they can write what they want, but nobody will react to it.

American Germanists interested in East German writers were restricted by GDR authorities to contact with those who most closely represented the GDR party line: that is, the cultivation of *Feindsbilder* (images of the enemy), which targeted Western capitalist societies; the advocation of world-wide revolution; and the exclusion of contact with and exposure to Western people and institutions. Moreover, writers belonged to the *Schriftstellerverband* (Writers Union), which met periodically to discuss and set policy, and membership in the union was a virtual requirement if one's work was to be published—a fact which gave the state vast and concrete censorship powers to go along with the subjective self-censorship necessarily exercised by the writers and publishers themselves.

It therefore became difficult for American scholars to extend invitations to East German writers other than those who had been approved by the Writers Union and who would therefore publish the obligatory scathing critique of corruption in the West after their return. After 1976, when the dissident poet and musician Wolf Biermann was expelled from the GDR, the ensuing international scandal brought enormous pressure to bear on the GDR Politburo, and some care had to be exercised afterwards on its part not unequivocally to restrict the travel of writers and artists who had attained global recognition. The Politburo was indeed negatively affected by the threat of such scandals and feared the continuing loss of credibility within the general population, a loss which had already occurred as a result of its mishandling of cultural affairs. It feared even more for the resulting loss of prestige and reputation on an international scale.

Christa Wolf and Heiner Müller were able to move about freely, but the Writers Union did not allow many others of their caliber and critical propensity to travel. It should be remembered that Hein, Müller, Braun, and Wolf were committed to what they understood as socialist ideals but that they were likewise aware of the discrepancy between such ideals and the actual conditions in their own country and in other socialist countries. Hein has argued that the repressive Stalinist style of government in East Germany contributed more than any other factor to the demise of the GDR and other East Bloc countries and prevented the possibility of a true democratic form of socialism ever coming into existence on German soil. Although Americans are generally not aware of this, that model, as described in public decrees by Neues Forum and other democratic movement groups in East Germany just prior to and shortly after the opening of the wall, would have included free elections plus critical argument and public debate as the driving wheels of progress. Public animosity towards the West would have no longer served as a scapegoat for personal inadequacies at home. Attempts to implement strikingly similar reforms were turned back with force in 1956 and 1968, and, finally, by the "velvet revolution," unification in 1989–1990.

Many writers before Hein had been thrown into prison for suggesting that criticism was necessary, most notably immediately after the 1956 invasion of Hungary. The pressure to express solidarity with the principles of socialism meant that everyone was required to denounce his neighbor, colleague, or friend if the occasion warranted, or risk losing his job or being reassigned to menial tasks. The endorsement of policy was to be unanimous in order to present a facade of strength to the outside world. Hein saw this not as a strength but as one of the key weaknesses in the socialist structure, and his early plays and essays pointedly allowed the readers to interpret for themselves whether the discrepancy between real progress towards the ideal and pretensions about reality existed or not. After the publication of *The Distant Lover,* Hein was watched closely and efforts at censorship were redoubled, especially for his dramas and for the novel *Horns Ende.* His stature on the European literary scene, however, made overt censorship an undesirable option, and the authorities tried a different form of chicanery.

The following is one incident typical of the kinds of harassment to which authors like Hein were subjected. I had met Hein in 1985 and invited him to come to the United States in April of 1986. On a Friday afternoon, two days before his scheduled departure, a telegram arrived stating that the American Embassy in East Berlin could not locate his passport. The Writers Union had forwarded it to the Embassy in January. The trip was canceled in an uproar of confused transatlantic telephone calls, which had to originate in the United States since it was virtually impossible to call from the GDR without a delay of somewhere between four hours and a week. Hein fell ill because of the incident and was told by doctors not to travel at all for six weeks. A few days later, the Embassy discovered his passport in a file used to discard unprocessed items for which no information was available.

That summer I visited both the Embassy and the Writers Union, where I learned that Karla Dyk, in charge of international travel at the Writers Union, had received the IAP-66 visa materials from Hein, but had not forwarded them to the Embassy. Hein had given the form to the Writers Union, not realizing this was unnecessary and being careful to follow what seemed to be the correct procedure. Dyk denied having seen the form, but bits of her conversation and her knowledge of details about the form indicated otherwise. She grew particularly enraged at the mention of a letter by Klaus Höpcke, the executive director of the Ministry of Culture, who had approved the plan to invite Hein to Kentucky, and she stated that Höpcke would not overrule decisions in the Writers Union. As I learned from the Embassy, the passport was useless for travel to the United States without the IAP-66 form requesting a visa, the form which had disappeared between the time of Höpcke's letter and the scheduled departure, coinciding, not incidentally, with the time when *Horns Ende* was confined to storage at the publisher's. The Writers Union had moved again to secure arbitrary control over who could travel and who could not travel.[7]

American Germanists interested in East German literature had always been obliged to take whomever the Writers Union would send, or no one at all. This time, however, the threat of another international incident loomed, and the U.S. Embassy, which I had questioned about misplacing the passport, stepped in with an offer to bring Hein to the United States on a special USIA exchange program. This was arranged, and Hein landed in New York in March 1987. The most the Writers Union could do was to delay his wife's efforts to obtain a separate ticket for her flight. She managed to pay for it with GDR money, as agreed, and was able to join him in New York. Hein went on to lecture and read from his works at the University of Kentucky, New York University, the University of Texas, and UCLA, leaving his mark as a modest human being and a brilliant and eloquent intellectual. A spark of interest in Hein arose in academic circles, not only among GDR specialists. He was later invited back by other universities and became an important new figure in literary and political discussions in the United States on contemporary German literature and GDR politics, which he explained articulately and objectively. When the Wall came down, I was told that Frau Dyk had attained the rank of Captain in the *Stasi*.

In his 1982 essay "Öffentlich arbeiten" (Working Publicly), Hein stated that in the future, literature would speak of that which affected individuals, of that which afflicted, struck and astonished them. It would be "autobiography, not in the sense of private autobiography, but nevertheless personal, not representative or paradigmatical, but rather a social autobiography" (öa 34). Hein saw literature as a communication about individuals in the world—about individuals who, as a result of an author's own knowledge, ability, and disposition, had become part of his own experience, had lodged themselves deep under his skin. In other words, the author found his literary material within himself. Later, Hein wrote that, as a chronicler using literary methods, it was his task only to report on the beauty and the sternness of the world, eschewing any moralization and ideological discourses about it. Readers are capable of using their own powers of reason, and "it would be a sign of tutelage if they were to need missionaries" (Als Kind 203). The facts, which may not have been presented accurately, are not always crucial, but the consequences and reactions to history by the observers, by the afflicted and the affected, determine how we think about history. The facts, if known, speak for themselves and contain self-evident moral judgements for each individual without need of a writer's commentary. Hein's often repeated statement that "literature has nothing to do with morality" should be understood in this context. Social autobiography can be understood to include reactions and internalizations by individuals and those individuals' interplay with the social, economic, and political mechanisms prevalent in society.

Courage and Integrity

No comprehensive biography of Hein exists, and he is reluctant to speak in detail about his life, seeming to fear a general propensity by scholars to degrade literary works by making incorrect connections between the work and the author's personal life. Hein is the first to say that authors always write about themselves, but he would be the last to provide details that would undermine the sociohistorical interpretation of his works. The following sketch of his biography is the most complete one available to date.

Born 8 April 1944 as the third of six children, Hein grew into the German Democratic Republic as it emerged, and his biography was that of an individual predestined for discrimination at the hands of the new social order. Heinzendorf, in Silesia (now in Poland), was overrun by the Red Army at the end of the war, and Hein's family fled his birthplace, taking up residence in Bad Düben, a small town near Leipzig. His mother, Lonny Hein, née Weber (born 2 November 1914), was a nurse and housewife. His father, Günther Hein (born 22 June 1912), an eloquent and resilient individual, became the town parson and began a long and distinguished career of resistance to the state's efforts to discredit and suppress religion. Hein attended elementary school in Bad Düben from 1950 to 1958, by the end of which time he already knew he wanted to be a playwright. One of Hein's most vivid childhood memories was the stationing of a single Soviet tank in the center of town on 17 June 1953, the year of Stalin's death and the date of the workers' uprising which almost brought down the GDR after just four scant years of official existence.

The GDR's early—and harsh—restructuring of society mandated the appropriation of private property, the establishment of economic and agricultural collectives, and the creation of educational institutions to develop socialist goals to the exclusion of all else. A Nazi, bourgeois, intellectual, or religious background was not to be tolerated. A key form of the discrimination which ensued from these policies was the restriction of educational opportunity. Children of clerics and of the bourgeoisie were scrutinized closely and were required, as were all young people, to join the *Freie Deutsche Jugend* (Free German Youth), a Communist youth organization, in order to advance in the educational system. Acceptance in the FDJ was marked by an oath vowing loyalty to the principles of the GDR and renouncing those elements it opposed, including religion.

For Hein, this was tantamount to renouncing his family ties, and he refused to join. Although he was one of the top students in his class, he was denied entry into elite preparatory schools. In the official language of the state, as Hein quotes it in his fiction, "It was inappropriate that [he] be allowed to attain the educational goals of an accredited high school in our Republic" (Dr 110) Hein recreated this incident in *The Distant Lover* as one of the key turning points in the development of the main character.

Günther Hein sent Christoph to join his older brother, Gottfried, at a West Berlin evangelical preparatory school which took the sons of East German pastors, doctors, and intellectuals who were not members of the SED, the Socialist Unity party that ruled the state. In his acceptance speech for the Stefan Andres Prize in 1989, Hein recalled a teacher who regularly invited interested students over for discussions about theater and literature. She used to lend them books from her personal library she thought they ought to read. And so Hein came into contact with authors he would otherwise have not known about at that age: Stefan Andres, Johann Peter Hebel (1760–1826)—known for the simplicity of his prose style and realistic, short narrative sketches—and Franz Kafka.

In 1960, Hein's father was called to Berlin to lead his church's youth organization, which he continued to do until his retirement in 1977. After a prolonged struggle with authorities to gain permission to take up residence in Berlin, the elder Hein eventually found an apartment. The move, however, caused his sons to become ineligible to live in the school dormitory in West Berlin. Hein moved in with his parents and commuted to the school until August 1961, when the construction of the Berlin Wall forced the family to make a decision.

Günther Hein chose to remain with his congregation in East Berlin, and Christoph elected to stay with his family—a decision, he maintains, which had nothing to do with politics, although it did have something to do with the idea of the shepherd remaining with his flock. He was again refused entry into the elite schools, and his application to learn a trade as a cabinet maker was rejected as well. In a state which ascribed to the dictatorship of the proletariat, trades in the crafts were as well paid as most professional employment, and this course was off limits to Hein as well. Between 1961 and 1964 he attended the Vocational School for the German Book Trade. He worked two years as an apprentice at various bookstores, including at Das gute Buch (The Good Book), a popular bookstore in the Alexanderplatz (Alexander Square), the center of the city. He enrolled in night school to earn his degree but was expelled at the order of higher authorities after only three weeks.

Not until 1964 was Hein finally allowed to attend an accredited evening school in East Berlin. Working days and attending school and studying for about five hours every night, he passed his final exams in 1966 at the age of twenty-two and, in May of the same year, married Christiane Zauleck, whose Jewish father had been killed while fleeing from the Nazis. Several months earlier, Hein had introduced himself to Benno Besson, a prominent director from Switzerland working at the Deutsches Theater. Hein quit working in the bookstore, and Besson took him under his wing at the Deutsches Theater. In the 1965–66 season, Hein worked eight months as the director's assistant without pay, scraping by with honoraria from literary contributions and feature interviews for weeklies such as *Sonntag* (Sunday) and *Junge Welt* (Young World). Besson told him there would be no pay in order to test the sincerity of his interest in the theater. Occasionally Hein picked up ten marks for bit parts or forty marks for small singing roles at the theater.

A new economic reform was instated in 1966, the key point of which was to allow factory managers more leeway in decision making and to reward workers in the form of annual bonuses for increased productiveness. The reform seemed to spread to cultural domains as well: selected works of a few "Western bourgeois" authors, including Kafka, were permitted to appear in East German publishing houses. Not much changed for Hein personally, however. In the summer of 1966, he had enrolled at the College for Cinema in Babelsberg, but the government ordered the school to invalidate his registration. This intrigue, poeticized later in his short story "Der Sohn" (The Son), continued when he switched to the College of Theatrical Arts in Leipzig, only to receive a letter of rejection directly from the central Ministry of Culture. Hein's first son, Georg, was born in October, and he moved to Leipzig to be with Christiane. He worked first as a waiter at the Gaststätte Intermezzo on the Martin-Luther-Ring, a restaurant and *Nachtbar* (a bar, usually with entertainment, open after serving hours), and then, from January to September 1967, as an assembler in an adding-machine factory.

This last course of action, common in the GDR, qualified Hein as a member of the working class and he was then able to enroll in the Karl-Marx-University in Leipzig. The spring of 1968 then brought the violent suppression of the Czechoslovakian attempt to democratize socialism. When East German soldiers and tanks were required to join other East Bloc countries, and hence German vows never to invade another country were broken, Hein's disillusionment with the real existing socialist state was complete, and indeed any hope among intellectuals for an effective reform of socialism faded. Hein recollected the impact of the Prague Spring on him (in a lecture in Dresden on 9 February 1992), in which he otherwise spoke about the difficulty both united German sides were experiencing in attempts to establish a basis for communication: "The collapse of the socialist countries did not surprise me all that much. After 1968, after the invasion of Czechoslovakia, this was a failed model for me and I have described this failure numerous times between 1974 and 1988, beginning with *Cromwell* and ending with *Die Ritter der Tafelrunde*. What did surprise me was the collapse of liberalism in Germany which soon followed."[8]

In Leipzig, Hein studied philosophy and logic, but his stubborn, outspoken adherence to his personal principles combined with his biting wit and masterful skills with the German language to cause an uproar among the faculty and the many conformist students in his department. The atmosphere became acutely tense when faculty who had criticized the invasion of Prague lost their positions. A cloud of silence descended upon both students—except for Hein—and faculty as it had done in 1953. After listening to an especially provocative oral report by Hein in 1970, his professors advised him to change universities before they were forced to expel him. He then completed his education at the Humboldt University in Berlin in June of 1971 with a senior thesis on pluralistic logic under Prof. Horst Wessel.

In December of that year, Erich Honecker had come to power and issued his famous statement that, from the standpoint of socialism, there should be no taboos in art or literature, either as to content or style. The tightly enforced dictums of socialist realism began to loosen with this edict, but the government

13

and the intellectual-artistic community interpreted Honecker's statement in radically different ways, as became eminently clear in 1976 with the Wolf Biermann affair. If anything, censorship after 1971 interfered even more in the production of good literature. Moreover, the theater, due to its German-European tradition as a public forum for contemporary issues, was subjected to local censorship if and when it had passed through the central censorship. Many plays were delayed by seven or eight years, or until the issues had become moot or the public had become complacent. Like many of his contemporaries, Hein had a long and arduous road ahead of him. Even Müller and Braun, with their base of international fame and success and their professed loyalty to the principles of socialism, had to wait until the last year or two of the GDR to see some of their works staged. It was during the 1970s that Hein realized his writing could not be linked to public success. "I am the reader I know the best" (Als Kind 201) he has often said, and he wrote and revised until he was able to satisfy his own extremely demanding standards, becoming himself his most unforgiving critic.

By 1971, Besson had moved over to the Volksbühne, where he and Heiner Müller were leading the venerable stage to its heyday. That fall, Christiane gave birth to their second son, Jakob, and Hein went to work as dramaturg and director's assistant to Besson. He translated and adapted several French plays for the Volksbühne, most notably Moliére's *Le médicin volant* (The Flying Physician) and Racine's tragedy *Britannicus* in 1975, the latter not published until 1990. He was promoted to house author at an unusually young age in the 1973–74 season, premiering with *Schlötel oder Was solls,* published in 1986 (Schlötel or What's the Use). Up to that time, he and his family had survived on an income of about 250 marks per month.

It was not impossible to get by on such an income in the GDR. Rent was extremely cheap, about 40 marks per month, basic requirements and food staples were inexpensive, and small subsidies were paid for each child. It made for a tight budget in any case, especially when compared with the normal pay of, say, a cabinet maker, which would have been 800 to 1200 marks per month. Eventually, Christiane's success in her job as a documentary film maker for DEFA, the East German TV enterprise, helped Hein to end his affiliation with the Volksbühne to become a self-employed writer in 1979. He had good reason to leave: not a single one of fifteen planned premieres of his plays was permitted to be performed on stage. Besson was tired of the constant interference with his program planning and left the Volksbühne along with two other renowned directors, Manfred Karge and Matthias Langhoff, and a number of other associates. Hein was compelled by the new director to leave as well. Although he was encouraged to disappear with the others to the West, Hein was both attached to his home and too stubborn to give up as long as his life was not disrupted so much he couldn't write.

Heiner Müller and Volker Braun were house authors at the Volksbühne as well, but it was Besson who exercised the greatest influence on Hein. Hein defended his master with an article published in France in 1978, "Besson ou le manque de gout" (Besson, or the Scarcity of Good Taste): "Besson's work was successful because it always had consequences, and this made it into a public affair" (öa 114)—a fact which, in turn, made it taboo. The essential concept of Besson's stage productions was the inclusion of elements which astonished and disturbed, which caused displeasure and indignation. For Besson, theater was a social instrument: "His theater negotiates public opinion, for him man is a political and historical communal being" (öa 114). Hein compared Besson's resonance at the Volksbühne with that of Brecht at the Berliner Ensemble, claiming that Besson's provocative productions had become a unique focal point in GDR theater. Besson's innovations indeed had a lasting impact on the way a number of great East German stage directors approached their work, including several who later staged Hein's plays.

Together with another family, the Heins purchased a farmhouse in Bergsdorf, about an hour north of Berlin. They renovated the house to some extent, and Hein began his writing career in earnest by withdrawing to the countryside whenever he was working on a text and returning to the Berlin residence close to Weißensee one or two days per week. Such houses were extraordinarily inexpensive—1500 to 3000 marks—but the local offices required the two families to establish residency in the town of Bergsdorf in order to own the house. Hein worked in Bergsdorf until 1987, producing a collection of short stories, essays, a novella, a novel, a children's book, and five plays. Disagreements with the other tenants led the Heins to sell off their share. In 1988, Monika Maron told them of an empty farmhouse much further north, near Krakow on the Polish border, and Hein has retreated to that location to write since then, enjoying a warm relationship with the local farmers, as he had done in Bergsdorf.

Working in a "Reader's Land"

The conditions for literary production in the GDR were complicated by censorship procedures, discrimination against writers who failed to conform to party mandates of form and style, prioritization for the allocation of paper, which was often in short supply, licensing agreements with Western publishers, the regulation of authors' royalties, and the authoritative control of the Copyright

Office. The Copyright Office was in charge of the export of cultural products, and it operated like a capitalist export business. Since GDR money was worthless outside of Eastern Bloc countries, the GDR took every opportunity to raise "hard currency." In fact, the monetary system in East Germany was three-fold: East marks, deutsche marks (West German), and barter. East marks were used in stores, but most East Germans earned far more than they needed to spend and had enormous savings by the time of German unification. Barter was unofficially practiced to obtain scarce goods and materials and was usually necessary in order to build a house or remodel a room. Deutsche marks were used to obtain scarce goods and services on the black market.

Many East Germans obtained deutsche marks—usually no more than a few hundred marks—from relatives and friends in the West or by providing scarce or emergency services, such as plumbing, which would otherwise take months to obtain, and then illegally demanding payment in "West marks." Possession of hard currency was against the law, and citizens were required to turn in such currency to the government. They could earn hard currency credits by performing special services, by attaining privileged political status, or by contributing to the export trade of the country. Individuals would receive an equivalent amount of Forumschecks (currency certificates), which could be spent in the Intershops—shops located throughout the country which sold Western items, mostly wine, candy, coffee, non-perishable foods, and clothing, for a profit.

For Hein and other writers, publishers signed license agreements with West German publishers, who then had the rights to sell the books in all Western countries. As much as eighty percent of the royalties for the writer could revert to the Copyright Office. The writer was additionally assessed income tax on the remaining income. The remainder was paid out in Forumschecks. These practices led to manuscripts' being smuggled out of East Germany into the West, particularly those which had not passed the censors. Writers such as Adolf Endler, who was not allowed to publish after he publicly criticized the handling of the Biermann affair, or Wolfgang Hilbig, whose apartment was searched and who was briefly jailed, had no choice but to sneak their manuscripts out if they were to be published. Hilbig and many others eventually could not cope with the harassment and moved to the West.

Hein did not leave in spite of the encouragement to do so, and he rarely published his works outside of the GDR without first having a contract with an East German publisher, although he occasionally accepted payment for short articles in literary journals in hard currency and probably agreed to have his West German publishers operate a Western bank account in his name in order to save some of his royalties. In essence the Copyright Office exploited the talents of its artists and writers to reap enormous profits. Hein and other writers whose works were internationally acclaimed were essentially robbed of many thousands of marks.

Hein's East German publisher, Aufbau Verlag, usually signed such license agreements with Luchterhand, a West German publisher that published a large repertoire of East German writers. The dramas were handled separately by Henschel Verlag. All dramatists were required to submit their manuscripts to Henschel. They were reproduced—rather painstakingly in the absence of functional copiers—and circulated among the theaters in East Germany to see who wanted to stage them. It should be noted that publishers like Aufbau and Henschel employed a group of competent individuals who argued for the publication of controversial texts in the face of possible reprimands from the central censorship authorities in the Ministry of Culture. Each text had to be scrutinized for political controversy, but the referees learned how to write their reports in ways to defend many texts successfully, including several by Hein.

Henschel sold the license to *Die Geschäfte des Herrn John D.* (The Deals of Mr. John D.) to Drei Masken Verlag in Munich and the rest of his plays to Kiepenheuer Bühnenvertrieb in West Berlin, which performed the same function in Western Europe to promote his plays on Western stages. Also at stake was the location of the premiere, which determined who would receive a percentage of the box office at other theaters where the play was later performed. The GDR would have been in a poor position to pay such royalties in hard currency if they allowed the premiere to take place in the West. Only one play of Hein's premiered in the West, and one of his plays was performed only once or twice in order to establish the royalty rights.

Another form of discrimination was limitation in the size of printings. The works of establishment writers like Hermann Kant were always available, but it was extremely difficult to obtain books by writers such as Hein, Christa Wolf, or Günter de Bruyn. It was generally necessary to order well in advance, to have a friend working in a bookstore who would set aside a copy, or to have connections in the publishing house. The size of the printings was nevertheless many times larger than in the West, often reaching 30,000 to 50,000 volumes for a first edition, compared to 7,000 to 10,000 in the West. Copies were circulated among friends who were unable to obtain them. When Christa Wolf's *Kassandra* appeared in East Germany missing a few paragraphs from the original which had appeared in the West German edition, copies of her book circulated with a typewritten page including the passages removed. Such was the burning desire of many East Germans to read the works of the writers on whom they did, in fact, often depend for enlightenment, information, and confirmation of values.

East Germany was known as a "reader's land," a place where literature was avidly read and, hence, where it played a greater role in shaping and informing society than at any time since the eighteenth century. The Enlightenment had resurfaced in the GDR in the form of its literature. The dialectical nature of that earlier movement manifested itself in the 1970s and 1980s in the critical rejection of literature's non-critical (and ineffective) earlier application as a medium for the transmission of dogmatic norms and their official justifications. When the Wall came down and the stores were inundated with all the Western magazines, weeklies, newspapers, trivial literature, and so on, that had previously been unavailable in the GDR, the reading public transformed into the same kind of reading public in the West: belles lettres became only a small part of the book trade, and East German authors, many of whose works constituted one of the strongest forces leading to the end of Honecker's regime, were lost in the shuffle of progress and transition in their own country and soon forgotten.

Only a few, very talented writers had the ability to be successful under the new conditions. The public no longer bought dissident works for the sake of confirming their own beliefs. Literature had done its part in the years leading up to 1989, and when the Wall was opened on 9 November, the rushing currents of history took over. Literature had been feared by the old regime, and precisely this fear gave it power it did not have in Western democracies. This power is now gone, and only good literature will survive. Hein is one of the talented few—uncompromising, unwilling to conform to market-oriented production—whose works already assure him a place in the canon of established German authors.

Notes

1. Christoph Hein, "Heinrich-Mann-Preis 1983," *Neue Deutsche Literatur* 31.7 (1983): 163.
2. Norbert Elias, *Studien über die Deutschen* (Frankfurt a.M.: Suhrkamp, 1992) 550.
3. Hans Mayer, *Der Turm von Babel. Erinnerungen an eine Deutsche Demokratische Republik* (Frankfurt a.M.: Suhrkamp, 1991) 261.
4. Wolfgang Emmerich, *Kleine Literaturgeschichte der DDR* (Frankfurt a.M.: Luchterhand, 1989) 270.

5. David Bathrick, "Kultur und Öffentlichkeit in der DDR," *Literatur der DDR in den siebziger Jahren,* ed. Peter Uwe Hohendahl and Patricia Herminghouse (Frankfurt a.M.: Suhrkamp, 1983) 57.

6. Andrea Jäger, "Schriftsteller-Identität und Zensur. Über die Bedingungen des Schreibens im 'realen Sozialismus,'" *Literatur der DDR. Rückblicke,* ed. Heinz Ludwig Arnold (Munich: Text + Kritik, 1991) 138.

7. Klaus Höpcke would have had greater authority than anyone in the Writer's Union, and it would have been odd that the Writers Union would act contrary to his will. His letter was dated 8 January 1986, sent by surface mail, and not received until 11 March. In it, he stated that he approved of Hein's trip and that he had consulted with the appropriate offices of the Writers Union. Letters from Hein during that time, however, indicte that the Ministry of Culture had withdrawn *Horns Ende* from circulation and that a struggle was under way to get it distributed (see chap. 3 below).

8. Christoph Hein, "Ansichtskarte einer deutschen Kleinstadt, leicht retuschiert," *Neue Deutsche Literatur* 40.4 (1992): 28.

CHAPTER TWO

The Invulnerability of Silence:
The Distant Lover

The key to *Der fremde Freund,* 1982 (*The Distant Lover*) is understanding Hein's use of short, staccato, matter-of-fact sentences relaying the thoughts of the first-person narrator about other people, her environment, and herself. Claudia, a physician, describes emptiness with the vocabulary of fulfillment, presents unlived life as existential happiness, and justifies a nihilistic attitude with the language of optimism. Her professed emancipation is reflected in her cynical manipulation of psychological mechanisms enabling her to repress inner moral guidance and to suppress affection or cordiality for friends, family, and acquaintances, and to facilitate the rejection of affection shown to her by them.

In the end she claims that she sleeps well, has no nightmares, but the book opens with a dream in which she experiences terror and helplessness. In the dream, Claudia finds herself—at least she thinks it is herself—together with a male friend whose face is blurred. They appear in her dream at the brink of an abyss. They try to inch their way across the broken ruins of a bridge when five runners come out of the forest and run silently and sure-footedly across the narrow beams spanning the chasm, leaving Claudia and her partner frozen in fear, unable to go back, hopelessly aware that they must go forward. The key elements of the dream consist of Claudia's desire for her frightened partner to stop clutching her—"everyone for themselves," she thinks (Dr 5)—and her unwillingness to plunge into what could be construed as the depths of her own being. Finally, she equates the dream with the anxiety of remembrance. Her spontaneous reaction is to paste daily routines over whatever reality might be revealed by memory, as a schoolchild would paste new stickers over old on a notebook. This ploy is indicative of her refusal to confront earlier traumatic experiences, fearing the damage such memory could do to her well-constructed shell of safety.

Following the introductory dream sequence, the novella unfolds in thirteen tightly-knit chapters. Chapters two through twelve describe her year-long affair with Henry Sommer. Chapter one portrays her attendance at his funeral, and thirteen consists of her reflections six months later. Claudia's encounter with

20

Henry is the point of departure for her break from her established routine to take a decisive journey into her past, culminating in a visit to the small village where she grew up. Henry's death marks her escape back into the routine and into her self-constructed fortress against the emotions of intimacy with other human beings.

Routines

Hein began writing *The Distant Lover* with the intention of telling the story of a man he had known who died as a result of unspecified but irresponsible or foolish actions that seemed like a trivial way to waste a life. Dissatisfied with the story's potential, Hein came upon the idea of portraying the man from the perspective of a second party, a woman. From this vague background, the woman, Claudia, quickly emerged as the central figure of the novella. Her description of Henry, the "distant [or "alienated"] lover," was extended to other characters and events as well, so that the narrative is related exclusively from Claudia's subjective perspective. She ultimately tells us a good deal more about herself than about other people. In fact, the reader must be careful not to assume that Claudia's opinions about people and events have objective value—they are usually revelations about Claudia. Hein never tells us whether her observations have any objective validity or which of them can be taken at face value. One aspect of reception aesthetics which Hein's writing entails is the obligation of the reader to exercise care in explicating the text. Hein releases the reader's thinking into an independent and highly subjective sphere, permitting a myriad of potential viewpoints, each of which acts as a continuation of a multi-faceted dialogue established between the written words of the author and the thoughts of the reader. This technique of drawing the reader into the inner thoughts of the narrator (with no chance to exit until the end of the book) can easily put the reader in a position of questioning one's own subjective reaction to the text and (unlike most of Hein's other works) tends to break down much of the traditional objective distance between reader and text. Hein establishes the reader's position with respect to the narrator in the opening chapters in the context of Claudia's self-described reactions to people and events encountered in her daily routines.

On the day of the funeral, Claudia demonstrates her self-imposed isolation from others on several occasions. In the dilapidated, unventilated elevator with speechless riders from her high-rise apartment, for example, she participates in their collective unwillingness to know each other, disgusted at the smell of too many people in the elevator. The atmosphere of the entire high-rise building is a mirror for Claudia's feelings, including her reflections about the concierge, whose only contact with the renters besides an occasional repair of a leaky faucet, according to Claudia's perception, is his obligation to deal with the apartments of those who have died.

At work in the clinic, she is annoyed at the head physician's request for her to accompany him to the mayor's office to ask for the restoration of their recently reduced contingency of available apartments, which they needed in order to recruit additional nurses from the province. (Although East Berlin was much too large for thorough or accurate controls, the state bureaucracy nevertheless tried to link housing permits for state-owned dwellings with work stations.) At the same time, Claudia is grateful she doesn't have to listen to the doctor's condolences when she begs off due to the funeral.

She also is irritated, as usual, by the chronic tardiness of her "cow-eyed" nurse, Karla, whose excuse is always her children. She uses this excuse, according to Claudia, "presumably in order to give her [Claudia] a bad conscience" (Dr 9) for not having any children herself—the reason her husband had supposedly divorced her. Claudia refuses to admonish a regular patient, a humorous and somewhat harmlessly perverse retired old man, for touching Karla, since she is old enough to take care of herself. Why should she help Karla? Karla annoys her by discovering her dark blue coat in the office closet and asking her if she were going to a funeral. Claudia's first thoughts in chapter one consist of her indecisiveness about attending the funeral at all. She had selected the coat because it could pass for black. Karla's question, intruding in the game Claudia has been playing in her mind, now determines that she will have to go to the funeral.

The routine lunchtime in the clinic's canteen includes a colleague's lament about his stolen car, a topic which is considerably more important than whatever sympathy the others might have felt for the fact that Claudia will be attending the funeral of a deceased friend. To be sure, the man had paid double the book value of the car, and the normal waiting period for purchase of a new automobile in the GDR was seven to ten years.

Claudia continues the day's routine by having coffee later with Anne—whose husband, Claudia reports, rapes her every other week. Their sex life is normal otherwise, and Anne is the mother of four children, but her husband seems to need to humiliate her once in a while. Claudia keeps her distance. Anne seems to be waiting for age to catch up with her husband, "senility as hope" (Dr 12). Claudia can only wonder if the new dress Anne's husband bought her—as compensation—would be more appropriate for the funeral than what

Claudia is wearing: "what do I have to do with her being raped. God knows, she deserves to bear her burden alone" (Dr 12).

It occurs to Claudia that she had not thought about Henry all day. As she drives to the funeral, she can only think of one thing: that she is supposed to remember him, to keep him in her memory. She's tempted to stop at home to pick up her camera and take advantage of the free afternoon to go somewhere and take pictures, her hobby. Funerals, memorial services, seem like a waste of time, a kind of "atavistic death cult" (Dr 13). At the cemetery, Claudia is uneasy to discover there are two funerals and she is unsure to which party she belongs. She doesn't like being stared at. At the ceremony she decides to join, she notices a woman with two children, evidently Henry's widow. After listening and thinking about the routine banalities of the rites, she finds herself in the absurd position of having to shake the widow's hand after tossing a handful of dirt onto the coffin. Thinking that Henry's widow hates her, Claudia is amused by the notion that she could have her face slapped at the open grave. Later, she stops in a café for a cognac and tries her best to think about Henry, the burial, the soft voice of the minister. Then she gives up.

Invulnerable

These descriptive reflections by Claudia at the opening of the book disclose how she trivializes meaning by ritualizing what might have otherwise been appropriate behavior. Although Claudia's exact relationship to Henry is not revealed until later, shortly after she gives up trying to remember him, a funeral is an event associated with the trauma of loss and the commemoration of an individual held dear or important. Claudia's behavior would indicate that she is attending the funeral of some acquaintance or colleague whom she didn't know very well rather than the funeral of her lover and that she is reluctantly doing so as the fulfillment of an expected social obligation.

Each of the incidents of the day represents what Peter C. Pfeiffer calls a "potential for the recovery of lost meaningfulness and fulfillment,"[1] a potential never realized by Claudia. She sees the funeral as an "excuse" to avoid helping to find housing for the nurses. She belittles Karla's need for personal interaction on the grounds of Karla's promiscuity. Claudia's interaction with other colleagues about the funeral is pasted over with the talk about the stolen car. Her reaction to Anne's trauma is diverted by thoughts of the dress Anne had received from her husband. Most important, as we realize later in the text, the funeral represents a potentially unavoidable trauma for Claudia should she have to shake the hand of the widow, the woman whose husband had cheated on her with Claudia. In her comparison of *The Distant Lover* with Camus's *The Stranger,* Brigitte Sändig states that the "consistent retention of the character perspective" and the psychological constitution of the figures provide meaning in the text: "Indifference and imperturbability permit both Meursault and Claudia to forego involvement with things and people. . . . But it becomes increasingly evident [that] this indifference is a protective mechanism against reality for both of them."[2]

The culmination of Claudia's alienation appears with her astounding words towards the end of the book: "I'm ready for everything, I'm armed against everything, nothing can injure me any more. I have become invulnerable. I have bathed in dragon's blood and no linden leaf left a vulnerable place on me. I will never get out of this skin. I will croak in my impenetrable shell out of longing for Katharina" (Dr 154). The last sentence, along with several others from the last chapter, reveals her vulnerability in the same breath she denies it. The imagery of bathing in dragon's blood refers to the famous medieval saga of the Nibelungen, of how Siegfried slew a dragon and bathed in its blood to make his skin impenetrable, how a linden leaf covered a single spot in the middle of his back, the spot struck by the spear which killed him in a cowardly act of betrayal. Claudia's childhood friend Katharina represents the vulnerable spot for her, the one spot she cannot cover, even throughout her continual posture of denial. Claudia's laconic, straightforward sentence structures appear together without necessarily containing a common sign of sense or coherence. As Sändig notes, "her reports are fixed in the structural syntax itself with the existential coercion to live in an alienated world and with her decision to confront this world with indifference."[3]

Claudia's meeting with Henry ultimately serves as a catalyst to her memory and the reawakening of her emotional capacity for intimacy, powerful elements which may be understood as the cause for her visit to the village where she grew up—a place which contains the remembrance of her self and the origin of her personality, molded by events and emotions she had suppressed for years. She attempts to keep a certain distance between herself and Henry and finds him very willing to collaborate. The distance provides an unyielding brittleness for the relationship and an uncomplicated familiarity for Claudia, who "had no need to open up completely to another person ever again, to be in someone else's power" (Dr 29).

Henry is sometimes mistakenly seen by readers as a Kerouac type—free, wild, and exuberant, an architect who likes fast cars and whose imaginary career would have been that of a race-car driver or a stunt man.[4] Although Henry may have generated this kind of perception in the forty-year-old Claudia, he describes his work complacently as building what he calls "useless nuclear plants" designed "sometimes for the river to flow on the right and sometimes on the left" (Dr 27), and his driving, during which time he "feels alive" (Dr 28), is just plain foolish and reckless, not adventurous or racy. It's also somewhat of a contradiction in terms, inasmuch as the vintage GDR cars were unable to go much faster than the official speed limit, about 60 mph, so that Henry's speeding is relatively tame, even on the narrow country roads. Not to say that he, like other East Germans, was not aware of the sleek, swift Western cars seen on television and on the autobahn connecting West Germany with West Berlin, and he too probably would have dreamed of driving over 100 mph on the West German autobahn as a participant in the psychotic German driving culture, just for thrills.

Henry is ironic and aloof. To him, life has no meaning; his outlook is pragmatically nihilistic. The love relationship is devoid of familiar admissions to each other of compassion and real intimacy. He and Claudia avoid exchanging biographical details most of the time, and when they do, it results in disaster. They first meet in the confines of the apartment elevator, and Henry shows up that evening asking to be fed, after which he climbs into bed with Claudia, to her consternation and amusement.

That weekend Claudia visits her parents, and we find that her family ties are weak, forgotten. Her mother talks about Hinner, Claudia's previous husband, and seems to want them to get back together. Her father is disillusioned by the lack of political engagement on Claudia's part and complains that she has no idea what is happening in the world, since she doesn't even read the paper—actually Claudia does read the paper, but only the personals and the classified ads. Claudia's parents' generation were the idealist socialists, strongly political and committed to building an alternate German society. Claudia's apolitical attitude is symptomatic of an important generational conflict in East Germany. The older political activists had been unequivocally committed to socialism and worked hard to build what they viewed as an alternate society after the war, while a large portion of Claudia's generation tended to withdraw into mundane private life and the generation after Claudia openly rejected socialist ideals and the hypocrisy they perceived.

In this context it is essential to understand that aside from their haunting ring of self-deception, Claudia's claims at the end of the book—that she has it made, she is a success, nothing significant remains for her to accomplish—all underscore a self-centered life, one conducted without contribution to the public or social sphere, an existence without expectations. Back home in the city, Claudia attempts to formulate some clear concepts about her parents. She is unable to do so. There is only a vague remembrance, nothing much; she soon falls asleep. The words echo her inability to remember Henry after the funeral.

The importance of history—how it is distorted, changed, and covered up by political constituencies—is one of the subjects of *Horns Ende,* published in 1985. In *The Distant Lover* the significance of personal history is also accentuated; Claudia omits details, suppresses key incidents, and endeavors to exist only in a present that she defines and that is without encumbrances from the past. The issues of social memory found in *Horns Ende* are preceded with issues of psychosomatic personal memory in *The Distant Lover.* According to Pfeiffer, these two novels and their portrayal of confrontations with the past articulate the precariousness of the national identity of the GDR, the lack of which identity helps to explain the collapse in 1989: "In the process of remembering, the sediments of the past suddenly become translucent in *The Distant Lover* and *Horns Ende,* revealing the petrified structure of the present both in the private sphere (*The Distant Lover*) and in the historical and social sphere (*Horns Ende*). The use of history and stories should provide the present with a renewed dynamic potential."[5]

Hein was strongly influenced by his readings of the Jewish social theoretician Walter Benjamin and of Marcel Proust on the subjects of history and remembrance. For both of these authors, the search for the past should be relentless and is central to a critical understanding of the present. Hein seems likewise to suggest that many of Claudia's internal deformities are related to her denial of the past and to her failure to come to grips with the totality of her being.

Avoidance of close contact with other human beings enhances Claudia's ability to stay out of their personal affairs, to remain ignorant of their personal lives. Each time an opportunity is presented, she manages to remain out on the beam over the abyss, unable to retreat, stationary, not moving forward, trapped in limbo.

When Claudia promises to use her connections to try to get a copper IUD for Karla from the West, Karla's gratitude almost leads to a closeness. They could have hugged, or shaken hands, an act that Claudia fears would lead to a daily rite, a friendly intimacy that she was relieved to have avoided. Why look for an explanation of this fear of touching in the vocabulary of psychiatry, she thinks, for her life was best seen as a clinical phenomenon: "expressions, movements, feelings, — merely false behavior in the face of the all-comprehensive termini of some abstract norm" (Dr 38). Even when she hadn't heard from Henry for a week, she recalled that they were not responsible for each other, they didn't owe each other anything. She was mildly annoyed to notice that she would have liked for him to have told her when he was leaving town for a few days.

It could also be that whole urban societies have, to some extent, "bathed in dragon's blood." A passage from Hein's "Worüber man nicht reden kann, davon kann die Kunst ein Lied singen," 1986 (That Which Cannot Be Spoken of Can Have a Song Sung about It by Art) indicates that Claudia may be seen as a representation of twentieth-century tendencies to respond to stress, trauma, daily routine. There, he argues that the drive of self-preservation, the conscious and unconscious reactions which help people avoid mortal danger is enhanced by the "ability to not perceive unbearable truth, to close one's eyes in its face" (Öa 50). The world itself has become unbearable: "If the world were constantly before our eyes, we would not be capable of reading a poem or even of relaxing when drinking a cup of coffee. The self-preservation drive guards us from really having to endure the world by covering our senses with a thick hide. A useful second skin, which protects us from the things which would make us unable to live, but a dangerous hide, because it permits us to bear the unbearable and to thereby endanger life itself" (Öa 50). The dangerous side of "invulnerability" had gained the upper hand in Claudia's life. The insensitivity that is detrimental to the development of society toward the more humane retards the individual as well. The narrow line between having too thick a skin and being too sensitive has become precarious and fragile in the twentieth century, and Claudia is not able to find an effective balance between the two, always electing to thicken her skin.

As somewhat of a (foolish) risk-taking pseudo-anarchist, spontaneous and indifferent, Claudia's friend Henry represents someone who might actually be able to rekindle in her the youthful anarchy or the energy to change her life which she still had at the beginning of her marriage to Hinner, but which has lain dormant for many years.[6] Claudia's encounter with Henry is a chance to overcome her apathy and indifference. At the very least, it represents an interlude of spontaneity, ultimately interrupted and broken by Henry's death. After the painful irritation of their encounter, she is able to return to the normal, painless, lifeless condition in which she previously led her life.

The Aura of Isolation

A key event in the novella, perhaps even a poetic turning point, takes place immediately following Henry's reckless driving and his run-in with the farmer on the tractor whose life he has senselessly endangered for the sake of a cheap thrill. The farmer gives him a black eye for his trouble. Claudia and Henry take a walk, and she comes to life—exulting in nature, taking pictures, enjoying herself even though she has noticed that Henry is too urbanized, bored, unenthralled by nature to share her feelings. Feelings begin to awaken in her. The sequence of events which follow her climbing up to a precarious position on the wall of some ruins to get a better angle to take pictures is quite possibly the literal enactment of the dream which opens the book.[7] Since she neither plunged (or fell) into the "abyss" nor made it safely across when the opportunity presented itself, her mental situation in the bad dream remained unchanged, stagnant.

The scene in the forest is the only time we actually see Claudia in the act of photographing. It is structurally linked with the opening dream sequence by the visual effects that Hein achieves with language. Like the dream sequence, events are accented as with a "camera zooming in" (Dr 5). Claudia's relationship with her photography is expounded at length in other passages of the book, revealing the distorted perspective that makes her refuse to engage in what Bernd Fischer calls "philosophical reflexions on the meaning-question."[8] A close reading of *The Distant Lover* compels the reader to apply Claudia's later expositions about photography to the incidents which occur in the forest.

She never takes pictures of people, only of landscapes, because—as she says—landscapes are always changing but people appear awkward and unnatural in photographs. The opening sentence of the book, the start of Claudia's description of her dream, stated almost biblically, is, "In the beginning was a landscape" (Dr 5). Photographing people is for Claudia an "indiscreet violation of alien life" (Dr 75). The idea that a person can be captured in a picture is nonsense: "Trees always remain themselves, they don't try to lie by giving a favorable image of themselves" (Dr 75). It may be what Walter Benjamin refers to as the "cult value" or "aura"[9] of portraits that makes Claudia uneasy. The cult value of portrait photography is connected to memory and remembrance. One is again reminded of Claudia's dream or "distant remembering," which she describes as a "picture, unattainable for me, in the final analysis incomprehensible" (Dr 6). Photography can also capture the aura of landscapes in a remarkable web of time and space: resting on a summer afternoon, watching a mountain top on the horizon or a tree limb whose shadow falls onto the observer, until the moment itself merges with the mountain or the limb to become part of its existence is, to paraphrase Benjamin, the experience of aura.[10]

On this day, climbing up the wall of the ruins, Claudia subconsciously senses the aura, and this moment triggers her anxiety, her sudden fear of falling. She breaks out in a cold sweat, afraid to look down, inching her way back to

Henry, clutching him in a role-reversal of the dream sequence. Her fear is dispelled by their closeness, and the aura is preserved in Claudia as they walk through the forest—that is, until Henry's unexpected revelation that he is married, that he plans to visit his wife and children on Sunday. Claudia's humiliation and feeling of betrayal reverse what might have been her first steps toward letting down her defenses and expedites her denial: "I didn't want him anyway. I never intended to have him for myself. I had decided some time ago to never marry again, to never again concede even the smallest power over me to another person. . . . I was convinced that I could never allow myself to give up my distance to other people, so that I would not be deceived, so that I would not deceive myself" (Dr 50). Henry's curtly stated piece of biographical information has paralyzed her, left her frozen on the metaphorical bridge of the dream, unable to move forward or backward, unable to merge with others or to escape from her neurosis.

Later, after Henry's burial, she begins to be afraid of her photos. She had filled her drawers and closets with her prints of trees, scenery, grass, country lanes, and deadwood—"a soulless nature, which I created" (Dr 155). Perhaps her fear is that her photos possess an aura of their own to which she cannot remain interminably blind, an aura over which she has no control and which could stimulate associations in her memory in spite of their lifeless objectivity. After all, "trees don't lie."

Hein returns to the issue of photography in the seventh chapter as Claudia develops some film and thinks about Hinner. Her thoughts reveal that she had been frigid while with him. The fact that her diversion, or hobby, is a compensation for her fear of creative spontaneity is illustrated by her fascination with photographs as they develop on paper in the darkroom, "a germination I cause, direct, that I can interrupt" (Dr 76). This she contrasts with the two abortions she had undergone while still married to Hinner because, as she says, her pregnancies were a spontaneous, creative process over which she had no control: "A monstrous violation, one that would determine my entire future, a violation of my freedom" (Dr 77). Claudia again uses the word *Eingriff,* or "intrusion"—which I have translated as "violation" in this case—just as she has done in her reference to portrait photography.

The disappearance of spontaneous interaction between Claudia and others enables her to remain free, unattached, and private, covering her vulnerability with everyday trivia, secure in the unvarying fixational quality of life. Her attempt to escape dependency upon other people (and them on her, even though she is a doctor) or circumstances helps her, she surmises, to determine her own needs and to follow her own interests or inclinations without external direction or guidance. However, this course of action ends on a fatally discordant note: she is not free; she is isolated.

The tight narrative perspective never permits the view of anyone besides Claudia and seldom even permits quotes from other people to be related in her reports. This technique enables Hein to create an "aura of isolation" around his character, as Sändig aptly points out.[11] Claudia's dilettante artistic endeavors with photography ostensibly provide a form of therapy in her view. But "art is in this case simply a defunct ersatz, almost a neurosis," according to Bernd Fischer, who points out additionally that Claudia's life consists of nothing but "ersatz" material and "art is one of the most harmless" substitutions for reality.[12] Photography, without Claudia's disturbing dilettantism, would have functioned to re-create an aura of memory instead of isolation.

Violent Intrusions

After learning that Henry is married, Claudia runs through the forest and, as he catches her, she breaks into hysterical laughter, uncontrollable. Unable to calm her down, he finally throws her angrily to the ground, himself on top of her. The description of the forced sex in the forest combines associations with the vulnerable spots left by the linden leaf on Siegfried's back and Claudia's exclusion from aura and intimacy. Throughout the sex, she feels a tree root rubbing her in the small of the back, rubbing her raw, and she fixes her gaze on an overhead limb which casts a shadow on her. Her rage and despair dissolve into "sudden carnal desire, into the dancing leaves overhead, into Henry's panting, into the feeling of terminal loneliness" (Dr 52), into a self-betrayal she refuses to acknowledge. In spite of this incident in the forest, Claudia remains with Henry. She does not protest when he shows up to join her while she is on vacation. They continue to see each other, usually in her apartment, two or three times a week. Every two or three weeks Henry visits his wife and children in Dresden, and Claudia and he simply don't pry into each other's private life.

Several of Hein's texts portray the act of a rape which leaves the participants or the victims unchanged—to the reader's shock—and which functions as a symbol of political or psychological unchangeability. When Hein's characters react emotionally to unimportant events and fail to react to events which are destructive to the integrity of human identity, the discrepancy between values and misdirected egocentrism (or helpless inertia) is made clear. The perversion of sexuality is a common denominator with which Hein degrades the standing of characters and creates antipathy. The rape of the nun in *Ah Q* is superseded by an alleged theft which did not take place. The two violent sexual acts in *Horns Ende* establish symbolically the continuity between fascism and Stalinism.

In his short story "Die Vergewaltigung" (The Rape)—published, significantly, in *Neues Deutschland,* the GDR equivalent of *Pravda,* on 2–3 December 1989—Hein describes a woman's speech at a ceremony to consecrate into the Communist fold youths who had come of age. Ilona R., a sincere and successful woman, describes the selfless aid provided by the Red Army at the end of the war, praising the GDR-Russian friendship. Afterwards, her husband asked her why she hadn't mentioned the rape of her sixty-four-year-old grandmother by two Russian soldiers in August of 1945. Her grandmother had hidden Ilona from the soldiers and attempted to soothe her afterwards: "What are you silly hens crying about? Did I break my leg?" Ilona doesn't think it appropriate to mention the rape on initiation day. It might leave the wrong impression, and, anyway, that was in the past. Her husband says that, if such is the case, she shouldn't have told the other side of the story either—a remark which seems almost to cause her a nervous breakdown—and she reacts by accusing him of being a fascist. Public acknowledgment or narrations of atrocities of the Red Army at the end of the war remained strictly taboo until the policies of glasnost and perestroika in the Soviet Union resulted in disclosures from Soviet news media, disclosures that remained unwelcome in official circles in the GDR. The women (the nun in *Ah Q* is dead) do not report the rape; they fall silent and go on as they had before. The self-imposed silence provides the connection between life experience under Nazi and Stalinist regimes.

The first structural study of *The Distant Lover,* by Hannes Krauss (1991), uncovered the theme more clearly pursued in *Horns Ende:* Hein's contention that fascism and Stalinism were inexorably linked in the GDR, even if the impact was lessened by the absence of overt terrorism. Krauss compares Claudia's journey into the past to restore memory with Christa Wolf's description of the same in *Kindheitsmuster (Childhood Patterns).* Both Claudia and the narrator in Wolf's novel are traumatized by recollection of their mothers' intimidating sexual education, including warnings about sexually transmitted diseases, which had been calculated to make them feel dirty and to instill fear to encourage abstention. Sexual taboos are connected with political taboos most clearly in the learned silence which causes the loss of the ability "to ask questions and to articulate desires for change."[13] The runic symbols on the shirts of the five runners in Claudia's dream are emblems which have been reinvented in modern form by the Nazis in their "research" to trace pure Germanness back in time and which represent the sport fetishness shared by fascist and Stalinist regimes.

These clues and fragments themselves, according to Krauss, were an early attempt to break the personal silence of a GDR author about the silence of the victims of Stalinism—individuals who had been conditioned to such acquiescence by the forces of intimidation which existed in Germany during the Nazi period.

Turning Points from the Past

The novella has been worked into a refined art-form in Germany, and Goethe defined its structural requirements as those of a story containing an unheard of, or remarkable, event. Of the many refinements of the novella, one of the most characteristic is the inclusion of a peripety or turning point, an incident which unalterably, often fatalistically, changes the course of the character's life.[14] The turning point in *The Distant Lover* is generally considered to be the scene in the forest. It would have to be understood as an intentional and bitter-ironic "anti-turning point," however, inasmuch as the opportunity for Claudia to change her life is wasted by her acquiescence to the non-committal relationship with Henry. Still, she has embarked on a course for change, and this turning point interrupts and diverts that course permanently.

A final chance presents itself when Claudia, against the advice of Henry, decides to make a trip to the small town where she grew up, "a journey into the past" (Dr 95). There she remembers the unheard of events which took place in her life. The actual turning point of Claudia's life occurred when she was twelve years old, not too long after the stationing of a single Soviet tank in the center of her town as a consequence of the strikes of 17 June 1953. Hein enables the reader to calculate the dates of the story by having Claudia mention the introduction of daylight savings time, which occurred in the GDR in 1981. Since she is currently forty years old, she would have been twelve years old in 1953. June 17th is a well-known date in Germany, marking the day of the violent suppression by Soviet tanks of an uprising. The working class had rebelled at demands to increase productivity without added compensation, and the farmers in the countryside were not cooperating with the effort to proceed with the collectivization of agriculture.

The most crucial source of understanding for Claudia's later behavior can be traced directly back to her experience with the public reaction to the political events associated with 17 June: at school, nobody spoke about the presence of the Soviet tank in town, and at home, her father urged her to avoid the subject. Claudia couldn't understand why the issue was suppressed, but since the adults were resolutely silent, she realized that "even a conversation could be something threatening . . . I learned to keep quiet" (Dr 108). The public reflex mechanism to suppress rather than to confront was internalized into Claudia's private personality.

Her life was fundamentally determined by political pressures. As Sändig has pointed out, the "emotional reactions [to political pressures]—internalization of problems, learning to remain silent, fear experienced in catastrophic situations—have become habitual for Claudia."[15] By avoiding public authority, she is able to remain immune to inclinations to become actively involved.

Because of the religious orientation of Katharina and her family, Claudia is further pressured by her own parents and her teachers and classmates to dissolve her relationship with her best friend, with whom she had sworn eternal friendship and loyalty. Claudia's parents are afraid that her association with Katharina—she was interested in Katharina's religious beliefs as well—would result in reprimands which could prevent Claudia from staying in school. The situation becomes tense after Katharina's three brothers go to the West.

In October of the next year, the administration of the school, in consultation with county officials, comes to the conclusion that Katharina will have to leave school after completing the eighth grade. It "was inappropriate that she be allowed to attain the educational goals of an accredited high school in our Republic" (Dr 110). Katharina then incurs the displeasure of the class by refusing to join the socialist youth club, the FDJ, and is criticized and badgered by the teacher. Finally, Claudia denounces Katharina, making a joke about the "Christian-superstitious views of a certain student" (Dr 112). Claudia and her classmates are irritated at being held after class because of Katharina's "stubbornness," i.e., her refusal to compromise her values. Already in the beginning stages of avoidance and denial, they listen, bored and uninterested, to the worn-out phrases as the teacher equates Katharina's decision with warmongering. The class is not concerned about the issues at all, although the socialist tradition of enforced solidarity—the reason the others are kept after school repeatedly until the issue can be resolved—represents a key dialectic and existential problem in that society. For the students, it is not a matter of denouncing one of the brightest among them in order to subjugate her to the political collective; they simply want to go home and not have to listen to the teacher's harangues anymore.

Katharina responds to Claudia's denunciation by slapping her face. Claudia kicks her in the shin. Both girls receive a reprimand. Claudia's friendship with a girl "she had loved so unconditionally, as she would never again be able to love another human being" (Dr 113) is finished. On the psychological level,

Claudia is not only under pressure from peers and authorities. The situation has been worsened by problems which are fairly universal to puberty and the fragility of friendships in the eighth grade: Katharina becomes interested in the precentor's son, a development which leaves her with less time for Claudia. Claudia feels a strange alienation when Katharina talks about her boyfriend; pangs of jealousy have disrupted her feelings for Katharina.

Claudia quickly represses the trauma of having denounced this friend she has loved so unequivocally. When she learns that Katharina and her mother have followed her brothers to the West, she proudly announces to her parents that Katharina has betrayed the country. It is evident to the reader that Katharina is a principled but vulnerable young girl and that Claudia has betrayed her, a betrayal not altogether unlike the betrayal of Horn in *Horns Ende*.

The psychological mechanism Claudia finds for neutralizing her trauma—her escape into daily routine—carries over into her adult life, where she masks her private feelings in a similar way. Superficiality has become a safeguard. Even on the day of Henry's funeral, she reduces the issues involved in the decision of whether or not she should attend Henry's funeral to the superficial question whether or not she would wear her dark blue coat, which could pass for black. Thus she diverts her attention away from her emotions, avoiding the risk of going out on the precipice where she could experience herself intensely and possibly have an opportunity to grow.

A second part of the turning point in Claudia's life takes place shortly after her estrangement from Katharina, when she discovers that her own uncle Gerhard, a grandfather figure for her, stands accused of having denounced his colleagues in the Social Democratic party during the war. Claudia feels that she, as the niece of a "Nazi criminal," has lost the right to be shocked or indignant about the injustice of the Nazi regime or to feel sympathy for its victims.

From this point, the story begins a frenetic rush to the end, like water rushing down the drain. Claudia visits the head doctor at home, visits her parents, takes pictures, follows her routine, even perseveres in her routine when her elderly neighbor dies, resisting the temptation to get emotionally involved. When her sister shows up with her ex-husband during a visit with her parents, she feels no envy; thinking that they probably deserve each other, she does not share her mother's distress at the situation. She continues dating Henry. They make no demands on each other; they are always happy when they are together; they avoid complications. On 18 April, she learns that Henry has died.

He had gone into a bar for a drink. A couple of youths made fun of his felt hat. When one of them finally grabbed it, he stood up and went outside to fight. Henry had been a boxer in his youth. He danced around like a professional. The boys laughed at him. Then one of the young men punched him; maybe he had some sort of metal piece in his hand. Henry fell to the ground, dead. Claudia does not break up her daily routine when her relationship with the aloof and self-alienated Henry ends. After the brief interlude of spontaneity and hope that the liaison has given her, Claudia's attempt to come to grips with the past also ends. She returns to her normal, painless, lifeless condition of pragmatic nihilism, cleansing herself with a cathartic experience. At home after the funeral, she tries to think about what kind of a man Henry had been, but she cannot really form an opinion.

Henry had been wearing the felt hat when she met him; he always wore it. A few days after the burial, a friend brings the hat to her. Henry handed the friend the hat before the fight. As soon as the friend leaves, Claudia takes the hat into the hallway and tosses it down the garbage chute: "I can't be filling up my little apartment with old hats" (Dr 155).

Text and Subtext

Readers of the English translation of *The Distant Lover* should be aware that it often fails to convey the irony and cynicism of Claudia's thoughts and speech and to capture the everyday routine of GDR life. The translator's language sometimes preempts the communicative process between the text and the reader, leading the reader into secure areas when it should have left things fragmented—a practice that would have allowed the reader to develop his or her own interpretive continuity of meaning. The *New York Times* review, superficial in scope, to be sure, referred to Claudia as a "competent" (but without compassion) professional, as a "dutiful" (but indifferent) daughter, and as a "courteous recipient of other people's confidences and untidy concerns."[16] Claudia's professional competence, dutifulness, and courteousness are all called into question in the text—a fact indicating that the American reader can be mislead by the translation. The translation was troublesome from the beginning, the rights having been sold to a British publisher who then relinquished them to Pantheon Press. Hein had no control over the translation, and the negotiations had taken place by the time he came to New York in 1987. He was pleased with Pantheon—before the small literary press was redirected to publish books of lesser quality, which sold more copies—and enjoyed an excellent relationship with Sara Bershtel, the senior editor and the driving force behind getting *The Distant Lover* published in English.[17] The translator, however, experienced considerable difficulty with the text, mistranslating a surprising number of words and phrases in the first draft and struggling to get the style under control. Bershtel realized that the style and use of language was absolutely essential for the success of the book and subjected the text to extensive editing. The manuscript took two years before it was ready to go to press, but it never reached the level of Hein's original and did not sell as well as could be expected when measured by its success in the languages of some forty other countries, a success which was by no means limited to academic and intellectual circles. The English translation is now out of print.

The difficulty lies in the communication of the subtext employed by Hein, who had modelled his use of subtext somewhat after Anton Chekov, of whose dramas he noted: "It is quite wonderful how the figures say something and the audience notices that they simultaneously are saying something else."[18] For his own part, Hein frequently pointed out that *The Distant Lover* was written with consistent use of subtext: "The figure states I feel well and every reader understands that she feels bad."[19] Chekov and Georg Büchner, for Hein, were capable of tossing out a half-sentence which would tear open a complete universe of meaning. The same is true for Picasso's paintings, "when he makes something with two or three strokes and one still has the feeling something is missing. Quite the contrary, it is absolutely finished, and one almost sees something more than he had painted. But he painted that along with it: this subtext or this un-painted portion is also painted in."[20] All of this writing technique certainly doesn't facilitate a translator's task, but the problems are not only to be found in the language of the text. Hein, who continually maintained that *The Distant Lover* was a GDR story for him, was initially surprised at its success abroad, in other German speaking countries as well as in Eastern and Western Europe and in South America. He attributes this success largely to what must be a reflection of the status of civilization in industrialized nations in the book, something which transcends political and cultural differences.

A Twentieth-Century Phenomenon

Both West German (*Die Zeit*) and American (*New York Times*) reviewers claimed that Claudia's self-alienation and ultimate incapacity for intimate relationships is a phenomenon of late twentieth-century urban life which occurs in cities like West Berlin or New York. Although this may be accurate, especially in terms of the structure of Claudia's personality and the description of her behavior, the details of Claudia's biography and the specific elements which lead to her state of mind are closely linked with the social and political circumstances associated with life in the GDR, especially between 1950 and 1980.

The reaction of East German reviewers, for example, centered around the disturbing question as to "whether this story is supposed to be the description of a general condition of our society."[21] This was a cultural-political question as much as anything, with implications for censorship practices as well, for Hein had not included a positive contra-figure, a hope for a social solution to the human condition embodied by Claudia. The answers, both pro and con, have generated heated discussion about the book, including charges that the story is not realistic—people can't turn out to be like Claudia in the socialist system— that the story is missing the promise of a social corrective.[22] But the outpour of mail Hein received, the majority of which came from female readers, attested that the story had struck a nerve in readers. Many people seemed to detect a bit of Claudia in themselves, and Hein was made uneasy when some of these women asked him for advice about how to conduct or change their lives. A large number of letter writers and critics both questioned and lauded his ability, as a male author, to probe so deeply into a woman's subjectivity.

By the 1980s, Western readers were not likely to be conscious of any blueprint for an enlightened and humane utopian society of the future which would also serve to fulfill a political mandate, to be applied collectively and universally by and for the population of a given country. In the GDR, the non-existence of the utopia was subsumed under the term "real existing socialism," which constituted the given current stage of development towards real socialism. This logic depends on the acceptance of utopia as a valid goal orientation. With such a postulate, whatever stage society finds itself to be in can be justified, regardless of the quality of life it happens to impose on its members.

It was difficult to get through school in East Germany without forming some commitment to the realization of ideals which measured progress towards the utopian ideal. The natural idealism of youth lends itself to an acceptance of these kinds of commitments, a fact which one should keep in mind when reading the passages in all of Hein's works that describe different, petty, and self-centered sources of motivation for action taken by his characters. Even though the population eventually came to view the socialist utopian concept with deep cynicism, it is an ideal which would have been an integral part of Claudia's education and that of Hein's readers in the GDR. Claudia's personality is influenced by a variety of occurrences in GDR everyday life. These forces negatively affect the development of her personality and alter her assumption of what her social and political responsibilities should be.

Her altered state terminates the possibility of the social corrective—a fact which GDR reviewers writing in state-controlled journals professed to have missed. In 1983 and until about 1988, the reviewers would have been required by their superiors to write some dogmatic criticism as a prerequisite to publish other, more positive and literary-critical oriented comments. Failure to accept such a commission could result in a demotion.

Many East German readers understood that controlled behavior and the restriction of creative thought can both mirror and cause social stagnation. The impoverishment of Claudia's personality and the alienation predominant in her everyday communication manifest a danger to social emancipation itself. The "Catch-22" dilemma in such a society is the circular argument that (independent) individuals are harmful to social progress and (collective) social progress is harmful to individuals.

Since the topic of alienation is familiar to readers of Sarte, Camus, Kafka, and contemporary American writers, it might be best to focus more on those aspects of *The Distant Lover* which anchor Claudia's experiences in the GDR and support Hein's claim that it is a "GDR story." Whether the text represents a condemnation of the politics of the GDR at that time is not the only issue at stake for a writer of Hein's stature; evidently conditions in other, Western societies could have had a similar alienating effect on a person like Claudia. Hein probes the specific conditions he knew contributed to Claudia's state of being and the subconscious blocking of contact with other people that it causes. Those conditions were created in the GDR by the Stalinist regime of Walter Ulbricht and continued after Stalin's death in 1953 in spite of initial efforts in the Soviet Union by Nikita Kruschev to reform the political structure and to do away with terror. Accepting 1953 as the turning point in Claudia's life and in the novella itself provides an important structural connection between the theme of alienation and the historical context. As can be seen in most of Hein's works, his modus operandi usually consists of incorporating history within the aesthetic framework of his writing.

Notes

1. Peter C. Pfeiffer, "Tote und Geschichte(n): Christoph Heins *Drachenblut* und *Horns Ende*," *German Studies Review* 16.1 (1993): 22.
2. Brigitte Sändig, "Zwei oder drei fremde Helden," *Sinn und Form* 45.4 (1993): 666.
3. Sändig 668.
4. See Bernd Schick's contribution to "Für und Wider," *Weimarer Beiträge* 29.9 (1983): 1634–1655. He sees parallels between Kerouac's Dean Moriarty in *On the Road* and Henry.
5. Pfeiffer 22.
6. The wedding portrait of Claudia and Hinner at her mother's house reminds her that they were once two "helpless, shy revolutionaries" (Dr 74) radiating hope and

the will to destroy the old order and improve social conditions. Hein does not explore what caused Claudia's transition from anarchy to apathy during the marriage, although her aversion to having children is linked with the failure of the marriage. The energy to change has been reduced to contempt and cynicism.

7. See Brigitte Böttcher, "Diagnose eines unheilbaren Zustandes," *Neue Deutsche Literatur* 31.6 (1983): 147f.

8. Bernd Fischer, "Christoph Heins 'fremde Freundin,'" *Chronist ohne Botschaft. Christoph Hein. Ein Arbeitsbuch. Materialien, Auskünfte, Bibliographie*, ed. Klaus Hammer (Berlin: Aufbau, 1992) 98.

9. See Walter Benjamin, "Das Kunstwerk im Zeitalter seiner technischen Reproduzierbarkeit," in his *Das Kunstwerk im Zeitalter seiner technischen Reproduzierbarkeit. Drei Studien zur Kunstsoziologie* (Frankfurt a.M.: Suhrkamp, 1977) 21.

10. See Walter Benjamin, "Kleine Geschichte der Photographie," in his *Das Kunstwerk im Zeitalter seiner technischen Reproduzierbarkeit*, 57.

11. Sändig 666.

12. Fischer, "Christoph Heins 'fremde Freundin'" 103.

13. Hannes Kraus, "Mit geliehenen Worten das Schweigen brechen. Christoph Heins Novelle *Drachenblut*," *Text + Kritik* 111, ed. Heinz Ludwig Arnold (Munich: Text + Kritik, 1991) 23.

14. Other traditional elements associated with the novella which are evident in *The Distant Lover* include the objective style of reporting with no intrusion by the author and the meshing of dramatic and narrative techniques. The "unheard of event," as spoken by Goethe to Eckermann 25 January 1827, is the existence of Claudia herself, a kind of person unheard of in the GDR socialist state.

15. Sändig 669.

16. Katharine Washburn, "A Confessor at the Funeral," *New York Times Book Review* 7 May 1989: 33.

17. See Hein's "Brief an Sara, New York," *Als Kind habe ich Stalin gesehen* 184–98, written in diary form describing Hein's daily reactions to the opening of the Berlin Wall and the events thereafter from 9 November to 20 November 1989.

18. Christoph Hein, interview, "'Dialog ist das Gegenteil von Belehren.' Gespräch mit Christoph Hein," *Chronist ohne Botschaft* 28.

19. Hein, interview, "Dialog ist das Gegenteil von Belehren" 28.

20. Hein, interview, "Dialog ist das Gegenteil von Belehren" 28.

21. Hans Kaufmann, "Christoph Hein in der Debatte," in his *Über DDR-Literatur. Beiträge aus fünfundzwanzig Jahren* (Berlin: Aufbau, 1986) 235.

22. See "Für und Wider," *Weimarer Beiträge* 29.9 (1983): 1634–1655.

CHAPTER THREE

The Museum of History: *Horns Ende*

As a boy of twelve, Thomas remembers standing in front of a triptychon mirror, making faces at himself and trying to see all three images of himself simultaneously. Squinting and turning his head sideways, he tries to see a scattering of many images. Thirty years later, he is haunted by the memory of Horn, a man whom he and a school friend had discovered hanging from a tree in the forest outside of town. It is an apparition which continually admonishes and exhorts him to remember what had happened—even to remember, if he can, some things which he hadn't seen. Only through the efforts of Thomas's memory can the circumstances surrounding Horn's life and death be kept alive and not be relegated to the silence of the stones.

The triptychon provides the unusual structural basis for this controversial novel. The mirror images in Thomas's eyes reflect the shattering of history into thousands of shards, creating the potential for unlimited perspectives about what is veracity and what is falsification. In *Horns Ende,* 1985 (Horn's End), Hein expanded the single narrative perspective so skillfully employed in *The Distant Lover* to include five separate individuals, four of whom relate the end of Horn from his or her own subjective point of view—each responding like a witness in a hearing, none able to provide a very clear picture about what specifically happened to Horn. As is the case with Claudia, each one reveals more about himself or herself than about Horn. But each one also reveals the historical milieu of developments in East Germany which affect all the characters, socially and psychologically influencing their progress into the present. A set of varying historical perspectives, which are at issue in this work, is related simultaneously in a multi-layered historical context: the Nazi period, the socialist rebuilding of the GDR in the 1950s—the focal point of the story—and the narrative present, in the case of this novel, the early 1980s.

Thomas's task is to burst open the continuity of history in Walter Benjamin's sense, to grasp a fragment from a "past loaded with the present time"[1] in order to "bring the present into a critical localization."[2] Benjamin, according to Hein, would not have accepted the notion of a *Stunde Null* (zero hour), the concept applied to the time in German history which began when the war was over (1945)—a concept which endorses forgetting and which, incidentally, experienced a rebirth in 1989 with the fall of the Wall and the end of the cold war.[3] Convergences from the past which disrupt basic continuity are established within the framework of three differing "philosophies" of history: those of Dr. Spodeck (cynicism), of Krushkatz (historical necessity), and of Horn himself—although he never narrates his point of view—(factual). The infinite number of images produced by Thomas's squinting in front of the mirror suggests an infinite number of ways to portray or interpret history.

Horn himself, who was denounced by his colleague Kruschkatz when both were still faculty members in the department of history at the University of Leipzig, represents the victimization of the many prominent intellectuals who attempted in good faith to democratize the socialist movement in the 1950s. Kruschkatz's second denunciation of Horn leads to his disturbing suicide, a "sacrificial death," as the former GDR Germanist Klaus Hammer called it in 1987, "in protest against a dogmatic historical determinism."[4] The suicide is also vaguely reminiscent of the real Johannes Heinz Horn, a Leipzig philosopher who hanged himself in a forest outside of town 8 January 1958, and whose fate was not mentioned publicly in Leipzig afterwards. Horn's tenure book, *Wiederspiegelung und Begriff* (Reflection and Concept), completed and defended in 1956, was published posthumously in 1958 by his widow with a generally positive foreword by his academic assistant, Johannes Förster—who nevertheless, and in all likelihood as an obligation insisted upon by his superiors, criticized Horn for drifting into bourgeois formalism (i.e., for failing to refer explicitly to the "superiority" of socialist dogma) on two issues and thus violating the party's monopoly on theories of knowledge, rather than remaining strictly within the concepts of Marxist-Leninist historical materialism.

Despite this indication of a connection to the historical Horn, it should be kept in mind that Hein explicitly rejected any direct relationship between his fictional character and the historical Horn in an interview with the Polish Germanist Krzystof Jachimczak in 1986 in conjunction with the translation of the novel into Polish. The real Horn, according to Hein, "had a completely different philosophical conception than Horn the historian,"[5] his title figure. Hein refers to a distant relationship, one which has something to do with the existence and the death of the real Horn, without its being a question of identity or identification with the title figure. Hein creates a new reality, an artistic reality in which Horn's function is to provide a metaphor for the social and political contradictoriness of the period of time framed within the novel.

Each of the eight chapters of the novel opens with a short exchange between the voice or apparition of Horn and the grown Thomas, the son of the town pharmacist, who was about eleven or twelve years old at the time of Horn's death. These passages are set off in small print in the GDR edition and in italics in the West German edition. Thomas fitfully resists Horn's urging not to let the past slip away and, indeed, provides only a relatively small portion of the re-membrance—but a crucial part since, due to his youth, he is the only link to a present that will extend into the future. For Thomas—and, by implication, for the (East German) reader—these memories rest "like a nightmare on his soul."[6] The same can be said of Kruschkatz, who is troubled by real nightmares, and of Spodeck.

The principle narrators include Dr. Spodeck, whose Nazi father had bought him a physician's praxis in Guldenberg, the village where the events of the 1950s take place; Kruschkatz, whose political career brought him to Bad Guldenberg for nineteen years as a party functionary and as the mayor; Gertrude Fischlinger, Horn's landlady in Bad Guldenberg, who struggles to run her shop alone and loses control of her son; and Marlene Gohl, the mentally impaired daughter of the local museum artist and restoration technician. They each take turns describing events, people, and themselves during the months before and after Horn's suicide, providing the (incomplete) historical and psychological exegesis for Horn's suicide.

The historical structure is woven into the narrative with their reports. Spodeck's story links the townspeople with Germany's Nazi past. Kruschkatz portrays both the oppressive nature of the socialist state being built in East Germany as well as the attempt to extricate East Germany from the past and to create a positive alternative. Gertrude Fischlinger represents the plight of the working class and the crudeness of lingering patriarchical attitudes. Marlene Gohl's story provides an unsettling link between the dark side of the German past and the present, demonstrating a German historical continuity which was officially discounted in the GDR and which was and continues to be problem-atical for West Germans and unified Germany as well.

Hein's novel is put together like a mosaic. Dr. Spodeck, Thomas, Kruschkatz, and Gertrude Fischlinger present a fragmented, non-chronological narrative in each of the eight chapters, creating a four-way balance in the structure which requires some attention by the reader to sort out the different perspectives. The mortar for these narrative pieces is the appearance of the Gypsies at the begin-ning of the novel. Actually, the Gypsies come each year around May, camping on the outskirts of town and loaning horses to the area farmers. However, this year they leave after Horn's death and never come back again, a fact which creates an impression of disquieting closure on the townspeople, who are por-trayed as having a racist attitude towards the Gypsies.

The other important revelation in the narrative—besides the political back-ground that seems to cause Horn's suicide—is the prejudice and latent Nazi attitudes which cause the tragedy of the Gohl family, revealed near the end of the novel when the reader learns that Marlene Gohl's mother had tricked Nazi police who came to take Marlene away towards the end of the war into believ-ing that she was Marlene. This cost her her life, and Marlene and Herr Gohl have lived alone and withdrawn from the townspeople since that time.

Although Hein regards himself as a chronicler and *Horns Ende* is clearly a historical novel, there is no beginning, explanatory narrative, and end. Chronol-ogy is less important than the diversity of understanding. It is not possible, for example, to single out all the passages narrated by Dr. Spodeck, whose reports both open and close the novel, and arrive at a clear impression of what the novel is about. Each narrator's contribution is necessary, and even then, the reader is left with a great deal of implied but unspoken text, and with the temptation to speculate about or to research the historical background. Spodeck, Kruschkatz, and Fischlinger tell the story of Horn. Fischlinger, who narrates two passages in chapter five, tells the story of Marlene Gohl, and in retrospect, it seems to be no accident that she, as the only unbiased adult in the story, is the only person who does so. All four of them have something to say about the Gypsies. Thomas usually narrates from the perspective of a twelve-year-old boy, one who would have been much too young to understand any context of the events which oc-curred in the 1950s or to comprehend the depth and complexity of the attitudes of the adults around him.

From Thomas we learn something about what kind of person Herr Gohl is, about Thomas's father, the pharmacist, and about other children. But Thomas's brief contact with Horn in the museum reveals that he knows very little of Horn. Thomas narrates twice in chapter three and three times in chapter four, giving him the most to say but still offering the least amount of concrete information for the benefit of the reader's understanding. Marlene Gohl's intensely intro-spective and highly poetical passages are limited to chapters two, four, and seven only.

There is more to the narrative technique: reading Hein's first full length novel is like observing an archeologist painstakingly fitting the shattered pieces of an ancient urn back together, just as Horn and Herr Gohl seem to be doing with their work in the town museum. Unlike in *The Distant Lover,* where the reader is drawn by the rhythmic quality of the prose to rush to the end of the book, one is forced here to proceed slowly, meticulously, to study the pieces and fragments of the puzzle as it is being assembled—presumably with occa-sional inaccuracies due to human error—by its five narrators. The result is a provocative fragment, and we are left to fill in the missing parts, those lost forever, with our own thoughts, and to contemplate whether the future is best served by digging up the past or by forgetting it.

Each ensuing generation, according to one recollection of statements by Horn himself, will assimilate whatever fragmented information is available, complete with factual errors or deliberate falsifications, and then create its own image of history anew. In this novel, Hein questions the ability of human beings to relate history with truth or accuracy. Each generation's attitude or partisan reaction towards history becomes substantially more significant than history itself in formulating consciousness. Since political history is written by the conquerors, a factual knowledge of the events—let alone some modicum of objectivity in the attitude of people towards historical developments—is difficult to come by.

Kruschkatz and Horn: Dangers of Forgetting and Remembering

Kruschkatz is the last of the four principal witnesses to begin his commentary, but by this time, his character has been seriously tarnished for the reader by Spodeck's short opening description of Kruschkatz's obesity and his self-ridiculing attempt to convince the Gypsies to vacate the meadow in the middle of town where they had camped. Spodeck even imagines Kruschkatz's death with great pleasure, thinking how, in his capacity as a doctor, he might prolong Kruschkatz's suffering by keeping him alive as long as possible, causing the reader to think that Kruschkatz probably deserves to suffer. As he had done in *The Distant Lover,* Hein takes advantage of the reader's natural inclination to form alliances with and against fictional characters by taking statements at face value. Hence, when it is Kruschkatz's turn, the reader expects to dislike the character and to be suspicious of what he has to say.

Kruschkatz is an opportunistic Communist bureaucrat who is painted as a monster by the others. For Hein, Kruschkatz became the most interesting character and the most suspenseful and challenging to write about. After providing the reader with a strong predisposition to antipathy, Hein took it upon himself to work against this prejudice by developing Kruschkatz into a complex individual personality. According to Hein, the "reader has a picture of a disgusting, obese, sweaty, obnoxious and opportunistic party bureaucrat. And then I put all my energy and affection into this figure, in order to make it into a human being . . . in order to show the human side of this monstrosity of a bureaucrat which the others had characterized."[7]

For his part, Kruschkatz's first comments demonstrate his annoyance about the fact that people still bring up Horn after all these years. To him, a good memory can be equated with sleepless nights, and sleepless nights can be dangerous to the mental well-being of the unfortunate insomniac. Every factual detail of Horn's case could probably be dredged up, but to what end? Speaking as a seventy-three-year-old pensioner, he reports that he can sum up his attitude towards the past, which he refers to as the culmination of his "life's experience," with a simple statement: "There is no such thing as history. History is a helpful metaphysics, used to reconcile us with the idea of our own mortality. . . . for no matter how many little building blocks from a past time we assemble, we order these small shards and faded fotos and breathe life into them with our own breath, distort them with the reason of our stupid brains and therefore misunderstand thoroughly" (HE 24). Unlike Horn, who believes that such fragments afford the only opportunity to know, Kruschkatz is convinced that people will not understand anything; they will only alter the meaning of the words he uses to describe his history by animating it with their own lives. It is therefore useless to attempt to understand what has transpired in the past.

Kruschkatz's rejection of the usefulness of history does not prevent him from doing his part to recount the past, but if all of his narration is put together in a single sequence, several things become evident. His principle purpose is to justify his own past actions with respect to Horn and to assuage his guilt. He makes the effort to remember "only in order to understand something about what others might presumptuously define as his life" (HE 25). However, he clearly never attempts to think about what Horn's perspective might have been, nor are there any direct conversations between him and Horn other than during Horn's appearance in the mayor's office to conduct museum business. Tight-lipped in his refusal to shake Kruschkatz's hand, Horn will have nothing to do with him beyond the minimum necessary. Although he is in a position to know Horn better than anyone else, he does little to inform the reader about Horn's life. Finally, Kruschkatz describes what appear to be genuine but largely unsuccessful efforts to improve the social and human situation in Bad Guldenberg and to overcome the corrupt provincial politics of the place.

Kruschkatz recalls precisely that the Gypsies appeared on 23 May, a Thursday, and that children (Thomas and Gertrude Fischlinger's son, Paul) had discovered Horn in the forest on 1 September, a Sunday. He disputes the connection made later between the disappearance of the Gypsies that autumn and Horn's death. Horn dies because that is his fate, and the Gypsies leave town just as they have done every other year previously. However, the fact that they never return after Horn's death causes the townspeople to make a connection that is really only a coincidence as Kruschkatz sees it and is anything but a coincidence as the reader sees it. Horn was a dissident, discredited and disgraced. The townpeople failed to defend or support him although they knew his transgressions were absurd. The mysterious disappearance of the aura-laden Gypsies seems to demonstrate that they sensed a revival of attitudes similar to those which caused their disappearance during the Nazi period. Hein himself had witnessed the Gypsies appearing in and then leaving Bad Düben and, as he has stated, he is simply describing something from his own his childhood.[8] There had been no explanation for the fact that they never returned again.

In *Horns Ende,* the Gypsies arouse the racial prejudice of the townspeople, and their disappearance, presumably, is directly connected to this. The city elders certainly are anxious to have them leave and are willing to use force, if necessary. According to Hammer, the Gypsies' very presence in the town questions the citizens' probity. They inject an incomprehensible alien presence into the "narrowminded and oppressive petty-bourgeoisie,"[9] disturbing the complacent flow of time by virtue of their identity as an ethnic group that had been persecuted by the Nazis.

Kruschkatz relates his visit to the Gypsies as a pure formality undertaken to placate the town elders and to avoid criticism from them for not acting. He knows that the Gypsies won't move, and he is satisfied to let them stay for the summer as they have always done. After the unsuccessful attempt, Bachofen, Kruschkatz's ambitious and antagonistic assistant mayor, urges him to send the police out to have them removed. Krushkatz refuses, and this begins a long intrigue by Bachofen to find something on Kruschkatz that would enable the city council to force him to resign, just as they have done with numerous previous mayors. Kruschkatz's position with regard to Bachofen and to his predecessor, Franz Schneeberger, is perhaps his one redeeming feature.

By contrast, Kruschkatz is willing to condemn Horn at the party commission's hearings in Leipzig in spite of the fact that he personally feels that Horn, "from a subjective standpoint, could not be ascribed any guilt" (HE 30). Although the details of Horn's transgression are left unclear, for the commission and for Kruschkatz, it is a question of *Parteilichkeit,* the principle of unity and solidarity with the socialist party line and with party interests that everyone is required to follow without criticism. Perceived contraventions against *Parteilichkeit* could lead to one's being expelled from the party or to demotion, and obviously opened the door to abuse and excess, both of which are sharply criticized in Hein's book.

Communist party dogma permitted substantial potential for abuse based on the arbitrary manipulation of the concept of *Parteilichkeit.* There can only be "bourgeois or socialist ideology," according to Lenin: "There can be no compromise here. Therefore every depreciation of socialist ideology, each deviation from its principles is an act of strengthening bourgoeisie ideology."[10] Groups of intellectuals who sought to work with alternative forms of socialism would be accused of sectarianism under this principle, and historians like Horn, who were unwilling to distort factual history in order to present events in a light ideologically favorable to socialism, would be reprimanded, expelled from the party, and assigned to a lesser, sometimes even degrading position. Horn thus lost his job on the university faculty and was "reassigned" to what amounts to demeaning work.

Kruschkatz, a friend and colleague of Horn's, must conform at the time of the party hearing in order to maintain his own loyal standing. The socialist structure thus practiced forced many thousands of people to make choices between friends or even family and party loyalty in order to preserve their careers. As can be well imagined, those who chose the party were despised by the population at large, inasmuch as basic human values of friendship and family could not be subjected to such injury without great cost—and ultimately great loss of credibility. This aspect of Kruschkatz's background does not seem to be a problem for most of the townspeople of Bad Guldenberg, but they do resent the fact that the authorities sent a party functionary (Kruschkatz) from the city (Leipzig) to preside over their affairs.

Kruschkatz's wife, Irene, reluctantly joins him in Bad Guldenberg, and he futilely promises to not let her be buried in such a nest. Kruschkatz, it would appear, must have also been "demoted" to mayor of a small town from his fairly prestigious position in Leipzig as a historian. Perhaps it is less of a coincidence than he thinks when he discovers Horn living in the same town.

Kruschkatz provides the reader with a sketch of his career path. He never had an influential uncle or a father with the right family connections and therefore began at the bottom, working his way up step by step. He attributes his success to the fact that he never made a (political) mistake. The choices he would have made between friendships and career to avoid "mistakes" discredit him in the eyes of the GDR public.

Kruschkatz hadn't realized that the office of mayor of a small town was to become a dead-end street for him. He thought it was simply another step, another level on his way to the top. He winds up living in Guldenberg for nineteen years—his wife dying of cancer after fifteen years. She used to go to the Thursday historical discussion sessions on the museum artifacts which Horn conducted for a small group in town, including Thomas's parents and Gohl. Kruschkatz realizes that Horn's suicide had somehow cost him his beautiful wife, whom he cherished and loved, and who was a supporter of Horn's point of view.

Shortly after Horn's death, Kruschkatz is lying in bed with his wife, caressing her with desire. She sits up and turns on the lamp and tells him, "I never would have believed it could have possibly come to this, but you nauseate me" (HE 53). These stunning words follow Kruschkatz interminably. He continues to love Irene, and she does not refuse his sexual advances, enduring his passionate embraces apathetically for years until, towards the end of his life, he discovers that he has begun to nauseate himself.

The thought of his wife's rejection causes Kruschkatz to provide the reader with a little more information on the incident in Leipzig. What happened was unfair to Horn, and Kruschkatz admits his part in it. But for Kruschkatz, the denunciation of Horn still constitues a higher moral, one which outweighs what is just and unjust, or at least reduces them to questionable value. It had been "an historically necessary injustice in the name of a greater justice, in the name of History" (HE 69). Horn, in Kruschkatz's view, could see only that his scholarly career was ruined; he was never able to understand that this was less important than the collective progress of socialist principles. As Kruschkatz saw it, Horn was unfit for society—the implication for the reader being that social survival depends on a willingness to sacrifice integrity or to compromise values in order to conform to political demands imposed by the party.

Kruschkatz reports on the fifth anniversary of the museum, which took place in March 1957. Horn's speech at this occasion, described without specific detail as a dry, boring explanation of recent archeological finds from an ancient Sorbian settlement (an ethnic minority still living in the Lusatian area of Germany near Dresden), is interpreted by Kruschkatz as a disguised treatise digging up something completely different: Horn's expulsion from the party in Leipzig.

In his speech, Horn pronounces judgment on Kruschkatz in the name of some private, abstract law, as Kruschkatz interprets it. Kruschkatz is not about to let this pass without a self-serving response and, indeed, gives a short speech of his own, likewise disguised around comments about an ancient society. He argues that each organized society must defend itself against its enemies, and in so doing, it sometimes also victimizes innocent individuals. Using a word from the rhetoric of the French revolution, he says, demagogically, that this is the "blood-toll which pays for progress" (HE 73). It does no good to take such tragic happenstances personally. It is better to not disturb the dead. The archaeologists of some future era can dig up the graves after this part of history has completed its cycle. Kruschkatz's view of history is the dialectical opposite of

Horn's concept. Remembering and forgetting are a conceptual pair in daily life for Hein: "Remembering in order to not permit forgetting"[11] is essential to overcome the suppression of misdeeds or misconduct from the past. *Verdrängung* is a word also applied in Germany to describe a national symptom of forgetting in order to not be reminded of the past—in the German case, the guilt and shame of the Nazi past. For the dead Horn—whom Kruschkatz does not wish to disturb—memory is the only possibility for the continuation of the values and the factual truth he represents. As Klaus Hammer has pointed out, the memory of Horn constitutes a burden for Kruschkatz, a nightmare.[12]

Later in his narrative, Kruschkatz gets around to mentioning some of the circumstances surrounding Horn's second hearing. The hearing took place in Horn's office in the museum with a lieutenant and two comrades in civilian clothes—all three would have been Stasi. When asked why he had trusted Horn so long and why he had not himself reprimanded Horn for his speeches and activities in the museum, Kruschkatz answers in the self-degrading language of capitulation to save his own neck: "It was a mistake, comrade. I underestimated the enemy. But I not only disappointed you, I am also deeply disappointed with myself. And I think I have learned a valuable lesson. Thanks to your help, comrades" (HE 75).

Afterwards, Kruschkatz excogitates that he had actually spoken the truth about Horn, but he nevertheless can't help but feel that he has defiled himself. Horn is sitting outside the room, and Kruschkatz walks past him without a word, embarrassed, but quickly rationalizing to himself that he has done all he can for Horn, that Horn will still feel himself unjustly accused and will not survive the second inquisition. Kruschkatz, however, will survive.

The events leading up to Horn's second arrest were precipitated by Bachofen, who rushes excitedly into Kruschkatz's office on 4 July with "incriminating" evidence against Horn. A document authored by Horn contains a short, vague historical-philosophical chronicle of the little castle which houses the museum, including references to how the "Wenden" had driven out the "Hermunduren," "Warnen," and "Düringer." The latter are pre-Christian Germanic tribes, and *Wenden* is the old Germanic term for Slavic tribes. It is unclear to what exactly Horn is referring, although his comments could be taken as fragmentary revelations of some actions taken by the conquering Red Army as it swept into Germany with a brutal vengeance. They could also refer to the loss of German territory to Poland after the war and the relocation of German citizens who had lived there. The latter circumstance was a forbidden topic of discussion in East Germany (it was the source of heated debate for about two decades in the Federal Republic), and many Red Army atrocities, as we have seen, were deemed best left covered up in view of the proclaimed eternal fraternity with the Soviet Union, a policy with which Kruschkatz agrees. This policy is again a practical application of the historical viewpoint which holds that the past should be forgotten in order for society to proceed unencumbered into the future. For Horn, it would be simply a matter of setting the record straight, as factually complete as possible, to create a more complete picture of history. Kruschkatz, after reading the document, condemns it as a "sorry banner of a fruitless, exhausted humanism" (HE 101), echoing party language directed at what it regarded as Western, bourgeois humanistic principles, which run counter to Marxist logic and which can only delay the inevitable onrushing world revolution.

We only have Kruschkatz's narration of the incident, a perspective which pointedly leaves the reader in the dark about the specific details of what Horn has written—just as does Kruschkatz's summary of Horn's speech at the museum and his vague references to the incident in Leipzig. We never learn anything more about them. Kruschkatz is, of course, the only witness available, but Thomas had been in the museum on that day, having sneaked away from home, where he had been confined as punishment.

Thomas manages to sneak up to the door of Horn's office and peer through the keyhole. He can see Horn but cannot hear him; he can hear someone asking him questions but not Horn's answers. He can see only a facial expression of agitation and a wounded spirit. Horn is asked about Marianne Brockmeier, his sister. Does she live in West Germany? Has she left the Republic illegally? Does he have any contact with his sister? Has he met her abroad? And finally, "For whom are you working, Horn?" (HE 224). These important shards of information comprise all that we learn about the hearing.

Bachofen had already supplied the viewpoint of the investigating committee at the time of his denunciation of Horn. Aware that Kruschkatz would prefer not to be forced to deal with the issue, Bachofen is adamant: "Horn is promulgating revisionism, sectarianism. He wants to drag us into discussions about an epoch we have already overcome. It is a regressive discussion of mistakes under the guise of objective science" (HE 102). At the same time, Bachofen admits that he hired Alfred Brongel as an informer to keep an eye on Horn at the museum and that Brongel brought him the incriminating document.

Two weeks later, Bachofen and Brongel find additional documents and send them directly to the district authorities without informing Kruschkatz. This puts Kruschkatz in an awkward position. He had no other choice, he says, in order not to put himself in jeopardy, than to welcome the disciplinary action against Horn and to wholeheartedly support the comrades conducting the hearing. The price he pays for his political loyalty, as we know from his wife's nausea, is to jeopardize and permanently damage his life, which itself becomes part of the "blood toll" of a perverted, monstrous "progress."

Bachofen's accusation contains language similar to that of Kruschkatz's response to Horn's speech in the museum: Horn has transgressed the principle of *Parteilichkeit*. He has been exposed as "a typical representative of the petite bourgeoisie and his lack of faith in the power of the working class and their party had caused him to make concessions to bourgeois ideology and, in chorus with other liberal twaddle, to demand a so-called expansion of democracy" (HE 104). Kruschkatz realizes that he has seriously underestimated Bachofen, which compels him to clarify to the reader why he felt obligated (to save his own hide) to make the self-degrading confession. And at this point, he again repeats to himself the devastating words of Irene, spoken exactly two months after Horn's body was found: "I never could have imagined it. You nauseate me" (HE 107). Irene fulfills the same narrative function for Kruschkatz in this novel that Katharina does for Claudia in *The Distant Lover.* Hein's juxtaposition of Kruschkatz's statements—that his actions were justified and he nauseates his wife—bursts open the barrier of principled forgetting with which Kruschkatz attempts to shield himself, exposing not only Kruschkatz but, more importantly, the dangers of suppressing memory and history.

Later, Kruschkatz recollects a house call by Dr. Spodeck when Irene was ill and the conversation they had afterwards over a glass of wine. Spodeck and Kruschkatz always let each other know what they think of one another. Spodeck repeatedly tells Kruschkatz that he is killing his wife, that Irene needs to live in the city. Kruschkatz responds seriously, telling him there's more to it than that. He can't allow her to leave him: "Believe me, doctor, if I were to lose Irene, nothing would remain of me but a pile of shit" (HE 197).

Kruschkatz gives some thought to the inhabitants of Guldenberg, and again, readers of *Horns Ende* should be tempted to think that Hein is using the image of the village as a capsule description of the GDR and its traditional German nature, its provincialism and its difficulty in effecting progress. Kruschkatz says that he was able to understand their "covetousness and envy, their pleasure at denunciation and suspicious spying on each other in order to not miss a chance to gain a little, self-serving advantage. I could also understand their willingness to help out, their genuine and naive openness and their careless waste of time, their strong sense of community morals and their unwavering support of principles of honor and tradition" (HE 152–53).

What disturbs Kruschkatz is the ability of the Guldenberg citizens unconscionably to follow up a gesture of selfless magnanimity with the most disgustingly shabby tricks as though there were no contradiction in their behavior.

They seem like cats who can egregiously torture a small bird after they have been purring to solicit affection or prancing to an elegant rhythm.

In retrospect, Kruschkatz finally does begin to faintly realize that he has been wasting his life all along; his efforts have been nothing but a handful of melting snow. It doesn't occur to him until the day of his early retirement, when he receives a ridiculous plaque for his service, a plaque he had designed himself years before and presented countless times in recognition of some trivial service to the city of Guldenberg. The only thing the city still tacitly credits him with is something he had nothing to do with: the permanent departure of the Gypsies after Horn's death.

Bachofen continues to press Kruschkatz on the Gypsy issue, and Kruschkatz continues to refuse to force the Gypsies to leave the meadow where they are encamped. There are no more laws that require him to drive out the Gypsies. That time is past. Bachofen maintains that at least there was order in the town in earlier days. And he punctuates this by saying, "I have nothing to hide, I was never a Nazi" (HE 156). Kruschkatz maintains that as long as he is mayor, the Gypsies will also have rights. Bachofen argues that there are plans afoot to restore Guldenberg's status as a health resort and that the townspeople want to dress up the city. People are boycotting the cleanup effort as long as the Gypsies are there. Why should they have flower beds and trash containers when they don't have a clean meadow? "People are saying, what kind of a health resort is that where Gypsies pollute the air!" (HE 156).

Kruschkatz is furious about this attitude, but Bachofen tells him to go ahead and speak with the townspeople. After all, they aren't Nazis. Kruschkatz's sarcastic reply once again provides a denied continuity with the past: "Of course not. No one here has anything to hide, Bachofen. There were never any Nazis in this town" (HE 157).

Bachofen uses a different argument, linked with the government effort to collectivize the country's agricultural base, an undertaking with which they continued to experience great difficulty. The rural population consisted and still consists of strong, independent-minded individuals who have plowed their land and plied their trades for centuries under a variety of government forms. They are not easily coerced, and it took until the early 1960s to move the majority of them into cooperative communal farms. The town elders have been putting together a report claiming that the Gypsies present the primary obstacle to the collectivization of the agricultural economy. The fact that they have provided horses for the farmers during the summer months has prevented the authorities from exercising adequate leverage to force them into a collective. Kruschkatz regards this as a lie and refuses to condone or allow the report. Bachofen, however, tells him they don't need his signature. He will simply wait until Kruschkatz is on vacation and they will forward the report at that time. Kruschkatz later takes a walk out to the meadow and thinks about the Gypsies. He realizes he won't take any action to help them. This is his last commentary on the Gypsies, who have provided Kruschkatz with an opportunity to redeem himself—but one that he fails to take, since it might cost him his job.

After Horn's death, according to Kruschkatz, Bachofen continues his efforts to discredit Kruschkatz and have him removed from office. Kruschkatz has opened the door with his "lack of alertness," for which he was reprimanded by the committee that conducted the second hearing against Horn and for which he had to make the self-effacing, self-critical statement.

Bachofen has worked on the other members of the city council to get their support, and his next step is to accuse Kruschkatz of being guilty of Horn's suicide. Horn's suicide was an admission of guilt, and Kruschkatz, according to Bachofen, could have prevented it had he not permitted Horn to continue his historical presentations in the museum. Appropriate and timely action by Kruschkatz would, presumably, have made it possible for Horn to have admitted his errors and done penance. Kruschkatz rejects this notion out of hand, but the irony remains in place—namely, that Kruschkatz bears the blame for Horn's suicide insofar as his narrative function is to represent despotic bureaucracy in the GDR. Horn, as Kruschkatz well knows, would never had admitted any guilt nor felt a need to do penance. It was not in his nature to make the "required" self-criticisms as had Kruschkatz done.

Bachofen's over-zealousness finally brings about his destruction. He writes one too many letters, in which he denounces Franz Schneeberger, the previous mayor and an old-guard Communist portrayed by Kruschkatz as a man beyond reproach. Bachofen claims that Schneeberger had "enriched" himself after he retired by illegally obtaining a set of china from confiscated possessions left behind by someone who had fled to the West. For this "transgression," Schneeberger, who must have been quite old, spent five days in jail, arrested in the night of 8 October (the GDR's national holiday commemorating the founding of the republic!) and released on 12 October. At the hearing, he was able to produce a receipt certifying that he had, in fact, purchased the china legally at a city auction of the property. Schneeberger had been treated as though he were living under a Nazi regime—his supposed infraction being a relatively trivial one at that.

In the 1950s, and for years beyond that, it was no trivial matter to be in possession of a TV. Older readers may recall that when TV ownership first became widespread in the U.S., programming was generally limited to the evening. More important for the GDR context is the fact that a TV enabled one in East Germany to view Western TV, especially the 8:00 p.m. news—something that was forbidden by an unenforceable regulation.[13]

One day before Schneeberger's release, Kruschkatz orders that the first television ever delivered to Guldenberg be sent to Schneeberger. He takes this action on his own in spite of the fact that announcements have been made about the arrival of the TV, which was to have been displayed in a publicly accessible place. No one objects to his decision. Schneeberger remains bitter, planting himself in front of his TV and speaking with nobody. According to East German critic Gabriele Lindner, Kruschkatz's actions in the Bachofen/Schneeberger incidents reveal characteristics of a dialectic problem involving conflicts between "individual willingness to act decisively and the subordination to social constraints," which provides space for exploring the "alternatives between human preservation at the price of martyrdom and conformism at the price of identity loss."[14]

Bachofen remains on the city council for another five years (this would have been 1962, one year after the erection of the Berlin Wall and the closing of the borders), and then he takes advantage of a trip abroad—for which his privileged status enables him to get a passport—and defects to West Germany. From the GDR perspective, Bachofen does not escape into freedom. He is a contemptible character deserting his country for the decadent West, where he is likely to make a small contribution to its corruption.[15]

Kruschkatz's final report substantiates the perils of remembering and forgetting for the present generation. It is a "lost" generation because it has no roots to its past. According to Hein, "understanding the immediate as well as the distant past" is "absolutely necessary if one wants to comprehend one's own situation. Without knowledge of my own history or of the history of my society I can in no way make any statements about my present time and certainly not about my future."[16] The danger of forgetting or not remembering confirms the well-known adage that whoever is unaware of history is condemned to repeat it.

Kruschkatz, confined to the retirement home, recalls an event years ago, when he was sixty-four, right about the time of his voluntary retirement. He had participated in a local festival celebrating the voluntary firemen corps which took place on the meadow where the gypsies had camped so many years before. Since Horn and Kruschkatz were in their mid-forties when they knew each other, the time would be late 1970s, perhaps as late as 1982. A lot of beer was consumed; people were telling jokes and enjoying a good mood. Kruschkatz was asked to speak, and he began to tell a group of young people about how he had come to the town of Guldenberg, about Schneeberger, Bachofen, Brongel, and others, and about Horn and the Gypsies. And even about Irene. Suddenly he noticed that the group had grown quiet, not because they were interested in his story but because they were bored. He stopped speaking and looked at them. He could see pity and indulgent apathy in their faces. He apologized for boring them. Their silence confirmed his words until one foolish young man wanted to show off a bit and said: "On the contrary, Mr. Mayor, it was very interesting for us. I remember it too. This man who hanged himself in the forest had a mentally handicapped daughter, didn't he?" (HE 259).

And thus the true story of Horn has been obliterated by the succeeding generation, the facts now falsified and the associations obscured. To these people, Marlene Gohl could just as well have been Horn's daughter, a mistake which negates the importance of the story of the Gohl family for the present generation, destroying their chance to alter their consciousness and change their lives and attitudes. There would have been no record of the events: after all, Alfred Brongel had become the caretaker of the museum of history. True to form, Kruschkatz let the matter drop. Two days later, he submitted his request for voluntary retirement and went to the rest home in Leipzig, where he remained silent and continues to remain silent. He wishes that he could drive away his memories, that he could go ahead and die and be freed of the dreams of the past which plague him every night: "Leave me alone, Irene, . . . I can't bear your dream face . . . which comes with the darkness like a horror and sits on my chest, grabbing for my heart, choking it, choking it. Go away" (HE 260).

We have Dr. Spodeck to thank for the only direct quotes of comments by the living Horn in the novel, the only chance for the reader to have a peek into his mind. On one occasion, Spodeck describes a walk home from a Thursday-evening session with Horn and Irene Kruschkatz. Spodeck is clearly fascinated by Irene's green eyes and by the strangeness of Horn's character. They stop for a time and look at the Gypsy encampment. Irene wonders if the Gypsies aren't like children who never wanted to grow up, a process whose value Horn questions.

Spodeck is devastated by Horn's repeated rejection of him personally. Horn fails to understand why Spodeck is so arrogant as to feel sorry for him and tells him that he is boring. Horn says Spodeck may think he is an independent person, but the truth is that he has become just like the town, that his soul mirrors the place itself. He asks Spodeck to give up his "interest" in him; it is despicable and indiscreet. Horn's language is always full of contempt when he speaks to Spodeck.

Dr. Spodeck later reflects on Horn's death and remarks that Horn's entire life was dishonorable. He feels justified in stating this, inasmuch as he readily admits that his own life is dishonorable too and inasmuch as Spodeck knows only a handful of people whom he regards as better than Horn. By this time, however, the reader is not as prepared to accept Spodeck's opinion at face value as he or she was when reading his statements about Kruschkatz at the beginning.

Spodeck describes a visit by Horn for a physical examination. Spodeck shows him an article on film technique with the title "The Broken Mirror, a Modification of the Schüftan-Variante" (HE 229). The article, as Spodeck describes it, refers to a couple of Soviet film technicians who devised a method to render useless any documentary value in film. Hein had heard rumors of such techniques and of the possibility that the inventors had been awarded a Stalin Medal for it. The original picture is placed on a mirror, which is broken in the middle, and photographed again. Based on the adjustment of the intersection of the mirror pieces, parts of the original picture can be made to disappear. With this technique, it is possible to replace undesirable elements with desirable elements so that the picture appears to be original and untouched. Thus, according to Spodeck, history loses another crown witness, and historians unknowingly have before them a falsification.

For Horn, Spodeck's views on historiography are nothing unusual. Such falsifications are the daily bread of historians. History is nothing other than the dough handed down—arbitrary or intentional artifacts from which each generation kneads an image in its own image. The falsifications and our own errors are the stuff which make these images tangible and kneadable, that which makes our bits of wisdom insightful.

Spodeck counters that he is more inclined to view memory in terms of genetics. His description is a nihilistic version of Thomas's experience in front of the triptychon. Our brain stores memories as though our consciousness were working with a thousand such mirrors, each of which is broken into thousandths. We perceive and remember only according to the genetically determined number of these mirrors and their breaks and angles. Consequently, everything is changed before it enters our memory to be stored: "We don't store an event, only our consciousness of or our thinking about an event" (HE 231). These are personal memories and cannot qualify as an image of the world because of their individualized omissions and additions to events and facts.

Horn stares at him, and Spodeck says that all he wanted to say was that "you should not trust your memory. These images deceive you" (HE 231). Horn's reply: "Does this mean, doctor, that you advise me to live without memory?" (HE 231). Spodeck claims that we can never be certain about the veracity of our memory and therefore should be aware that we cannot know if our memory deceives us. For Horn, it is a "terrible thought to live without memory. We would have to live without experience, without knowledge and without values. If you extinguish the memory of human beings you extinguish humanity" (HE 232).

In spite of Horn's argument, which is a key philosophical statement not only for Horn but for the gist of the entire novel, Spodeck stays with his argument and maintains that experience is incomplete, that we complete the missing parts unconsciously according to our limited ability to comprehend, and that, furthermore, we always run the risk of getting lost. Horn still would like to know what Spodeck's advice would be as a logical consequence of his thinking. Spodeck quotes a seventeenth-century Spanish philosopher, Baltasar Gracian: "In all things try to get time on your side. If you can succeed in adjusting your memories according to this, then it will be easier for you to live" (HE 232). Such an elimination of historical time, an attempt to get time to work for you, based, presumably, on Spodeck's theory of the acceptance of the fragmentation of memory is not palatable to Horn. Even though he works with similar limitations, it does not prevent him from continuing to seek the truth rather than to manipulate it into a comfort zone for practical living. Horn's reply reminds us of Kruschkatz's fate without Irene: "Doctor, in that case life is nothing but a pile of gilded shit. . . . With such wisdom, doctor, you can live to grow old" (HE 232–33). Spodeck responds that he is aware of this. Horn's parting words: "That makes me want to throw up" (HE 233).

Dr. Spodeck: Damaged Psyche

Spodeck's relentless spite, we learn, is directed equally towards his wife, his daughter, the citizens of the township of Bad Guldenberg, Kruschkatz, and, above all, himself. He regards his own misanthropic life as a living penance to the town for the evils committed by his capitalist Nazi father.

Spodeck describes the humiliation he suffered as the illegitimate son of Dr. Konrad Böger and his own helpless acquiescence to his father's control of his life. Spodeck's account of the arrogant, authoritarian, patriarchal, and exploitative nature of his father—honored as a benefactor to Guldenberg—provides a link with the town's Nazi past. It is not too much of an exaggeration to see the patriarchal relationship between father and son as paradigmatic of the relationship between the Nazi elite and the German population—in particular, that segment of the German population which felt devastated by guilt after the war. Spodeck's guilt originates in his inability to rebel against his father or to create an independent life, capitulating instead to a sullen obedience. Silent obedience to an authority is symptomatic in the continuity of German history, it manifests a pre-condition necessary for authoritarian systems to succeed under either fascist or socialist regimes. Spodeck's mother lives in poverty, affording Böger more leverage for coercing his bastard son, who would otherwise be economically and socially deprived.

Spodeck's father pays for his entire education, and Spodeck dutifully studies medicine in order to fulfill his father's plan to present him to the town of Guldenberg to atone for his excesses. Spodeck actually becomes interested in psychiatry, but his father responds to his request to change major fields by telling him that he "will live off of sick people, not crazy ones" (HE 87). Spodeck is held in a state of subjugation at the completion of his studies: his father purchases a physician's practice for him in Guldenberg, completing the defeat of his will. His acceptance ends forever any chance of creating a life of his own. As his father tells him, it will be easy: "Your bed has been made for you, you just have to lie in it" (HE 90). Spodeck's shame and self-hatred, along with the degradation he feels from his father's brutal scorn, scar his life permanently.

Spodeck's life provides further structural continuity between the authoritarianism of the Nazi period and of the socialist period in East Germany without obscuring the obvious differences in content between the two. Spodeck does not see much change around him, and the reader can imagine that he despises Kruschkatz because Kruschkatz, too, has laid himself in a made bed: Kruschkatz accepts the party directives to move to Bad Guldenberg and has no courage to stand up (and put his career on the line) for Horn or for the Gypsies. He tries to help Schneeberger, but it is too late, and he is only able to replace Schneeberger's injured honor with a television set.

Dr. Spodeck only sees patients one day a week. Otherwise he works on his pet projects. One is a collection of case notes from previous patients who are either dead or have been sent to a sanitorium in Leipzig. He has eleven bound volumes, and he avails himself of his short study of psychiatry and the scholarly literature of his professor from that time and of other published works which he studies and compares with his notes. He has no intention of publishing this work. His second project is the history of Bad Guldenberg. But this is no city history or vain homey chronicle: "What I am writing down in these pages are quite simply the vile affairs and the base actions with which my honorable fellow citizens have distinguished themselves. . . . It is a history of human cruelty" (HE 133).

He is, understandably, particularly vituperative in his description of his father—whose grandiose plans to expand the train station and develop a renowned health resort around the hot springs and to become the principal citizen of the city had collapsed in a few days one spring after the economic explosion. Spurred on by the town's greed, the scheme fell like a house of cards. Yet instead of taking this man as the cause of their ruin and shame and beating him to death in the market square or hanging him from the 400-year-old oak tree, the citizens of Guldenberg had honored him with a medallion as a "Beneficiary of the City" (HE 134). The economic expansion and the collapse of the health resort suggest a reference to the pre-Nazi era of the Weimar Republic—a reference which also occurs in one of Thomas's discoveries in his father's study.

Spodeck describes the town during the time of the Brown Shirts, the Hitler troops—how the population cheered them. Spodeck directly disclaims the official GDR historical view that the Nazis counted really as the "other," somehow infiltrating and suppressing the good Communist core of citizens. The denouncers and murderers didn't come from anywhere else, according to Spodeck. They lived in Guldenberg; they were citizens of this sleepy little province. His father had sent one of his half-brothers to join the brown storm troopers and then celebrated his "heroic death" with a grandiose funeral procession. He regrets that his father died before the end of the war because he would like to have seen how cleverly his father would have exploited the new circumstances to his advantage (as many ex-Nazis successfully did). The pages of Spodeck's history of human cruelty will be filled with his own observations at the end—commentaries on all the many human transformations, the sad comedy and pitiful opportunism which ensued as the citizens of Guldenberg masked, hid, and destroyed evidence of their past.

It may be, according to Spodeck, that the new people who came to take over the offices of government agencies had the best of intentions, but they were helpless and politically naive, incapable of recognizing the back stairs, rooms, and doors of the town hall or of avoiding or extricating themselves from the old intrigues. Guldenberg had had sixteen mayors since the war—an observation which sheds light on how difficult Kruschkatz's task really was.

Spodeck plans to make three copies of his history and present one to Kruschkatz, one to the town pastor, and one to the museum director. He expects the mayor to burn his copy. Now that the cowardly Alfred Brongel is the museum director, Spodeck expects that copy to go up in smoke as well. He doesn't know what the pastor will do. He might not even read it; he might burn it too. The three key elements of GDR society represented are the official bureaucracy, the petty opportunists—including the element of the IM's, or *inoffizielle Mitarbeiter* (unofficial collaborators with the *Stasi* who acted as informers)— and the church, which eventually became the base of dissident activity in East Germany.

At any rate, he plans to write his history until the day of his death, unwaveringly, objectively, as a chronicler. He plans not to leave his own baseness out as well, his cowardice in not standing up to his father and his affair with Christine, his devoted housekeeper and secretary. His unmerciful self-castigation and Horn's disdainful rejection of his ideas on history create insecurity for the reader who otherwise would be inclined to take Spodeck's chronicles of human cruelty at objective face value. We are left with a dialectical character who is discredited by Horn and who discredits himself but relates facts with meticulous accuracy.

Dr. Spodeck relates, as promised, what he regards as a dark page in his own biography. The Eastern portion of Germany had no Marshall plan to revive its economy; instead, the Soviet Union either assumed ownership of industrial plants or dismantled them and transported them to the Soviet Union as partial payment of reparations. During the resulting period of extreme hardship immediately following the war, people had to make do as best as possible. Spodeck agrees to take in a young girl who was essentially being abandoned by her parents because they could no longer afford to care for her. Christine helps out with the housework and becomes a nanny to Johanna, the daughter. Spodeck notices that her presence has softened his quick temper and relaxed him. For her part, she remains singularly devoted to the family and visits her own family less and less, even preferring to spend Christmas with the Spodecks.

When she is seventeen, Spodeck hires Christine as an assistant in his praxis, and pays for her additional training at a professional school. He feels guilty that she comes home to continue her work there after spending six hours in his office. He encourages her to take advantage of free time and to go out and meet people, but Christine responds that she enjoys what she was doing very much and desires nothing more than to remain with the family on the same basis permanently.

Christine is nineteen years old when Spodeck's mother dies. Although his wife sobs over it, she refuses to accompany him to the funeral or to allow Johanna, who is nine years old, to attend. Spodeck reacts with quiet rage. He knows his wife's expressions of condolence are a lie; she had despised his mother from the first time they met, despised her for her simplicity, her poverty and awkwardness. All of this reminds Spodeck of his own shame about his origins as a bastard child. He had always remained fiercely loyal to his mother.

His wife suggests that he take Christine to the funeral. After the ceremony, Christine and Spodeck drive home, talking about their mothers. Christine's mother was talented. She could paint and draw, but her talent was wasted by her labor in the business of the farm and household. Christine thinks she should have run away from it, and Spodeck realizes that this is what Christine has done herself. Indeed, Christine's talent seems to be that of caring for other people—having patience, possessing a rare, selfless naivete. The car breaks down—an occurrence which would be a trite fictional device except for the fact that poorly manufactured East German cars frequently broke down and which thus replaces triteness with humorous irony—and the two of them wind up making love. Christine tells Spodeck she loves him, but Spodeck is overcome with the self-hate which still permeates his being as a result of his hatred towards his father. His father's worst sins, in Spodeck's mind, consisted of his womanizing, and now Spodeck finds himself no better than his father.

This conclusion is evidently not true for the reader, in spite of Spodeck's miserable personal futility in taking the situation at face value. Christine was nineteen and Spodeck fifty-one: "I was almost an old man when I lived the hour of my life which could have freed me from my hate and my raging despair" (HE 174). He orders her to forget him and to leave and get married and have children. She replies that she will forget him but she will stay there and not leave him. Over the years, Spodeck is never able to talk her into going away, and he is not able to allow himself to pursue a meaningful relationship with another human being—something that might have cured his misanthropy. He has been damaged like Claudia, although for different reasons.

Spodeck's wife senses the attachment one day when she, surprisingly, goes up to Spodeck and gives him a kiss, causing Christine to drop a tray of dishes. His wife tells him with manifest cruelty that she knows they love each other and adds: "But I also know that I will outlive you and that you will never dare to divorce me or separate from me and your daughter. You don't have the courage to do that. You are a coward. You will never have Christine. I promise you that" (HE 177).

On 30 September, not long after Horn's suicide, Spodeck closes his summer residence to return to Guldenberg. Spodeck is in a good mood and jokes with Christine as they go through the house closing the windows. He touches her cheek with his hand. She grabs his hand and kisses it passionately and then places it on her breast. They look each other in the eyes, and Spodeck says, "Please don't." "Yes, doctor," she responds, and lets his hand drop (HE 266). That was Spodeck's last chance. On the way home, they pass the Gypsies, who are leaving the town in a caravan, signifying the end of Horn, the end of Spodeck's chance to transcend his bitterness and the stagnation of the town itself, and the opportunity—since the presence of the Gypsies will no longer remind them—to forget the past and avoid confrontation with the confusing, self-incriminating emotions they feel towards the Gypsies. Spodeck's cruelty toward himself is the equal of the cruelties he describes. Kruschkatz is punished by Irene's nausea, and Spodeck punishes himself—both of them doing so for their lack of courage to do what is right.

Clarity: Gertrude Fischlinger and Marlene Gohl

The one character whose reports are never clouded by self-serving subjectivity is Gertrude Fischlinger, and Hein portrays with great care her immense suffering and stubborn ability to work and stay alive under the harshest of circumstances. Gertrude Fischlinger is the only character in the novel representative of the working class, and nobody suffers more than she, with the possible exception of Gohl. In the dictatorship of the proletariat, the "Worker and Farmer State," the bitter irony of Gertrude Fischlinger's lot constitutes in itself a condemnation of the hypocritical standards of the socialist government in its East German form. Hein never speaks such words, but we know that she runs her small, drab shop alone, putting in twelve working-hours a day and being afraid to allow her son to mind the store because he might steal money. She has only a single friend in town and does not appear in the narratives of anyone else except Thomas—a fact which leaves the impression that she is as isolated as the others.

Gertrude Fischlinger's description of her wedding night sets the tone. She is reminded of it by her constantly swollen legs, which she even had then. She remembers her anxiety and being ill from the alcohol they had drunk. Her husband shows no consideration for her condition. She has to get undressed, and he places the exquisite wedding veil over her and then gets on top of her. "The next morning, when he saw the torn, bloody veil, he smiled and said: you were the oldest virgin I ever had. But better late than never" (HE 55).

She returns the borrowed veil to the mother of her friend, Juliane, a couple of days later. The veil had evidently been in the family many generations. It was intended for Juliane. As it turns out, Juliane, her lifelong friend, never marries. But the mother's cold, silent reaction to the stain turns the blood in Gertrude Fischlinger's veins to ice. When she is five months pregnant, her husband moves in with a younger woman, and finally, when her son Paul is four years old, her husband and his lover move to another town at her request, since it was difficult to live in a small village under such circumstances.

Gertrude Fischlinger describes how her husband returns for one last visit shortly after Horn's funeral in order to pick up some of Paul's things. Paul's father has found him an apprenticeship, and Paul has moved to the town where his father lives. Frau Fischlinger is unhappy about the prospect of her son's education being continued by his father, but she has not done very well in this respect herself and has no control over him. The husband shows up at her house with his girlfriend, a bleached blond in red heels with a red fake-leather purse, articles which seem in their poor taste and quality to somehow represent a kind of GDR would-be nouveau petite bourgeoisie. He seems to regard himself as a self-made man, the owner of a junkyard. Her husband is brash enough to ask her to fix dinner for them, during which he blithely carries on the conversation alone, his girlfriend passively giving signs of approval to everything he says. Although we may anguish over Frau Fischlinger's passive behavior and her inability to throw them out of her house, a powerful value structure is established with this passage. The silent, inner strength of the women in this novel—Frau Fischlinger, Christine, Marlene Gohl and her mother, and Irene, all of whom exhibit passive behavior traits which contribute to their unhappiness—is repeatedly contrasted with the cowardly, self-serving, denunciatory, and impassive attitude of the male characters.

After the bizarre couple leaves, Gertrude Fischlinger breaks into tears and thinks a bit about Horn—about how he never really felt affection for her, how he was only polite and friendly. Nevertheless he is the only man she has ever known who gave her the feeling that she almost meant something to him. Taking place shortly after Horn's death, her husband's visit rounds out an oppressive phase in Frau Fischlinger's life, and after he leaves, she notices, in spite of her tears and her aching legs, a new strength and "an unrestrainable desire to live" (HE 204). Frau Fischlinger is the only person in the novel to express the will and the strength to live, not exactly what might be expected from her after all she has been through and after everyone has left. But her husband, Paul, and Horn as well, have been burdensome to her, and now she is free emotionally.

Gertrude Fischlinger reveals in bits and pieces, without regard for chronology, how Horn approached her, after living in the house for about two years, and began the intimate relationship which lasted six months. He would come into her bedroom two or three times a month, and they would sleep together. They spoke softly, but very little. He was gentle, but he avoided caressing her legs or looking at them. Horn ended the relationship with his apology, which Frau Fischlinger rejected as unnecessary. He liked her but was not in love with her, he said, and he knew the feeling was mutual. He just felt it was wrong. Although Frau Fischlinger came to feel like the "widow of her tenant" (HE 204), the contrast between her husband's crass insults and Horn's forthright honesty are important.

She recalls feeling some relief at having her room back after Horn's burial. She originally agreed to let Horn rent a room in her apartment in the hope that he might exercise some positive influence on Paul. Horn was correct and polite, but never permitted himself to become involved with her son. After the first week it was evident to Frau Fischlinger that she could have expected more human kindness had she "put a sack of wood in the room" (HE 21).

Gertrude Fischlinger reports that Horn came to her a week before his suicide to break off their affair. She told him that no apology was necessary, that she was a grown woman and was responsible for her own actions—perhaps as the only character in the novel capable of assuming some responsibility for herself. Horn explained that somebody had reported on his activities at the museum and that he was going to be in trouble, he would have to defend himself again. Frau Fischlinger suddenly realized that Horn was far more alone than she.

Her descriptions consistently differ from those of Spodeck and Kruschkatz, both of whom seem to be trying to persuade or to defend their point of view. By contrast, Gertrude Fischlinger seems to be the most objective and, hence, the most reliable witness. She does not editorialize, not even with respect to Horn after he broke off their short affair. From her perspective, appropriately, we learn about the Gohls. According to Frau Fischlinger, Herr Gohl lives a little outside of town with his daughter, Marlene, now a grown woman who, however, rarely leaves the house.

Herr Gohl has no friends or acquaintances in the town. Nobody visits him, and he speaks to no one outside of the museum. Before the war, he was a painter and sold his pictures to the wealthy guests at the health resort. Now he earns a few marks at the museum and receives a pension for his daughter and a supplementary pension as a Nazi victim. The only people he associates with are the Gypsies. In spite of the language barrier, they would drink schnapps together, and the Gypsy women would sing ethnic songs. Gertrude Fischlinger regards it her right and duty to sell her wares to the Gypsies and regards it as Gohl's right to associate with them if he wishes, no matter what people say. She thinks perhaps the Gypsies regard the insane as holy ones.

Frau Fischlinger and her friend Juliane knew Gohl's wife as Gudrun Stephanski. She was their teacher in elementary school before she married Gohl and gave birth to Marlene. She quit work when she discovered that her child was sick and would never be quite right. Only toward the end of the novel does Frau Fischlinger finish telling the terrible fate of Gudrun Gohl. Although her narrative reveals what Spodeck would regard as a story of human cruelty, she does not allow this story to be jaded in any manner, as Spodeck surely would have.

In May of 1943, the daughter was taken away. The Gohls had succeeded for a long time in keeping Marlene away from the intervention of the government, which officially placed such sick individuals in special homes "in order not to endanger the life of healthy citizens" (HE 181). The Gohls had hidden their daughter a number of years at home when, finally, an anonymous, written note to the government offices exposed them. In May, she was taken away forcefully, and in September, they received a notification of death and an urn with her ashes. The official cause of death was given as a lung infection.

The issue here, immediately evident to Germans, refers to the Nazi practice of euthanasia for all citizens classified as "unworthy life" (*unwertes Leben*). This included the mentally ill and the physically handicapped. It also applied to groups who were the object of racial discrimination besides the Jews, to other minorities like the Gypsies, although such minorities were usually pressured to move away. Often lost in the well-documented holocaust in American histories is the fact that some 300,000 human beings were destroyed under the rubric of *unwertes Leben*.

The Gohls rarely left the house after this. Whenever Gohl displayed his pictures for sale he had tears in his eyes and spoke with no one from the town. In her inimitable, objective style, Gertrude Fischlinger recalls that about a year before the end of the war, a terrible rumor sprang up that people had seen Marlene Gohl playing in the garden. Apparently the officials had taken her mother. Mrs. Gohl must have succeeded in tricking the officials into thinking she was Marlene and allowed herself to be brought into the sanatorium where all people were sent for whom a fatal sentence had been passed: *unwertes Leben*. Gohl's daughter Marlene was alive. In the urn in the forest cemetery were the ashes of Gudrun Gohl, the mother of the mentally ill Marlene.

This knowledge left the town thunderstruck: "The relief which manifested itself after the denunciation and the presumed transportation of the sick individual to the sanatorium was suddenly transformed into silent horror" (HE 182). The shame and horror continued to the end of the year, and Gohl and his daughter were left undisturbed in their house. Even though many were aware of the truth, no one dared to speak out. Even the most fanatical Nazis kept their mouths shut. Hein's description is devastating on this point: "The bad war news, the advancing Russians and the nightly bombings of German cities by English planes made it apparent to those who had heard or seen something to not dare make a second denunciation" (HE 183). This is an ominous implication that, without the impending loss of the war, the citizens of Guldenberg may have reported it a second time.

Gohl kept to himself after the war, only accepting the offer to work in the museum. The same year he began working there, the Gypsies appeared in the town again. The Nazi regime would have never allowed them onto German soil, having driven them out in the first place. As the town developed its irritation with the Gypsies, covering this racial prejudice up with the claims that they prevented the collectivization of the farms, the townspeople gradually came to resent Gohl's socializing with the Gypsies, and according to Frau Fischlinger, virtually the entire town regarded his behavior as a betrayal. Gohl was not interested: "It was for him as if nothing had changed since the end of the war" (HE 185).

This is clearly one of the most incriminating statements in the entire novel, a statement incongruous with socialist positivism and precisely the kind of statement for which someone like Horn—who is not an untouchable like Gohl—would be ostracized and even imprisoned. The implications go well beyond the historical issues, as important as these themselves are, demonstrating the link between two totalitarian states, one Nazi and the other Stalinist, both employing similar authoritarian structures with which to manipulate public opinion and knowledge. Those in the GDR, in fairness, never included such innovations as mass euthanasia or genocide. On the other hand, the Gypsies first returned to Eastern Germany after the fall of the Berlin Wall, appearing out of Romania and other Eastern areas, sending their wives and children to beg in the downtown streets of Berlin and making Germans uncomfortable and resentful once again.

Gohl remained unapproachable and isolated. On the white gravestone in the cemetery he had a name inscribed after the war: Gudrun Gohl, born Stephanski, 1901–1943. Otherwise no history of her existence would have ever been documented. But now it is written in stone.

The powerful affinity between Gertrude Fischlinger and the Gohls is elucidated in Marlene Gohl's reports, which take the form of imaginary conversations with her mother, almost in stream-of-consciousness style. She dreams about the Gypsies, and the next day, they are there, to her delight. The Gypsies provide a carnival atmosphere for her, and she says that they call her princess and that Carlos will be her groom. She knows the people say she is crazy, but "they only say it because I see and know much more than I am capable of telling" (HE 46). The people are only envious that she sees things they don't, and they are the crazy ones, not her. There is more truth in her statements than she is capable of knowing.

Marlene Gohl relates the shocking story of why she no longer can marry Carlos: she is now already married. The whole experience had been so painful and bloody she can't understand why people even wanted to get married. Her new husband did not kiss her or caress her; he just threw her to the ground and tore off her clothes because he wanted to get to her *Muschi*. He said he doesn't kiss crazy people and punched her with his fist until her mouth was full of blood. Why didn't her mother come to the wedding, she wants to know. She didn't know this man wanted to marry her, and now he is gone. He never told her his name. He smelled like schnapps. At night she walks in the park, hoping to see him again. She just wants to know his name because a married woman ought to know her own name. She can hear the Gypsies singing and Carlos's voice downstairs with her father. She can't go to Carlos. She is already married even though she doesn't know her husband's name. Carlos will never be able to call her princess again.

Marlene fulfills the role of naive seer (the insane are holy, according to the Gypsies) with her ecstatic language: "Why are you lonely when you get married?" she wonders; "Tell me, Mama, how come so much pain and so much blood is beautiful if I'm not even caressed? And why can't you tell about it, why are you not supposed to tell the truth, instead you should lie and claim that it was beautiful? Or does beautiful mean for you Crazy Ones that it is terrible? Have you gone and made the words crazy?" (HE 234). This is part of the last entry by Marlene Gohl, the only narrator who seems to have had no direct contact with Horn. Once again, an anonymous individual from the town has violated the Gohls in the most despicable manner, confirming Gohl's opinion that nothing really has changed since the war. It happened while the Gypsies are camped on the meadow, after the townspeople once again have become annoyed with Gohl for his disloyal socialization with the undesirable Gypsies.

The victimization of the two key female figures in the story, the grisly association established between wedding night and rape, heightens the clarity of vision expressed in their words, rendering the arguments about historical theory mute and trivial—except for the fact that Fischlinger and Marlene Gohl are ignored, are outcasts, yet they are far better conveyors of history than anyone else. Heinz-Peter Preußer's article on *Horns Ende* is the only one which focuses principally on the figure of Marlene. What Marlene thinks, what she knows, and what she says transcend what can be communicated with ordinary language; she is the medium for those things which speak to and through her with "specific immediacy." As Preußer has written, "She exists outside of all time. What she has experienced is virtually still present, hardly gone by and does not need to be remembered."[17] In the narrative structure, Hein achieves the timelessness of Marlene by making her the only figure who is not reminiscing; she speaks during the summer of 1957, in the present tense, before Horn's death. As a timeless figure, she keeps the alarm sounded. Her personal physical humiliation is, asserts Preußer, "irradicably written" into her senses, "not to be forgotten and not to be palliated and, above all, not to be concealed."[18]

Hein does not likely wish to establish a blanket incrimination of the entire town, or of the entire country, by creating fragmentary links between past and present in the framework of the mortifying biography of the Gohl family, but the existence of such links is undeniable and irrepressible for Hein. As a chronicler of the time in which he lives, Hein refuses to let what is known, what is still accessible through memory, be washed over by Spodeck's cynical resignation or Kruschkatz's pragmatic forgetting. Let the facts speak for themselves is Hein's view, and in this novel, none speak so devastatingly as the story related by Gertrude Fischlinger about the Gohls and the story related by Marlene Gohl in her blunt, mentally impaired statements as she wonders if the people have not just "made the words crazy."

Memory: Thomas

Thomas's remembrances are relayed through his mind as a child, not through his adult memory. There is no attempt to analyze his recollections, as is the case for Spodeck and Kruschkatz. As a child, Thomas would not have always been aware of connections between events and people in the adult world, a bit of realism which Hein retains in the structural balance of the narrative perspectivism.

For Thomas, the Gypsies have an exotic quality about them, not lessened in his mind by the racial slurs of his classmates or of his father, the respected pharmacist, who forbids him to associate with the Gypsies so as not to tarnish the family image. Thomas liked to pick up odd jobs with the Gypsies, and he also worked part-time in the museum, where Herr Gohl worked as a painter and Horn looked after his archeological artifacts. Thomas states that he feels pressed in by the past. He did not like the small village and would have preferred to get away from it. The voice at the beginning of each chapter presses him to remember, but he's not sure he can. It seems that the only positive relationship he had was with Herr Gohl in the museum.

"You cannot forget, my boy. If you forget me, just then will I really die. But then Hell will awaken the dead. I live only in your memory" (HE 59–60). Such are the words Thomas hears, urging him to strain his memory. Thomas remembers the first time he was at the museum, remembers thinking that he most of all wanted to completely forget the first eleven years of his life; he wanted to grow up, to be independent, to forget all the insults and humiliations he had experienced in that town. Thomas exhibits a natural inclination to forget and to suppress, a characteristic which Hein uses to underscore the dialogue between

Thomas and Horn. Historical veracity appears to be dependent on the resolution of this dialectic situation.

One day when Thomas is hanging out at the museum Horn enters the room and opens a glass case. He takes a blackened piece of metal from his jacket pocket and places it between the fragments on display. To Thomas, he says: "Have a look around. This is all very old. Too old to lie. A couple of stones, a couple of shards, but the truth. That is not insignificant, my boy" (HE 65–66). Thomas then tells a lie to Horn, saying that when he grows up, he wants to work in the museum too. Horn decides to let him come by and do little jobs. Maybe Thomas will become a person who grows up to become a caretaker of truth also. "It's only a small museum that we have," says Horn, "but nevertheless we write history too. We are the ones who have to see to it whether truth or lies will be reported" (HE 68).

Thomas's life is touched by his pre-puberty fascination with Elske, a girl four years older than he is. He visits her a few days after she had cleaned up his bloody nose with her perfumed handkerchief. After that, she stays in his fantasies for some time and allows him to visit her, leaving the bashful Thomas always wondering what he would be saying to her if he were four years older. Elske also serves as a narrative vehicle to demonstrate the continuing prejudice of the townspeople towards the Gypsies. To her, the Gypsy girls are filthy, and she wishes they would all disappear, although she doesn't really know why. Her prejudice has been socially inherited without serious reflection of the consequences or meaning, predetermining future attitudes which will not easily be overcome.

Thomas renders another account of his fascination for Elske, the feeling of inadequacy he feels around her as a result of their age difference, his sexual fantasies about her, and his inability to express himself to her about what he is really thinking. The humiliation Thomas had experienced growing up in Bad Guldenberg is embodied in the figure of Elske. Once, he manages to tell her he wants to caress her after they return from a bicycle outing. She allows him to caress the hair in her armpit, but she grows bored of it and sends him home.

The day Paul and Thomas find the body of Horn is mixed in with Elske's final humiliation of Thomas. Hein constructs these events as a minuscule example of the conversation between Horn and Spodeck about misperceptions of history. Paul takes Thomas into the woods to show him Horn's body. When they finally locate the police—it is Sunday and the station is closed—Paul makes it clear that Thomas's presence is unwanted. Paul wants to make sure he gets all the credit for finding the body, and when he leads the police to it, Thomas is left behind. Thomas goes over to Elske's house, and she uses him to take a letter to Klemens, an older student from Munich visiting his grandmother in the East. Klemens, who is talking to a couple of girls when Thomas delivers the letter, gives him a reply and calls him Elske's little boyfriend. He makes Thomas promise not to read the letter and to be sure to tell Elske to be punctual. Thomas runs home, tearing the letter into pieces, and goes into his room. His father calls him in to reprimand him for associating with children like Paul, and Thomas blurts out that Horn has hanged himself and bursts out crying. His father hugs him and says that was terrible; he hadn't realized that he had cared so much about Horn. But Thomas was crying about Elske's betrayal.

At the beginning of the eighth and last chapter, which contains the description of the boys' finding Horn, Thomas wants to just forget and to sleep, but the apparition will not permit it: "If you remain silent, then the stones themselves will scream" (HE 249). Fabrizio Cambi has pointed out that the figure of Horn remains puzzling and distant throughout the novel, manifesting the power, however, to cause reflection about the past—the use of "sober memory" to re-experience a "difficult historical and political moment," which Cambi describes as the "therapy of memory" for Thomas.[19] The psychological sense of therapy is evident in Thomas's confrontation with his humiliation at the hands of Elske, misunderstood out of ignorance by his father, and associated in Thomas's memory with the suicide of Horn, which had less of an impact on his consciousness than his interactions with Elske.

In his published interview with Jachimczak, Hein stated: "Without some knowledge of my own history or the history of my own society I cannot possibly make any statements about my present and absolutely none about my future."[20] This statement does not imply a thorough, factual knowledge of the past, but it does entail the effort to understand one's identity in the context of history. "Memory creates a bridge," according to Cambi, "by means of which the prejudices, the expectations, the disillusionments, and the indolence of the people of a faraway and puzzling village are transported" into the present.[21] The moral and traditional imperviousness which is correspondingly transported into the future exists in the fragments of history. The examination of these fragments is the only opportunity to avoid repeating an identity locked in the social and political structure of the past. The therapy to which Horn forces Thomas to subject himself gives Thomas a chance which his childhood companions Paul and Elske will not be capable of having.

Thomas's forays into the past include a discovery in his father's den. Behind the row of impressive editions of German writers—cloth bound, thick, inscribed with gold letters and never used or read—Thomas finds a collection of ragged paperback novels and magazines with half-naked women on the covers, some of the volumes with a stamp proclaiming "Only for Mature Gentlemen" (HE 121).

For Thomas, it is both mysterious and inexplicable that an older man like his father—with a wife and children, well-respected and honored in the town— could own such questionable books and pictures. He suspects that his father's unknown past is much more heroic or terrible than these things might indicate. His imagination associates his father as being mixed up in the stories in these books he read when he sneaked into the den, fully aware of the awful punishment he would receive if caught. Thomas remembers one of the illustrated stories, which is difficult to interpret. The title, written in Sütterlin script, is "The Prostitute's Lover." It depicts a woman holding a cigarette in a cigarette holder, with a bobbed hairstyle and a dress reminiscent of the late 1920s or the early 1930s, the pre-Nazi period at the end of the Weimar Republic. A man appears in a smoking jacket with a thin mustache. He gestures, and the woman puts her legs up on the arm of the chair and laughs. He pulls out a revolver. She attempts to get away. There is a chase through the room, each picture showing her with less clothing; underwear is scattered around. She fearfully covers her breasts with crossed arms; he is pointing the gun; then she is lying on the bed looking both defiant and despairing. Then the man stands in front of her and points the gun at his own head. She, completely naked, grabs his knees. The last picture shows her on the carpet in an alluring position, her hand on her breast a few centimeters from the bleeding, mortal wound.

Thomas thinks of his father as somehow being aware of the crime depicted in the story of the prostitute's lover, although Thomas doesn't identify him with the murderer. He identifies him, instead, with a character in another book: an epistolary romance novel that has a Swiss heroine named Bella and contains photographs in the same old-fashioned style as those in the family album. In Thomas's imagination, the stern, pedantic man, who left punctually every morning for his pharmacy, had led a wild and bizarre life earlier—one connected with prostitutes and criminals. Hein does not clarify the vague references in this passage, leaving it as yet another shard from the past that combines sex with violence. There is an inclination to associate the generation of Thomas's father with this passage in the book, a generation which was anxious to forget its past. The soft-porno images suggest the Nazi wartime subjugation of other countries, such as Belgium, or the Nazi propaganda depictions of injustices being perpetrated against the Germans by their enemies. However, there is nothing to substantiate such references, and the passage can be understood in general terms as an attempt by Thomas to reconstruct—on the basis of small pieces of information which in themselves are perhaps quite misleading—a past about which he knows very little. In an adult's mind, the books are fiction, cheap paperbacks; but in a child's mind, they constitute evidence of reality.

This "evidence" has been carefully hidden behind the volumes of classical works. Thomas sees a connection with his father during the times when he and his brother are to be punished: "Father became a man without a past, the strict and quick-tempered man who was just my father, nothing more, who could punish his children, but could never be sought out by a Bella or by a murderer" (HE 130). Thomas then describes his father's behavior when punishing him and his brother, evidently not an infrequent occurrence. His father's stern authoritarianism is the principal character trait remembered by Thomas. One of the pharmacist's principles was to punish both sons equally, regardless of who was at fault. He was not interested in having them tell on each other and felt that his principles served as a good pedagogical tool for developing a feeling of solidarity between them. Consequently, the innocent were always punished together with the guilty, as had been the case in *The Distant Lover.*

The punishment of the day was directed at the son (Thomas) who had been fraternizing with the Gypsies, doing odd jobs for pay, and this in full view of his "patients"—his father referred to his customers as "patients" as a way of adding dignity and prestige to his station in life as a pharmacist. Thomas's father told them that his profession was the pride of his life, the fulfillment of the dream of a farmer's son who had been able to study at the university. The father's portrait here is a mixed bag of a self-made man, one who benefitted from the socialist policy of sending children of farmers and of the working class to the university, and of an individual who has himself become a sort of nouveau riche bourgeoisie whose social standing in town was of extreme importance and whose children were to manifest exemplary behavior at all times. Indeed, party members and socialist elite became the new upper class and enjoyed a variety of privileges unavailable to others, privileges which remained a point of resentment throughout the short history of the GDR.

Moreover, this patriarchal authoritarianism documents a lack of change in human character between historical periods in Germany and provides a perception of hypocrisy, inasmuch as the "new person" (*der neue Mensch*) of socialism was portrayed in socialist ideology as cooperative and kind (but not letting down his guard towards the outside enemies). The pharmacist is an enigmatic figure, one who cannot be classified in terms of sympathy or antipathy. He and his wife also belong to the small group, along with Irene, which attends Horn's Thursday-night meetings, and this action tends to give them a certain amount of integrity in the reader's mind.

Just as Hein had structured the parallels between Gertrude Fischlinger and Marlene Gohl, the authoritarian aspect of Thomas's father and the solidarity employed in punishment of the brothers can be understood as a paradigm for the structural parallel between Kruschkatz and Horn. The authoritarian state punished Kruschkatz—who had denounced Horn—to establish solidarity between the two ex-Leipzig historians. It is a ploy destined to failure, one which contributes to lack of understanding and to the antagonism between the two. For his part, Kruschkatz never understands that he, too, is being punished. Even when he realizes he has come to a dead end in his career, he never permits himself to take that fact as the devastatingly personal defeat that Horn does. However, his suffering is connected with the punishment of living on, his nightmares and the memory of Irene gnawing at his soul and creating an anguish equal to or worse than that which drives Horn to suicide.

At the beginning of chapter seven, Thomas sheds some light on the second interrogation of Horn, about his sister living in the West. Before Thomas steals his glimpse of the proceedings, Gohl prevents him from going into Horn's office, where the interrogation is taking place. Since Gohl is never forthcoming with speech, it takes Thomas a while to find out that Horn is in some kind of trouble. He wonders if it has something to do with the Gypsies, an idea negated by Gohl but an example of associative thinking about the past.

Thomas observes how Gohl had painted a background mural behind some bushes and plants they had installed in a corner of the museum, a mural which blends in so well that Thomas's admiration prompts him to say that one can hardly tell where the real grasses stop and the painting begins. "Quite simple," replies Gohl, "I deceive the eye. The perspective fools us. . . . It's just a principle, a trick of art ["Kunstgriff" might be better rendered as "artificial trick"]. . . . Nothing more. And then we can't detect the difference. The human eye is no good. Lets itself be too easily fooled" (HE 221). With his metaphorical comments, Gohl has described the difficulty of discovering and preserving history. Too many artificial colorings have obscured the real history of the human race, and that procedure continued during the time of the GDR and continues today—as, for example, the "conquerors" of that country, the West Germans, rewrite its history once again from a different perspective, perhaps not in as distorted a fashion as the GDR "historians" had done but a slanted one nevertheless.

The unstated political history represented by the interrogation of Horn in Hein's novel was equally unstated by the GDR media or official histories. Thomas's glimpse into the room provides the reader with a small glimpse into GDR life under the socialist regime in the 1950s, which is somewhat reminis-

73

cent of the McCarthy era in the U.S., but even more importantly, it provides an insight into the family tragedies which became such a common experience to a significant percentage of the population. Anyone whose family member(s) left for the West was ostracized, their careers were fundamentally terminated, and they were employed in an often demeaning situation outside their educational background or preference. This is the second time for Horn. Both cases against him seem trivial and without much substantiation, mostly circumstantial to us. Yet this was the shape of the society in which people lived their daily lives—a society whose members had learned, as had Claudia during the 17 June 1953 episode, to keep quiet, to suppress or ignore the small pieces of history unfolding beneath their eyes, for fear of becoming victims of a situation which so easily lent itself to abuse. Hein's fragmented chronicles urge the reader to remember—even to remember things which they hadn't seen, just as Horn's apparition does with Thomas.

History and Censorship

A good example of fragmented information in literary form is *Horns Ende* itself, which languished over a year on the publisher's shelves while the censorship office struggled to keep it off the market. Aufbau Publishers had completed the printing and agreed with the West German publisher Luchterhand on the license edition for the West when the Ministry of Culture ordered the book held up. Censorship documents which surfaced after the fall of the Wall indicate the extent of the difficulties with which Hein—who by this time was writing *Die Ritter der Tafelrunde*—was faced. The book was screened by Klaus Selbig and two female associates, whose names are given as Fuckas and Horn(!). In his letter to Klaus Höpcke of 10 May 1984, Selbig wrote:

> We have doubts that this novel can be published here because it is— due to the inclusion of the Party niveau—in our opinion much more explosive than *The Distant Lover,* and makes clear that the author is defending his humanistic message from a non-Marxist position. Even taking into consideration that the existential viewpoints (Dr. Spodeck) and the skeptical formulations, historically-philosophically speaking, of the main characters cannot be equated with the standpoint of the author, a differing position is nevertheless not easily discernible and the impression remains that the story carries over into the present as a history of human cruelty. To be sure, the

dialogues which precede the individual chapters and the concluding dialog provide a kind of contrapunkt, but it requires an extremely thorough reading and a great deal of good will not to interpret this novel in the aforementioned sense. . . .

It seems to us that Christoph Hein will not write any differently in the future, so that the question arises: What shall we do with the literary works of this talented author?[22]

The letter went on to call attention to the fact that Hein would undoubtedly proceed with a West German publisher if his manuscript was turned down in the GDR.

From Elmar Faber, the chief of Aufbau publishers and a long-time friend of Hein's, the censorship authorities learned that Hein would not be prepared to make any changes with the possible exception of "partial cuts which we would have to insist upon, if we decide to go ahead with the publication of the book on author-political [*autorenpolitisch*] grounds."[23] *Autorenpolitisch* would have to be interpreted to mean that Hein's global fame and international prestige would bring them more grief if they censored the book than if they approved it. Selbig asked Höpcke to read the manuscript so they could come to a collective decision (i.e., not jeopardize their own jobs), and he included a positive recommendation by Jürgen Engler, who argued, dialectically, that the novel needed to be published in order to provoke argumentive reactions from the Marxist standpoint. Engler—who belonged to a circle of younger intellectuals who were friends with Hein—presented an argument which had begun to gain a foothold. It was the same argument which Dieter Schlenstedt used to ultimately help move Braun's *Hinze-Kunze-Roman,* a book likewise being held up at this time, through the authorization process: critical and argumentive discussion in a public forum was necessary to break the stagnation created by the stubborn dogmatism of "real existing socialism."

From the editor's office at Aufbau came a note dated 17 December 1984 and signed by Günter Drommer, Hein's editor, which described the extent of editorial cuts being made in close cooperation with the author—a task which had now been going on for almost a year. According to Drommer's note, the title was changed from *Horn* to *Horns Ende* in order to disrupt the historical continuity between fascism and Stalinism which comes to light in the novel. The end of Horn signifies that the conditions which may have existed in the 1950s to support this continuity were no longer in effect in the present. Drommer stated that the changes made left them with two distinctive versions of the novel:

On the basis of various changes in the dialogues between Thomas and the dead Horn it was possible to emphasize that aspect of the situation which could not be generalized. The last dialogue was cut. That causes the events described in the manuscript to have a more contained effect, more in the past. The errors of those years no longer tower so provocatively into our present time.

With respect to the Schneeberger-episode Hein made considerable changes. In the first version the untenable comparison between justice and punishment of the 50's with the Nazi period . . . had already been removed.[24]

Drommer concluded by mentioning how the episode describing Bachofen's career in the West as a recreational-vehicle leasing agent and then as mayor of a town would function as a socialist provocation to Western readers. This episode seemed exaggerated and almost absurd in the text of *Horns Ende,* which otherwise adheres strictly to Hein's principles of non-editorializing chronicles, but the point Drommer was making for the officials at the censorship bureau was that being a criminal by socialist standards constituted a success story in the West.

Hein may have intended the Bachofen episode to be ironic, or he may have known such a character, or more likely, he focused on opportunism as a character trait—one which he frequently criticized. In any case, Hein made a stunning disclosure in a letter of 13 September 1993 that the Drommer letter and Elmar Faber's note to the Ministry of Culture were both part of tactical rumor-spreading on the part of the publisher, intended as a diversion in order to get the novel through the approval procedure: "They reported to the Ministry again and again that I was working on it, that I had been working on it, etc., in order to signal that I was ready to compromise. That was the tactic of the publishing house, but none of it is true."[25] Hein stated in his letter that only one single change was made in the entire manuscript (which was retained in the West German edition as well). In chapter seven, narrated by Kruschkatz, he relates his visit to the Schneebergers after delivering the TV and his conversation with Mrs. Schneeberger, who says, "They were brutal" (HE 242). The original sentence was: "They were worse than the Nazis." In reference to the actions of the GDR police who arrested Schneeberger, this latter sentence, of course, was politically brutal, and Hein was unable to prevent the change. Additionally, there was never a change in the title of the novel, as Drommer's letter stated, although he had earlier toyed with the possibility of *Die Zigeunerwiese* (The Gypsy Meadow).

A certain amount of fiction has broken into reality in this remarkable case, inasmuch as the letters discussing *Horns Ende* uncovered and published by Ernst Wichner and Herbert Wiesner as part of their exposé of GDR censorship were themselves a clever ploy. Having thus been deceived by intentionally falsified information, Wichner and Wiesner—and the readers of their intriguing collection of censorship documents—became themselves victims of the theory of the *Schüfftan-Spiegel* in the case of *Horns Ende.*

Luchterhand went ahead and published the new version, and the Luchterhand text does correspond exactly to the one which was finally released in the GDR. The publication of *Horns Ende* in the West added pressure to the GDR agencies, and the Minister of Culture, Hans-Joachim Hoffmann, wrote to Kurt Hager in the Central Committee of the Politburo that the controversy surrounding Braun's *Hinze-Kunze-Roman* was acting as a further catalyst for potentially more bad publicity for the GDR from the *Horns Ende* controversy and that it was best to go ahead and publish Braun's book before this happened. This letter was dated 16 December 1985, and two months earlier, on 28 October 1985, Hoffman had written up a pleomastic official party opinion on Hein's novel:

> The problematical aspect of the book derives from the fact that the author attempts to trace historical processes within the framework of their complexity and contradictory structure with examples from individual life destinies, omitting, however, a dialectical view of the functioning of human beings within the context of their social conditions. A concept of human history emerges in the form of a culpable entanglement of an inescapable metaphysical self-determining course.
>
> This book will not and cannot be understood as a representative literary portrayal of a piece of GDR history. It can nevertheless not be ruled out that the currently submitted, repeatedly revised version will not engender flawed interpretations and intentionally misconstrued representations.[26]

In spite of Hoffman's apparent endorsement of publication of the book, *Horns Ende,* according to Hein, never received official authorization. Elmar Faber released it anyway after what had amounted to two years of negotiations. Hein: "*It is therefore, to the best of my knowledge, the only belletristic book that ever appeared in the GDR without this essentially indispensable authorization*"[27] (my emphasis). Faber experienced extreme difficulty after this and was able to survive only due to the fear of a powerful reaction from the Western media (a reaction which, by means of TV, was always accessible in the GDR).[28] Among other things, the *Horns Ende* incident reveals the surprising power of Western foreign media to influence cultural events in the former GDR.

Not only had Faber released the novel without authorization, but the release had been preceded six months earlier by an illegal edition, which was claimed to be an odd error at the bindery: the binder "mistakenly" covered a number of *Horns Ende* copies with the cover jacket of a Karl May volume (*Der Geist des Llano Estacado*). May, who wrote tales of the American West somewhat after the style of James Fenimore Cooper, was and still is the most popular writer of tales for children and early teens in Germany, and few German children grow up without reading Karl May. Aufbau was printing an edition of May's works at the same time, and the two books were "temporarily mixed up." Hein was unsure who had actually done this, and no one knows how many copies were thus illegally circulated. However, in all certainty, the *Horns Ende* episode demonstrates that there still remains a highly intriguing chapter to be written in the history of culture, censorship, and subversive activity of the intelligentsia in the GDR.

Historical Context in *Horns Ende* and the 1957 Show Trials

In order to understand *Horns Ende,* it is necessary for one to be aware of key political and cultural events of the 1950s, and especially of the year 1957, the year of Horn's death. Most English-speaking readers will not be aware of the impact of several key historical events on East German society. Nor are they likely to be cognizant of the totalitarian government's specific attempts to coerce belief and attitudes regarding such historical events by re-stating and re-writing those occurrences, by disclaiming and ignoring other events, or by demanding and enforcing a unified view of history as a show of solidarity and resolve towards the "enemies" in the West, sacrificing factual truth when such was deemed necessary.

East German history was so consistently obscured and manipulated that it became increasingly difficult to know the facts. Although their leaders' atrocities could be considered mild compared to those of the Nazis,[29] many Germans had their careers (rather than their lives) destroyed, and many others were imprisoned (rather than being sent to concentration camps). Because the 1950s were a period of transition from the Nazi past to a form of socialism, the Ulbricht leadership justified the secrecy of their repressive actions as necessary to national security—generally defined as anything deemed essential to the attainment of Communist goals. *Horns Ende,* in masterful literary form, may well be the best historical document of the GDR in the 1950s, when read at face value, and it becomes a penetrating critique of the failure to de-Stalinize socialism in the GDR when read between the lines.

A standard East German history published as late as 1986 by Heinz Heitzer—although it admits to some mistakes by the Central Committee which contributed to the revolt of 17 June 1953—makes no mention whatsoever of the impact of Stalin's death on socialist countries, on the reform movement triggered by Nikita Kruschev's relaxation of hard-line party controls and his denouncement of Stalin, of the Polish unrest and the reasons for the Hungarian revolt in 1956, or of the imprisonment of reform-minded intellectuals in the GDR in 1957, all of which are indirectly reflected in *Horns Ende.*

When Khruschev came to power after Stalin's death, he began a series of reforms which left the Communist party elite in a state of confusion and uncertainty. His reforms came during a period of time between 1953 and 1956 known as "Tauwetter," (thawing weather) from the title of a novel by Ilja Ehrenburg. At the Twentieth Congress of the Communist party of the Soviet Union in Moscow, Khruschev gave a secret speech denouncing the personality cultism nurtured by Stalin and the terrorist methods he employed. Khruschev had already freed hundreds of thousands of prisoners from the Gulag system and begun a tentative policy of "peaceful co-existence" with the West. The speech took place in February 1956, and in it he denounced the crimes and errors of Stalin while pointing the way towards a democratization of socialism. Although Khruschev stated the cleaning of dirty laundry should only take place internally, the speech was published as early as 20 March in Yugoslavia, and the U.S. State Department released a version for repeated broadcast over Radio Free Europe on 4 June. Parts of the speech were read at the end of March at the third conference of the Socialist Unity Party in East Berlin, but they were never officially made public in the GDR.[30]

GDR intellectuals, politicians, and writers proceeded to develop thinking for what became known as *Der dritte Weg* ("The Third Way"). According to Hermann Weber, this oppositional group was independent of other, earlier such groups. The circle was "antistalinistic but not anticommunist, rejecting both capitalism and the structure of power in the GDR" in favor of democratic reforms which would create a "humane socialism." Weber's accurate assessment of the group points out that the "marxist education in the GDR" produced not only "true believers in the system, but also marxist rebels who worked within" the party structure.[31]

Walter Ulbricht seemed to permit some independent thinking about "The Third Way," generating a widespread dispute which attracted, among others, Walter Janka, the director of Aufbau Publishers; Gustav Just, editor of *Sonntag,* the weekly cultural feuilleton; and Wolfgang Harich, a professor of philosophy, editor of the *Deutsche Zeitschrift für Philosophie* (German Journal of Philosophy), and a senior editor in Aufbau Publishing House. This group of "Third Way" discussants took an active interest in heretofore unheard-of measures which they regarded as necessary to reform the socialist movement: the de-Stalinization of GDR socialism, the dismantling of the repressive bureaucracy, the elimination of the secret police, and the establishment of a civil rights code.[32]

The reform movements gained momentum on the strength of initial successes in Poland and Hungary, but after Soviet tanks put down the rebellion in Hungary in 1956, the situation in East Germany changed swiftly. Ulbricht had never renounced his authoritarian-Stalinist methods and invited Harich to discuss his reform ideas. Ulbricht and a few close allies essentially played out enough rope for the entire group to incriminate itself and, after giving Harich a harsh prison term in March, staged in the summer of 1957 a Stalinist show-trial for the rest of the so-called Harich-Janka group. Harich himself, in order to have a portion of his sentence commuted, became the crown witness for the prosecution in the July trials. Harich's self-denunciation at the end of his own trial demonstrates with a stunning reminiscence of language from George Orwell's *1984,* written in 1948, showing the extent to which human dignity was denigrated in show trials where the accused actually declared themselves ripe for the gallows. Harich's statement could easily have been Hein's model for the cowardly self-criticism exercised by Kruschkatz in his second denunciation of Horn. It is a chilling reminder of the period of history captured in *Horns Ende* and is worthwhile repeating here in order to put the novel into historical perspective:

> I would like to express my thanks, and especially to the State Security Police of the GDR . . . and I have come to the conclusion, that they are quite correct and decent. . . . I had gotten, to be sure, out of control. Politically I was a runaway horse, which could no longer be stopped by calling to it. . . . If I had not been arrested, then I would not today be ripe for the 10 year sentence, which Herr Attorney General has requested, but for the gallows, and therefore I state . . . my thanks to the Secret Police for their alertness.[33]

All the central figures were given hard prison sentences. Janka—part of an old line of German Communist party members, wounded three times and awarded a medal of honor in the war against Franco's Nazi Spain—spent five years in isolation in Bautzen, in the same prison where he had spent time as a victim of Nazi repression. Others were booted out of the party. Sympathizers or independent thinkers like the Leipzig professor Ernst Bloch, widely regarded as one of Germany's outstanding twentieth-century philosophers for *Prinzip Hoffnung* (The Principle of Hope, Written in Exile in the United States) 1938–1947, was forced into early emeritus, eventually leaving the GDR for a position at the University of Tübingen in West Germany.

Bloch has a remote connection to *Horns Ende*: he had secured a position in the philosophy department in Leipzig for Johannes Heinz Horn, chiefly on the basis of the latter's dissertation, "Lenin as Philosopher." But the "thaw" was emphatically over and with it, the possibility of critical discussion on a political plateau. The rule of party unity and solidarity was reaffirmed with a vengeance, and once again, those who had anything to say publicly which might not conform to party dogma knew they had better remain silent, the silence which Horn insisted that Thomas break in the early 1980s.

A few months before the Wall came down, Christoph Hein had offered to hide Gustav Just's manuscript of his silenced memories of those events in the 1950s. When the book was finally published early in 1990, Hein wrote in his foreword:

> Just's book [*Zeuge in eigener Sache* (Witness in My Own Case)] destroys a mendacious and inhumane view of our world, a viewpoint of which so many had partaken who knew the truth even in those days, but who were unwilling to stand up for it. Participating and also sharing in the responsibility were those unable to muster the courage to free the truth from the stranglehold of the corrupt people in power. Just's book helps us to destroy a view of the world which many, which all of us accepted passively, more or less aware of its mendacity, knowing that it was directed at us, and that it sought to discipline us. They wanted to kill our memories and our capacity for remembrance in order to win our souls.[34]

Horns Ende is much less a story fitting together pieces of the real Horn's fate (J. H. Horn died 8 January 1958, and the fictional Horn, 1 September 1957) than it is a story determined to recall what effect the unjust fates of those who struggled for truth and integrity in the socialist world had on them and on society at large, on the history of what Hein calls "social autobiography" in East Germany. For Hein, there is no direct relationship between the real and fictional Horn: "It is a novel about history, about historical understanding and about writing history."[35] The censorship authorities must have recognized immediately the implications of dredging up the injurious memories associated with the time of the Harich-Janka trials and of the Stalinist measures which impeded any sort of rational progress. Their resistance to the restoration of history incorporated in the figure of Thomas demonstrates Hein's point that little had changed by the early 1980s with respect to the recognition of factual history.

The show trials had forced active intellectuals into silence and the population into a thoroughly monitored state. The measures taken against "revisionism" in the fall of 1957 ended open discussions with what amounted to a witch hunt against "revisionists": to succeed it was, once again, necessary to be silent on the issues unless voicing the party line. From the sensational show trials, the reprisals spread throughout the country in a quieter but equally effective manner. Those who had spoken less convincingly or were guilty by association received lesser punishments: they were demoted to museum work or to less important political functions. One of the important social repercussions to be kept in mind when reading many of Hein's works is the fact that this situation created the possibility for opportunistic individuals to discredit their rivals and advance—or protect—their own careers by doing so.

Another important aspect of the novel, briefly mentioned earlier, is the question it raises about historical continuity, a point Hein later elaborates in his 1989 lecture in Essen. Whereas West German historians viewed 1945 as a "zero hour" marking a new beginning in time, East German historians regarded Hitler as a usurper who disrupted the evolution of socialism in Germany, which dates back to the early nineteenth century. In his lecture, Hein reminds us that Germans were still living on German territory—both East and West—after the war, as they had been living there before the war. However, East German historians, while acknowledging the enormous campaign to de-nazify the East, nevertheless maintained that the war was a victory of socialism over imperialism and (as proof of the success of their pedagogical efforts) that there were no Nazis in East Germany (hence Kruschkatz's cynical remark to Bachofen), only victims of nazism, members of the antifascist resistance movement and old Communist party members. According to the party line which eventually evolved, as preposterous as it sounds, whatever Nazis had remained had allegedly all moved to the West. A significant portion of the displeasure expressed by censors with the novel can be traced to Hein's portrayal of attitudes and behavior which bear strong resemblance to the Nazi period, in spite of the omitted comment by Mrs. Schneeberger. The advocation of denunciation and informing on one's neighbors and associates to coerce citizens is a continuation of a form of Nazi mental terrorism, and it was encouraged and utilized in the GDR right up to the last day before the Wall came down.

Guldenberg can be understood as a microcosm of the GDR: Horn's death plagues the people of Guldenberg even as they ignore it, a corresponding parallel to the unwillingness of GDR citizens to acknowledge the past they knew about, in spite of the party's demand that they forget. Hein began writing the book shortly after the time period of Kruschkatz's final report, around 1980–1982, and he seemed to express the fear that time was running out, that it would be too late to remember if nothing was done.

During that time (1981), a book by the renowned Kirgisian (Soviet Union) author Tschingis Aitmatow, translated as *Ein Tag zieht den Jahrhundertweg* (One Day Pulls Away the Century), was immensely popular in East Germany and, ultimately, in West Germany and Europe as well. The most powerful passage in the book is the telling of the legend of the Mankurts, captives of a conquering tribe of the Sary-Ösek Steppes. After shaving the heads of their prisoners, the tribe would slaughter an adult camel and slice the skin of its neck into strips. These they would stick to the captives' heads in layers while still warm and then leave the men in the field, arms and hands bound, under the hot sun without food and water. Those who didn't die became Mankurts—slaves who could no longer remember their past. Their memory having been destroyed, they were concerned only with physical necessities and were absolutely obedient. The mother of such a Mankurt makes a trek across the Steppes to find her son. She finds him and attempts vainly to get him to remember his name and the name of his father and who he is. But he cannot remember, and instead, at the exhortation of his masters, he kills his mother. The legendary cemetery where she is buried, and where her memory is honored and preserved, is threatened with destruction in the novel by a relentlessly advancing technology.

The importance of history to Europeans should not be underestimated. It constitutes a mentality which perhaps does not exist very strongly in our own society. For Christoph Hein, the self-described chronicler without a moral message, knowledge of history is crucial in order for us to know who we are. Unlike those of whom he spoke in his preface to Gustav Just's book, Hein did not wait to speak out until after the Wall came down, and he consistently displayed the courage to stand up for truth. Hammer maintains that active commemoration of the past leads to the necessity of internalizing the contradictoriness of historical processes. For Hein, according to Hammer, "historical consciousness is the condition of humanity and human progress," which corresponds to "Aitmatov's idea that the loss of memory is the most terrible of all imaginable crimes."[36] Freedom is the responsibility for choosing between truth and lies.

A Note on the Gypsies

Some background information on the collectivization of the rural economy in the GDR is helpful in understanding the implications of the debate between Bachofen and Kruschkatz, who would have been under some pressure at the time to improve the number of agricultural collectives. There was considerable resistance between 1956 and 1958 to the process of the collectivization of farms into communal operations. When Kruschkatz tells Bachoven that they both know the real reasons for the farmers' reluctance, he is referring to the fact that very few of the collectives up to that point were able to show any profit and were, in general, only able to maintain their existence on the basis of government subsidies. The average annual income for member farmers was around 3,400 marks, which did not compare favorably to the 6,100 marks earned by workers in a heavy machinery factory. Moreover, independent farmers were earning between 20,000 and 25,000 marks.[37]

The state political machinery began a tough agitation to persuade more farmers to join. They particularly felt that if the stronger farmers were to participate, the collectives would be strengthened and made profitable. The political argument was very similar to the argument used (unsuccessfully) in *The Distant Lover* to coerce Katharina to joining the youth group: joining was a contribution to peace, to making the GDR a strong country which protected peace. Failure to do so was condemned as sabotage of the peace effort. Nevertheless, it was not until an intense and forceful campaign in 1960, prior to the erection of the Berlin Wall in August of the following year, that GDR officials—probably aided by the global negativity which arose out of the Castro assassination attempt by American-based Cuban exiles and the shooting down of American U-2 spy pilot Gary Powers over the Soviet Union—succeeded in collectivizing the majority of farmers and rural workers. By the time the Wall went up, there were only about 10,000 independent farmers left, and this number would dwindle as well, inasmuch as the option to leave home and move to the West had been eliminated.

In this context, and with particular reference to the comparative income structure, Kruschkatz was clearly behaving as a realist, and Bachofen's ludicrous analysis is exposed as an additional manifestation of his opportunistic attempts to advance his own career at Kruschkatz's expense and to restore a symbolically questionable town landmark from the past: the health resort. On the other hand, Kruschkatz's capitulation in the end and his unwillingness to stand and fight for principles—to defend the rights of the Gypsies—exposes him as both a spineless victim of the political system and a perpetuator of it. Forgetting, which was Kruschkatz's philosophy of necessity, also includes forgetting everything which cannot be forgiven, reproducing the conditions which in turn generate new injustices. The memory of the Gypsies and of Gudrun Gohl, as Preußer has pointed out, serves as a point of departure "for self introspection, self accusation and the sorrow of a neglected opportunity for a totality in life," causing "private and political spheres to flow together"[38] in the narrative typology of Hein's novel.

Hope for the present and for the future rests in the remembrance of the sufferings from the past. Walter Benjamin held that the "historical articulation of the past does not constitute the recognition of what really had taken place. It means to take control of a remembrance in the way it flares up during the moment of danger." Hein clearly attempted to wrest control of remembrances from the 1950s away from a rigid political monopoly and place them into a flexible and viable poetic dialogue, where danger could be recognized and hope could replace complacency. "Only the writer of history," wrote Benjamin, "possesses the talent to kindle the spark of hope from out of the past . . . : the dead are not safe from the enemy who conquers them and this enemy has never ceased to conquer."[39] Both Thomas and Marlene communicate with the dead in order to restore their memories, and the Gypsies are the medium through which these memories pass.

Notes

1. Walter Benjamin, *Illuminationen* (Frankfurt a.M.: Suhrkamp, 1977) 258.

2. Walter Benjamin, *Das Passagen-Werk,* vol. 1 (Frankfurt a.M.: Suhrkamp, 1983) 588.

3. See Christoph Hein, interview, "Dialog ist das Gegenteil von Belehren. Gespräch mit Christoph Hein (February 1991)," *Chronist ohne Botschaft. Christoph Hein. Ein Arbeitsbuch. Materialien. Auskünfte. Bibliographie,* ed. Klaus Hammer (Berlin: Aufbau, 1992) 35.

4. Klaus Hammer, "*Horns Ende.* Versuch einer Interpretation," *Chronist ohne Botschaft* 129.

5. Christoph Hein, interview, "Wir werden es lernen müssen, mit unserer Vergangenheit zu leben. Gespräch mit Krzysztof Jachimczak. Nach dem Erscheinen von *Horns Ende* (1986)," *Christoph Hein. Texte, Daten, Bilder,* ed. Lothar Baier (Frankfurt a.M.: Luchterhand, 1990) 58.

6. Claus Leggewie, "Wie ein Alp auf den Seelen," *Christoph Hein. Texte, Daten, Bilder* 148.

7. Hein, interview, "Wir werden es lernen müssen, mit unserer Vergangenheit zu leben" 63–64.

8. Hein, interview, "Dialog ist das Gegenteil von Belehren," *Chronist ohne Botschaft* 31.

9. Hammer, "*Horns Ende,* Versuch einer Interpretation" 126.

10. Lenin, *Kleines Politisches Wörterbuch* (Berlin: Dietz, 1986) 724.

11. Hein, interview, "Dialog ist das Gegenteil von Belehren" 34.

12. Hein, interview, "Dialog ist das Gegenteil von Belehren" 34. Hammer's conversation with Hein includes his own observations as well as the questions he put to Hein.

13. In the 1960s, the Free German Youth group—the group which Katharina in *The Distant Lover* had refused to join—went around tearing down antennas from houses in order to police the population's viewing habits. Their action was short-lived and ineffective.

14. Gabriele Lindner, "Ein geistiger Widergänger," *Christoph Hein. Texte, Daten, Bilder* 159.

15. Bachofen returns to Bad Guldenberg years later, driving a large, American-made automobile and bragging about his success. It seems that in the West he managed to succeed where he failed in the East: he had become mayor of a small town. The passage ironizes the West, of course, indicating what type of person is capable of having a success story there. The passage departs from Hein's normal dry, objective prose and loses its verisimilitude.

16. Hein, interview, "Wir werden es lernen müssen, mit unserer Vergangenheit zu leben" 57.

17. Heinz-Peter Preußer, "Hoffnung im Zerfall. Das Negative und das Andere in *Horns Ende*," *Chronist ohne Botschaft* 139.

18. Preußer 139.

19. Fabrizio Cambi, "Jetztzeit und Vergangenheit. Ästethische und ideologische Auseinandersetzung im Werk Christoph Heins," *Chronist ohne Botschaft* 110.

20. Hein, interview, "Wir werden es lernen müssen, mit unserer Vergangenheit zu leben" 57.

21. Cambi 107–8.

22. Klaus Selbig, letter to Klaus Höpcke, 10 May 1984, in Ernst Wichner and Herbert Wiesner, *Zensur in der DDR*. Ausstellungsbuch (Berlin: Literaturhaus Berlin, 1991) 102.

23. Selbig, letter to Höpcke 102–3.

24. Günther Drommer, Notiz ze Christoph Hein: Horns Ende, 17 December 1984, in Ernst Wichner and Herbert Wiesner, *Zensur in der DDR* 103.

25. Christoph Hein, letter to the author, 13 September 1993.

26. Hans-Joachim Hoffman, letter to Kurt Hager, 28 October 1985, in Ernst Wichner and Herbert Wiesner, *Zensur in der DDR* 104.

27. Hein, letter to the author, 13 September 1993.

28. To add a personal note here: Hein's passport had been sent over to the U.S. Embassy in January of 1986, presumably around the time of Höpcke's letter to me of 8 January, in which he approved my invitation to Hein to come to the United States. On the basis of the letters from the Ministry of Culture translated here, it is evident that the mix-up with his IAP-66 visa form is clearly linked with the government's displeasure over the publishing of *Horns Ende*. That summer, after my conversations with the *Stasi*

agent at the Writers Union in charge of travel, I wrote an article on *Horns Ende,* disguising it with a sprinkling of *Sklavensprache,* but making the link between Stalinism and fascism as clear as I could by using the common-denominator denunciation. A mutual friend, Stefan Dietzsch, working in the philosophy section of the Academy of Science, arranged for the editor of *Sinn und Form,* the most critically reputable international journal in the GDR, to look at it. When this editor expressed interest, I showed the article to Hein, and he responded by stating in a letter that he would not meet any further requests which he might receive to publish in *Sinn und Form* until my review essay appeared. This proved to be unnecessary. The review was promised for the fall of 1986, but it was delayed until the March/April issue of 1987, reaching newstand circulation precisely while Hein was in Kentucky. That issue is more notable for its publication of a speech given by the prominent Germanist Hans Mayer on the occasion of his first visit back to the GDR since he left his professorate in Leipzig some twenty-three years before to move to the West, but the acceptance of the article in *Sinn und Form* re-opened the possibility of discussing Hein's novel in public in the GDR, and more reviews followed. The publication of *Horns Ende,* the lifting of the review ban, and the visit to the GDR by Mayer all constituted a major shift in the relationship between the state and the cultural community, a shift which expanded rapidly thereafter.

29.   An estimated six hundred East Germans lost their lives attempting to escaped from the country after the Wall was built—an atrocious figure. The Nazis, it is estimated, destroyed the lives of some six million Jews and of another 300,000 minority and handicapped people.

30.   See Dietrich Staritz, *Geschichte der DDR 1949–1985* (Frankfurt a.M.: Surhrkamp, 1985) 101–7 for a summary of Kruschev's actions during the Twentieth Congress of the Soviet Union.

31.   Hermann Weber, *Geschichte der DDR* (Munich: DTV, 1986) 286.

32.   See Weber 288.

33.   Walter Janka, *Schwierigkeiten mit der Wahrheit* (Hamburg: Rowohlt, 1989) 89.

34.   Hein, ". . . und andere (Für Gustav Just)," in Gustav Just, *Zeuge in eigener Sache* (Berlin: Buchverlag der Morgen, 1990) 6.

35.   Hein, interview, "Wir werden es lernen müssen, mit unserer Vergangenheit zu leben" 62.

36.   Hammer, "*Horns Ende,* Versuch einer Interpretation" 124.

37.   See Staritz, *Geschichte der DDR 1949–1985* 128.

38.   Preußer 140.

39.   Benjamin, *Illuminationen* 253.

CHAPTER FOUR

Homesickness for the Cell:
Der Tangospieler

The spring 1989 publication of *Der Tangospieler* (*The Tango Player*), translated into English in 1992, completes what could be designated as a trilogy of historical prose writings by Hein, each of which focuses on a time during a key historical turning point in East Germany: *The Distant Lover* on the revolt in East Germany of 17 June 1953, *Horns Ende* on the impact of the Hungarian revolt in 1956, and *The Tango Player* on the "Prague Spring" of 1968 that led to the fall of the Czech party chief and head of state Alexander Dubcek and the elimination of democratic reforms in Czechoslovakia.

Reading *The Distant Lover* in 1982 shocked people; reading *The Tango Player* in 1989, whose main character reminds some critics of Claudia (neither is interested in a close relationship or in politics),[1] provided ironic amusement. Hein captures the mood of the changing times: the situation had become so absurdly pathetic in the minds of many people that it deserved ridicule. A few weeks after the appearance of *The Tango Player,* the mass exodus by GDR "vacationers" through Czechoslovakia and Hungary began the final stage before the fall of the Wall. But in 1968, the main character's behavior was not amusing. The political situation was deeply serious.

None of Hein's books actually present an intense direct interaction with these historical events on the part of any of the characters. Such happenings are kept in the narrative background, but they are undeniably important in the lives of the characters, even though the characters often tend to discount their significance. For Hein, as we saw in *Horns Ende,* an individual's attitude toward history is the crucial point, and these varying attitudes comprise the level of reality he explores and intensifies in his fiction.

The three books were written throughout the decade of the 1980s, and each traces not only steps in the gradual easing of censorship in the GDR during this time—measured in terms of reduced need for *Sklavensprache*—but also those specific earlier historical events which most caused disillusionment and loss of faith in the system, and apathetic withdrawal into private life by ordinary citizens.

The Tango Player opens with the release of Hans-Peter Dallow from prison in February of 1968 after a twenty-one-month internment. Now thirty-six years old, Dallow had been a junior faculty member in the history department of the Karl-Marx-University in Leipzig, specializing in nineteenth-century proletarian history. He had been nearing promotion to *Dozent* (equivalent to associate professor with tenure) when a group of students talked him into providing the piano accompaniment for their cabaret show. Their regular pianist was sick, and they had only two days before the first show. Dallow agreed and played an old tango number from the 1920s, "Adios Muchachos," to which the students, having altered the text, performed a witty persiflage of Walter Ulbricht.

Dallow claimed to be innocent. He had not paid any attention to the text; he was only the tango player, and a fill-in at that. Nevertheless, he was sentenced to twenty-one months in prison with the others for "defamation of character of leading personalities of the state" (Ta 71). The story concludes seven months later with Dallow's return to the university with the promotion just a few days after the repression of the Czechoslovakian reform movement by Soviet tanks and Warsaw Pact troops. Dallow replaces his rival at the institute, Dr. Roessler, who is demoted for having accidently misread the situation in Prague. During the seven months, Dallow tries to put his life back in order by establishing his old routines.

He picks up women at different bars each night until this becomes boring; he visits old colleagues and acquaintances, pays a belated visit to his family, starts an affair with a single mother, and spends most of his time in disgruntled thought about the unfairness of his imprisonment. There are some encounters with his lawyer and the judge. The tango number is played again in the cabaret bar (without Dallow this time) by the same students as an ironic joke, and Dallow is followed by two *Stasi* agents whose purpose is to "rehabilitate" him and to entice him to return to the university and re-enter socialist society. Dallow has enough savings to avoid work during the seven months, but the judge finally orders him to obtain work. After Dallow's failed attempts to get a job as a truck driver, a bartender friend finds him a job on a resort island as a waiter. There, he occupies himself by sleeping with vacationing young girls, avoiding political involvement, and continuing his withdrawal, until the events of the Prague Spring provide him with the opportunity to return to Leipzig.

As usual, Hein does not pretend to be more clever than his readers and does not directly attempt to establish Dallow as a representative of society around 1968. His writing thus causes "reader insecurity" which leads to a "heightened tension."[2] Unlike in *The Distant Lover,* Hein does not employ a first-person narrative and hence creates more distance between the reader and the main character. Familiar short sentences like those seen in the *The Distant Lover* create a neutral zone, and then the narrative switches to long, introspective sentences when Dallow's reflections about his innocence and his future are related—a thought process which reveals his guilt for not assuming responsibility for his actions or for his life. Consistent with Hein's objective use of language, interpretive adjectives are seldom used; there is seldom a change of perspective and a "minimum of ironic fracture."[3] His dramatist touch with language and dialogue readily lent the text to a screen adaptation by Roland Gräf later in 1989, the first DEFA film produced after the opening of the Wall and one of the last major films produced in the GDR before unification.[4]

When Sara Bershtel moved over to Farrar, Straus and Giroux in 1990, she took the rights to Hein's works other than *The Distant Lover* along with her. Plans were in the works to translate *Horns Ende,* but little progress was made, possibly due to less-than-expected sales of *The Distant Lover.* When *The Tango Player* appeared, a decision was made to proceed with it first. The translation by Philip Boehm is a marked improvement, but it still fails to replicate much of the essence of Hein's precise descriptions of humdrum every-day existence, or his use of dialogue to define his characters' mentality in a nutshell. The translation doesn't provide the reader with the intermittent sardonic chuckle that Hein's blend of ironic humor with banal reality produces. The severity of this shortcoming may, however, depend on the reader's lack of common cultural reference points regarding life in East Germany and an unfamiliarity with the kind of creative, ironic-bitter wit which ordinary East German people added to their everyday language to buffer themselves against the world around them. Few in the United States have ever lived behind the iron curtain, and any translator is faced with difficult barriers when attempting to find common parallels in linguistic expression—especially one who has not spent time in the GDR as more than a hostile tourist. To his credit, Boehm at least tries to avoid finding common American cultural equivalents as reference points: they seldom exist.

A Little Progress

When Dallow gets out of prison, he finds that things have changed: "Wir sind ein Stück weiter gekommen" (we have made a little progress) is a phrase used as a leitmotiv throughout the novel. Dallow hears these words several times in conjunction with the news that he would not be sent to jail for playing the tango nowadays. Under the new constitution, enacted in 1968, it would be a simple misdemeanor.

This change adds insult to injury for Dallow, causing him to act defiantly towards the system which ostensibly attempts to rehabilitate and reintegrate him. By the time of the publication of the novel in 1989, a large segment of

GDR society had resigned itself to the situation, looking upon the aging members of the government with disgust and ridicule. East German readers would have reacted positively if Dallow had at least had the fortitude to stand with the other members of the student cabaret group, if he had at least bothered to pay attention to the text and therefore had been "unjustly" imprisoned for having knowingly participated in the caricature of Ulbricht. The fact that he continues to maintain his innocence (by reason of ignorance) makes his situation ludicrous and demonstrates that he has no backbone. His persistent resistance to being reintegrated does offer some hope, however.

When Dallow gets out of prison he returns to his apartment in Leipzig, cleans it up, gets resituated as quickly as possible, and establishes a routine. His previous girlfriend has left the apartment quite some time ago, and she never appears in the story. He checks out his car, fills up the battery, and hooks it up to a charger. He speaks to his car, "I missed you, you and the ladies" (Ta 12).

After cleaning up, he goes into town for a walk to see what had changed, to check out his old haunts. Even by GDR standards, Leipzig itself was not a very typical large city even though it boasted over 600,000 inhabitants. A source of constant irritation for the Leipzig inhabitants was the preferential treatment given to Berlin for scarce building and renovation funds. The fact that Leipzig was left in a state of dilapidation throughout the existence of the GDR fueled old antagonism between the Saxons (Leipzig) and the Prussians in Berlin, a city which was rebuilt as a "showcase" to the West. Leipzig's town center was shut off to traffic, a situation that generated an atmosphere more of a small town than of a big city. It was not unusual to bump into friends and acquaintances in the city center in spite of the size of the population.

In a café bar, he discovers his former defense lawyer sitting at a table with the judge who had sentenced him, Dr. Berger. That the judge, the ex-prisoner, and his lawyer all patronize the same bar underscores the provinciality of the city—a resistance to change and a small-town sense of boredom. Dallow shakes hands with the attorney and reminds the judge that he had sentenced him to twenty-one months in prison. The judge tells him that he is welcome to make an appointment if he has any questions or complaints, but Dallow says he was just saying hello to his lawyer, Kiewer.

Observing Dallow still taking his first gingerly steps after his release from prison, the reader is expecting substantive encounters and significant actions by the character. Dallow goes up to the bar and asks for his friend Harry, the head waiter, who is not scheduled to work until later that evening. Dallow has a conversation with the barmaid, who doesn't find him very pleasant. Some men next to him are discussing Dubcek and the situation in Prague. This annoys Dallow—they are speaking so loudly that it disturbs his concentration on the breasts of the barmaid. This minor glimpse into the workings of Dallow's mind defines the characteristics of his non-political personality and exposes his sense of priorities, personal self-gratification being at or near the top. Hein juxtaposes Dallow's particular chauvinistic and degrading attitude towards sex and his political disinterest from the outset of the narrative.

When Harry shows up, the conversation of the two men centers around small talk and women. They joke about the barmaid. Maybe she's the type for Dallow. Nothing of substance comes up, in spite of their not having seen each other for almost two years—not even any description of life in prison. Dallow hangs around the bar until midnight, drinking and looking over the women. He can't help but think to himself how harmless looking and suburban the judge, who is having a bit too much to drink, appears. He now makes a different impression on Dallow than he had wearing his formidable robes at the hearings. The reader begins to sense banality but, is, at the same time, willing to allow Dallow some time to get his bearings.

The next day, Dallow tries to sort things out during a walk outside of town. He finds that the only conclusion which presents itself is for him to cease thinking about what happened—a narrative construction of anti-identity, on Hein's part. He realizes that he has no desire to speak about it with anyone: "He wanted to wipe the time out of his memory in order to free himself of it" (Ta 21). It was incomprehensible to him that the imprisonment could have been a punishment; for him, it was an unjust theft of his time and a personal insult. He is happy that his car motor still runs without missing a beat, and he (ominously) resolves that the machine can be an example to him for how to continue with his life.

That night, he goes to a different bar and picks up a young woman. She has to move her small child into the hallway—she doesn't want it sleeping in the kitchen because of the gas stove—so they can use the bedroom. Although there is no description, the GDR reader would know that her apartment would have been crowded and small; she would have been assigned space which included a hallway, a narrow bathroom, a small kitchenette, and a bedroom/living room.

Dallow is noncommittal about whether he will return. She tells him there is a key on the kitchen table. If he plans to come back, he can take the key along; otherwise, he should toss it through the mail slot after locking up on his way out. From a telegram delivered to her that morning, he learns that her name is Elke Schütte. He is amused that the telegram is from a male friend. He changes his mind and leaves her a note with his name and phone number, writing that he will drop by in a few days. He keeps the key and, since he doesn't come back for a long time, for Dallow Elke is not much more than a woman in reserve, a potential piece of the routine he has begun to re-construct for himself—an "object" to fall back on in the event someone else doesn't pan out. Since Elke stands apart in the novel from the one-night-stand ladies (mentioned with no description or names), she represents both a failed opportunity for love—and meaning—and a yardstick by which Dallow's human worth can be measured.

In some respects, Dallow has emerged from an incubation period—a Rip Van Winkle theme commonly used in European literature. Poor Rip, of course, is estranged and disoriented by the changes he perceives. In Max Frisch's novel *Stiller* (1954),[5] the main character retells the legend of Rip Van Winkle as part of his struggle to create a new identity for himself. His denial of the old identity ultimately is overpowered by the forces of society. Dallow is exactly the converse of Stiller: although presented with the opportunity to establish a new identity, he struggles to get back inside the skin of his old identity.

He decides to try out his phone and unconsciously calls up his old work number in the history institute, where his former rival, Jürgen Roessler, answers. They agree to meet, an idea which amuses Dallow, since he thinks it will make Roessler, whose career moved forward when Dallow was arrested, uncomfortable. The phone rings, and a man who identifies himself as Schulze asks him to come to the district court for a meeting at 2:00 p.m. It could be a full day for Dallow.

He encounters Sylvia at the institute, a former student who has become an assistant professor. Instead of congratulating her, he reminds her of a pajama party he was supposed to attend at her house the night of his arrest and alludes to sexual activity with her. She discounts any importance in what he says and claims, prophetically, that he just seems to want to return to the way things were. Hein leaves the impression that the content of Dallow's identity was and is to be a womanizer (he missed his car and the ladies) and that his profession as a historian has been more or less inconsequential to him. Dallow then listens for a few moments through the door to Sylvia's lecture and to the student discussion and recalls how tiresome it was to teach, underscoring his alienation from his profession, from the importance of history and passing it on to the next generation. Dallow is much different from any of the historians of *Horns Ende;* even Kruschkatz has at least wrestled with the importance of social historicism. For Dallow, a scant decade later, history has no intrinsic or social significance; it simply provides the means for his career. The "little progress" takes on an ironic characteristic.

Outside Sylvia's lecture hall, he recalls having suffered through listening to nonsense from the students, "nodding approvingly or rolling his eyes" (Ta 32). He remembers the "contempt he felt when he gave praise, acknowledged an achievement with goodwill or respectfully accepted a week-long effort by a student to finish a paper. And the same repeated student questions every year about all the possible riddles of the world, naive, cute little questions, each sentence a testimonial, statements of belief and hope not yet damaged, awaiting fundamental, all-encompassing explanations" (Ta 32).

He found that his answers had to be devoid of sarcastic comments, and "the corners of his mouth hurt from forming smiles which glossed over everything" (Ta 32). It was nothing more than a question of discipline for Dallow to maintain his posture over the years, to meet the necessity of such "stupidity" by pretending that their questions and his answers were meaningful. The cynical attitude expressed by Dallow's not-too-subtle choice of words regarding his pseudo-professional life as a teacher is highly reminiscent of Claudia's non-committal and routine job performance as a doctor and healer. Both occupations suggest the need for dedication due to the important role in society which they represent. If teachers (historians) and healers perform their tasks with only mechanical routine, serious problems exist within the structures of the society which they impact and from which they originate.

Dallow could not have taught at the university without having joined the party—which he clearly would have done as an act of pretention, without conviction. He would have been required to reiterate the party line. History is not important to him, but he is a professor of history. History, too, is nothing but a formality for Dallow. If we recall Horn's thoughts, humanity ceases to exist when history is wiped out. Hein's choice of profession for Dallow is integral to the "social autobiography" he constructs in *The Tango Player* to reflect society's widespread degeneration into apathy. "The legitimate child of dictatorship," as Barbara Sichtermann wrote in her review of *The Tango Player,* "is apathy."[6]

Roessler is now head of the history section, aware that this is a job to which Dallow would have been promoted before his transgression in the student cabaret. At stake is Dallow's future, now that it has been altered by the fact of his imprisonment. Roessler advises him to forget what happened: times have changed, "we have progressed a little" (Ta 36–37) since then. Nowadays he would receive a mild reprimand, nothing more. The best thing for him to do is to start over and to orient himself towards the future.

"The word future frightened him" (Ta 37). Dallow cannot conceptualize what it means for him. For him, the "future was a large, white, frightening piece of paper" (Ta 37). It would help him to think clearly if he were only capable of drawing just a couple of lines on this paper. He doesn't understand why this word future renders his brain lame. The future seems to Dallow to be a linear continuation of the past and the present. Just as Roessler sat on the chair in his office, Dallow can go on doing that day after day, and his future will be secure. Dallow's past was the prison cell, not so comfortable as the office, but nevertheless he discovers that his release from prison was actually an interruption of the linear quality of his future and his security. Dallow is trapped between future anxiety and a return to "normalcy."

The meeting comes to an awkward and unresolved end. Dallow leaves, flirting with the secretary a bit, and then heads to the district court building to see what Schulze wants. As he approaches the building, two men appear behind him and introduce themselves as Schulze and Müller. These names have a comical ring. On stage, they would probably be shown not to be threatening evildoers from the all-powerful secret police but slightly inept, albeit dutiful, bureaucrats doggedly pursuing their quarry. Evidently they have been following him, although Dallow isn't sure from which direction they came. The word *Stasi* is never used in the book, but it is clear from the beginning that Schulze and Müller hail from the secret police. They have come to help with his rehabilitation, as the new constitutional laws had provided. Thematically for Dallow's important day, they will attempt to find solutions for his dilemma as Roessler has done.

Schulze and Müller also engage in "soft terror" to counterbalance the rehabilitation effort by playing mind games with Dallow. One asks the other if he locked the door to the office, and the other answers, "Of course not. What gives you such an idea?" (Ta 45). Dallow recalls that one of the men had stood at the door for a while after they entered the room, and he wonders whether the door is locked or not. He asks if he can leave, and the reply is yes, of course, any time—they just would like to chat with him.

The chat eventually gets around to Dallow's plans for the future, and he answers the same as he had with Roessler. He didn't have time to think about it in prison. They wonder how he had spent his time in prison. He invents a story, telling them he wrote a novel there. He says on the last day before his release, the authorities took his manuscript and tore it up. Schulze and Müller know that none of this is true. They wonder if Dallow isn't interested in going back to work, and they tell him they can help him. Dallow asks them why they want to help him. They reply, "Because we are convinced that your sentence was a silly mistake. Today that wouldn't happen. We have made a little progress" (Ta 50). Dallow wonders if they can give him the two years of his life back, and then he gets up and leaves.

A Historical Digression

One can gain a better understanding of this notion of "a little progress" by taking a brief look at the historical period in question, 1966–1968. A period of mild liberalization accompanying the "New Economic System" of 1963—which placed more responsibility on management to emphasize plant profitability and rewarded workers with bonus incentives—came to an end around 1965–1966. Symptomatic of the accompanying cultural freeze was another notorious case which led to the official discrediting of one of the GDR's most prominent intellectuals, Robert Havemann, a professor of physics at the Humboldt University in Berlin. Havemann had been a member of the KPD (Communist Party of Germany) since 1932 and was sentenced to death by the Nazi government in 1943 for his involvement in the resistance movement. However, he survived to the end of the war in the Brandenburg prison. In East Germany he had a distinguished career as a member of the People's Parliament and received the National Award of the GDR in 1959. Havemann began to distance himself from the party in 1956 and eventually became the new principal spokesman for those efforts aimed at the democratization of socialism. When these ideas became evident in his lectures on philosophical problems of natural science and in essays he published in the West, the tolerance-wave came to a halt. Stefan Heym, who was closely associated with Havemann and Wolf Biermann for a time, summarized Havemann's controversial thoughts from 1963 in his autobiographical work, *Nachruf,* 1988 (Obituary):

> It is no easy task . . . to bring people to believe in socialism without satisfying their material interests immediately. These material interests are in a state of contradiction . . . with the interests of the overall development. If, moreover, a man like Stalin assumes the leadership and creates a manifold hierarchy, a huge political bureaucracy, which exercises airtight supervision of each individual, then it would be almost unavoidable in such a system for people in public functions to have come into their jobs by virtue of their abilities, instead of by virtue of a single, indeed disgusting ability, namely, the precise ability to obtain such a position within such a system. Nevertheless, the essential problem is not one of persons. The internal structure needs to be changed. Democracy, without which, as Lenin repeatedly emphasized, socialism could not be realized, was suffocated during the period of Stalinism. . . . Only the reinstatement of democracy . . . will convince the mass public of the necessity to struggle for a socialist society."[7]

Havemann was excluded from the party in 1964 and forced to leave his position at the Humboldt University. In January of 1966, he was relieved of his position as director of the Institute for Photochemistry, and his name was struck from the rolls of the Academy of Science that spring.[8] The repercussions were felt deeply throughout the cultural and intellectual segments of society.

Havemann's public calls for opposition parties within the socialist structure had all been serious enough to have caused his arrest, but his antifascist background and national prestige apparently sufficed to cause authorities second thoughts. In some respects, the loss of profession instead of imprisonment may have been an indicator of a change (a little progress) in the instruments of repression employed in the GDR since the time of Harich and Just. But, on the other hand, the leadership of the SED was once again sensitized to criticism and moved to suppress it in cultural-intellectual spheres—an example of which could be an incident such as that in the student cabaret in which Dallow found himself inadvertently entangled. This cabaret, unnamed by Hein in the novel, would have been the popular *Pfeffermühle* ("Pepper Grinder"), located in a side street adjacent to the main lecture halls of the university, a cabaret bar which came under repeated scrutiny and was frequently closed or had its programs altered by the state for lack of "political-ideological responsibility."[9]

A noteworthy phenomenon of GDR society which began to permeate behavior in the 1960s, especially at school, could be called the "as if"[10] clause of the social contract. Students, unlike Claudia's friend Katharina, adapted to the lesson plans by repeating the socialist creed as a mindless formality in order to assure their grades in other subjects. The building of the Wall had necessitated a certain amount of adaptation and conformity. The convention of recognizing authority was obeyed as an exchange for advancement of personal goals and, more importantly, as a concession tacitly made for the right to be left alone in private life. This social phenomenon sheds some light on why Dallow joined the party.

The younger and middle-aged functionaries and representatives of state authority—of which Dallow is clearly an example—more often than not had grown up within such conventions themselves and accepted this pro forma behavior in lieu of meaningful content as long as their concession to this type of behavior did not cause them to harm themselves and their own careers. Such circumstances helped maintain the somewhat enigmatic order peculiar to GDR society and created the atmosphere for what became known as *Nischengesellschaften,*[11] private niches of citizens leading their lives without conviction or interest in GDR politics.

Dallow is a prime example of such a citizen—as is Claudia, for that matter. Nevertheless, the ruling Central Committee of the GDR remained irritated at the thought that its society could contain alienated citizens. The writings of Kafka, for example, were banned until the mid-1960s due, in part, to his representation of alienation in society. In *The Tango Player* the appearance of Schulze and Müller to "help" Dallow get back on his feet comes across as quite

Kafkaesque and also as a reminder of Kafkaesque situations existing in the 1960s while the famous Prague author was, ironically, still banned.

The state, in return for this lip-service acknowledgement from its citizens, maintained and enforced its policy of strict totalitarianism and viewed the liberalization process in Czechoslovakia with alarm, expressing strong public disapproval. Whereas the GDR repeatedly emphasized that the centralized power and legislating body could not be limited by any person or entity, Havemann published an essay in a Prague newspaper in 1968, in which he stated that the determining principles for the ultimate success of socialism consist of democratic control of the government from below, including the right of opposition, not only in the general public domain, but in press, radio and television as well, and including a call for secret ballots for parliament and other governing bodies whose members were "elected" by the people. (In the GDR, elections always finished with about a ninety-eight percent majority for the unopposed SED candidates. The voting choice was "yes" or "no").[12]

Precisely these formulations and other democratic notions, which Dubcek was attempting to implement in Czechoslovakia, caused the most fear among the bureaucratic leaders of the SED as well among those in Moscow. For a short period of time in the summer of 1968, Czechoslovakia actually enjoyed freedom of the press, and its population was able to travel as well. In retrospect, the institution of democratic reforms, which would have led to a socialist government of consent—and which quite predictably would have taken several different directions—is the one serious step that could have possibly rescued socialism from its total demise. GDR citizens were able to follow the developments which inspired them with hope on West German TV and radio.

Though the population of East Germany and of other East Bloc countries was highly sympathetic to the events taking place in Prague, the invasion with tanks and troops put an end to hope, marking a permanent civil resignation and withdrawal. Most demoralizing of all for East Germans was the inclusion of their own troops and tanks, breaking the solemn promise that German troops would never again invade foreign soil. East German officers had been included in the joint command, and on the home front, Czech flags and pro-Czech slogans displayed by GDR citizens were removed by the *Stasi* and a number of individuals were arrested.

A second important piece of background information for understanding *The Tango Player* is the rewriting of the country's constitution in 1968, mentioned several times in the novel, which was passed in April, only a few months prior to the invasion of Czechoslovakia at the end of August. New emphasis was placed on crime prevention and on the rehabilitation of political offenders.

Some aspects and methods of the Stalinist era were therefore improved upon, and additional emphasis was placed on the individual rights of citizens. Some of these rights were essential to socialist ideology and included freedom from exploitation, equal rights for women, and the right to work for all—the latter of which plays a role in *The Tango Player.* Additional statements of rights evidently were written as pro forma only—freedom of the press and other media, for example, was a phony piece of legislation, mere "lip service" to Havemann's proposals. The SED took special care to solidify and clarify its position as the sole ruling party of the working class and therewith thoroughly eliminated any potential for the kind of democratic reform taking place in Czechoslovakia. Individuals opposing this concept would continue to evoke a harsh reaction from the law. The new constitution, although it was backed by government attempts to reduce the crassest of contradictions between its professed standards and reality, greatly solidified its power by "neutralizing the population."[13] Contrasting this "little progress" with the example of the Havemann affair (not mentioned in *The Tango Player*) and the ensuing invasion of Czechoslovakia, Hein's persiflage of the trumpeted social progress of the 1960s becomes a document of the time, a representation of history in the Benjamin sense.[14]

Living Outside the Cell

Eventually, Dallow receives a letter from his mother wondering, as he then does himself, why he hasn't called or visited since his release from prison. He sends her a telegram saying he would come for a visit. It appears that Dallow has been avoiding visiting his parents as part of his overall reluctance to put himself in a situation where he would have to explain his recent past: why he was put in prison and what it was like to have been there. Dallow begins to think about his situation some more and realizes how much he dislikes coping with problems, especially when these problems include the painstaking need to find appropriate words to express excuses or reasons for his actions or behavior.

In prison he never had appointments, duties, or meetings. He now realizes "that he must learn how to live outside the cell" (Ta 58). For him, this task means that he has to reshape his attitude, but it also seems to mean only that he has to find new forms for the expression of the inconsequentialities of life which make up its routine. "The cell, he concluded, had been a familiar environment, a home in which he was safe and secure, and freedom, so desired and longed for as it had been, had become alien and eery" (Ta 58). Dallow realizes that he has now been busily constructing a new cell for himself, shut off from the outside, a place where he need not receive guests, need not answer any questions about his time in prison, need not tell anybody about it. Prison will always carry a social taint, no matter how sympathetic some of his friends and acquaintances may feel about it. An interpretation which suggests itself is that his reluctance to speak about prison is not associated with the social taint, but with the feeling of child-like security he has about it, a feeling he might understandably be unwilling to disclose.

At the same time, it is easy for the reader to think that the cell is a microcosmic description of the condition of life in the GDR—which left its citizens feeling locked in. Symptomatic of this feeling could be the emergence of a need to organize one's own life in accordance with the kind of consciousness which develops in individuals who are locked up. Long-term helplessness and dependency experienced within the confines of the cell could be metamorphosed internally into the supine comfort and security found in a life of subordination. Dallow leaves the reader with the impression that he is a typical case of such psychological self-manipulation and, for the East German reader in the late 1980s, having lived since 1961 in a "cell" defined by the country's borders, this impression was unsettlingly familiar.[15]

During the visit to his parents, Dallow experiences an evening of depression and confusion. He can't seem to get a sense of direction. He had thought that he would resume a life very similar to that before his imprisonment, that he could return to familiar relationships and structures, to old habits, to the security of an everyday routine. On the other hand, he keeps telling himself that this is a chance for a completely new beginning, a rare quirk of luck enabling him to start over altogether, a new direction which he only needed to recognize.

From this mid-point in the narrative, Hein seems to dangle the chance of a new beginning like a carrot on a stick in front of the reader, who hopes that Dallow can overcome his lethargy and do something sensible with his life. In prison he never had to think or act for himself; his daily routine was prescribed for him by others. His essential struggle now is to assume the responsibility for his own life and future. Any renunciation of this responsibility leaves him no alternative but to live in a cell, "not the cell in prison, from which he cannot extricate himself, but the one of his old, comfortable life story."[16]

One Foot in Prison

At home in the small village where his parents live, Dallow is obliged to recount to his father the events which caused him to be arrested, at last providing the reader with the details. He says that the students had assured him that

100

the texts were approved by the authorities. During the interview with Kiewer, his lawyer, he had been shown the texts, which he claimed all along to have ignored, and had commented that the texts were miserable. His lawyer advised him to say that to the judge, but then Dallow, naive about the charges being leveled against him, explained that the problem with the texts was that they "were without wit, they were missing esprit and bite" (Ta 72). Because of this remark, Dallow's lawyer changed his mind and advised him to reply with only "yes" and "no" answers.

Nevertheless, Dallow had elaborated to the judge about how he had concentrated on trying to get the students to comprehend the least notion of musicality and rhythm, of which they seemed not to have much understanding. He still seems blithely unaware that his narrow, pedantic focus on the aesthetic quality of the music and lack of attention to the satirical content was self-incriminating. His father does not respond much to Dallow's description of the events and his continued claim of innocence. But for his father, it is too late for Dallow's innocence or guilt to make any difference: the family has been disgraced. Hein seems to imply here, as in other works, that both the older generation of the GDR founders and the younger generation born into socialism felt betrayed by each other.

At the local train station, Dallow places a long-distance call (there would not have been many private telephones in a small village) to his sister, and the railroad official (doubling as telephone operator) utters a statement which can be understood as paradigmatic for life in the GDR: "In my profession you always have one foot in prison. Forget to give the right signal and you're out of here" (Ta 79).

During an evening with his sister and her husband, who seem to be the only people in the story with whom Dallow has a genuinely relaxed relationship, they drink and joke into the night about the tango. He should have used a bandoneon to play it, not a piano. That's probably what the judge objected to, the brother-in-law jokes. According to his brother-in-law, "You can read in the statistics that each one of these old, sad tangos has more suicides on its conscience than all the virgins made into whores in the entire country" (Ta 84). He goes on to tell about when he drove an ambulance, a precarious job: they would be fined if they drove too fast, and the patient would die if they drove too slowly. This left them with "one foot in prison." Dallow says he has heard this before: "it appears that the entire country has one foot in prison. Except of course the prisoners and the guards" (Ta 84).

The ambulance (rescue) team hated the tangos. The brother-in-law figured they should just drive up and down the streets on Sunday afternoons and break down the doors wherever they heard one of these old, sad tangos being played.

Maybe they could still rescue someone from a noose before the person expired. But their boss insisted they would just be interfering with some couple in the act of conceiving a new human being. Discrediting oneself (as Dallow had done) could result in depression and, as we have seen, loss of employment, imprisonment. A silly mistake and the choice was suicide or one of the above. The best choice would be the conception of a new human being. Make love, not rebellion, they conclude.

The word-plays on "tangos" can be understood as political satire on all the old, sad figures in the political leadership from mid-level on up, not just Ulbricht, whose era was nearing the end. It was a popular way of joking that was widespread in private parties with friends, but certainly not much appreciated by those who were the butt of the jokes, as Dallow well knew. More directly, "tangos" constitute a dissident activity, from which one needed to be "rescued." Of course, if everyone "has one foot in prison," then everyone lives with an Orwellian fear of being caught with a dissident attitude. Even if one is not a dissident (like Dallow!), the danger is not diminished. There's some hope evident in these passages that Dallow can shake himself loose from his brooding about the imprisonment, but on his way back to Leipzig the next day, he gradually feels relieved to get away from his parents, the village, and his family, happy to return to the city.

Dallow decides at last to drop in on Elke again. This time, the two get to know each other a little better. Dallow's primary interest is still to sleep with her without feeling committed. She begins to realize that he probably wishes to live his entire life with no commitments or obligations, and he confirms her suspicions by telling her about his profession. Dallow tells her that his job consists mainly of an anecdotal form of historization describing how illegal social-democratical newspapers of a hundred years ago were printed and distributed, how workers and craftsmen bravely attempted to defend and define class conflict. Dallow's failure to take history seriously in his conversation with Elke continues to call his character into question and, at the same time, exposes the shallowness of force-fed, dogmatic versions of history, to which he passively and cynically allows himself to ascribe.

Elke had gotten a divorce two years earlier, having grown tired of supporting her husband. She is uneasy about Dallow's obvious lack of interest in going back to work. Elke is perhaps typical of thousands of female single parents in the former GDR, struggling to make ends meet, living in a tiny apartment, working and taking care of a small child. The right to work for everyone, coupled with the tacit demand on the part of the state that everyone work, including women, created an economic independence for women unmatched in other modern industrial societies. In addition, the state paid for day-care centers to make it possible for women to work, provided an extra monthly subsidy for each child, and supported a liberal abortion law. Many couples actually married early in their lives order to gain access to a decent apartment. All this led to the tiny GDR's having the world's highest divorce rate for a period of time—a situation exacerbated by the resistance of the men to adapt to the principles of equality inherent in these new socio-economic structures. The man generally left most of the housework, cooking, and child care to the woman anyway, even though she worked the same hours on a job as he did. Since Elke had divorced her husband to establish her independence, the reader tends to wonder exactly why she puts up with the likes of Dallow, who never helps her with the chores; perhaps she is drawn to him only because of the extreme physical passion with which they make love. However, Hein makes no effort to explore the character of Elke in depth; the focus is more on the fact that Dallow is content to regard her merely as an object of his sexual desires.

When he gets up the next day, he reads disinterestedly in the paper that the country has passed the new constitution—the draft of which, he recalls, had led to sarcastic comments by his fellow prisoners when they first saw it. The early draft was circulated throughout the country, apparently even to prisoners. He also notices two short articles about Prague and Warsaw (Poland was also experiencing considerable unrest), but is unable to discern what it is all about. The editors seem to manifest a deep concern about the monumental events taking place in those cities. The key word is "disinterestedly." History is poised to intrude in Dallow's life in the form of the Prague Spring, and it has already done so subtly in the form of the new constitution, but he fails to acknowledge or realize its significance. When pressed to do so, he will simply say that he is just a piano player, not an historian. He accompanies whatever song is being sung; the content is unimportant.

Dallow has gained a freedom that he is incapable of exploiting and which he can hardly bear, an experience that surprises and depresses him, for he now knows "that all the tracks for his life had been laid, by himself or by someone else, and that he could now only proceed along the prescribed path to the end, unable to change anything" (Ta 110). Prison had only been an accidental interruption of his journey along this path; it has not changed anything, it was just a trivial error by both the judge and himself. He had "taken a few punches," according to Friedrich Dieckmann, and would now just "crawl wordlessly back into himself . . . into the emptiness of lost identity." [17]

Present circumstances might offer Dallow the one chance to break free of the tracks, but "he now suspected that he would not understand how to take advantage of the opportunity" (Ta 110). It had all been in vain: "Like a little toy electric train he had been lifted off the uniform, monotonous tracks and now he would be capable of nothing other than making the effort required to place the wheels of this little toy train back onto the old tracks without further bumps and disturbances, fitting as best as possible, so the toy train could resume chugging imperturbably along the infinite loop" (Ta 110).

Dallow thinks about looking for work the next day, and then he thinks about sleeping with Elke. He would go back to see her and then, sometime soon, the decision about this relationship would be made for him as well. He would simply keep on seeing her because he saw her the day before, or two days before. Dallow goes to bed and pulls the covers over his shoulders and thinks to himself: "The toy train locomotive, the little model train with the name Hans-Peter Dallow, would run interminably straight ahead and yet always in a circle" (Ta 111). With a sneering, self-mocking smile, Dallow falls asleep.

The next evening is not much better for Dallow as he proceeds more rapidly into his impending crisis. He begins to be tortured by a feeling of homesickness. He is homesick for his cell. He misses the special sheltered security, the totality of provisions, the completely regulated life. He never had to make decisions in the cell. Not having to make decisions was a deliverance. "And now he missed the pre-ordained daily routine and the directions, he missed the thoughtless and decisionless mundane existence" (Ta 115). He admits to himself that he never really left the cell: "I, too, obviously still have one foot in it" (Ta 115).

The Job Search

Dallow really does begin a job search. He has made up his mind to work as a truck driver. But as soon as prospective employers learn that he is an intellectual, they tell him the advertized position has been filled. They don't need historians from the university working in the transport of goods. They show little concern about his prison record, but they are unwilling to facilitate the integration of intellectuals and workers—a symbolic rejection of fundamental communist principles by the proletariat itself, and a realistic reflection of unchanged and unchanging attitudes, especially the working class's traditional mistrust of intellectuals. After a month-long, fairly intensive search, Dallow becomes discouraged and gives it up. He wonders if Schulze and Müller have had anything to do with the situation, especially towards the end when the rejections come much more quickly.

Dallow pays another visit to the bar where his friend Harry works and again bumps into the judge and the lawyer. This time, the judge approaches him and mentions what an amusing evening they have just enjoyed. Dallow, who is drunk, fails to understand what the judge is talking about. The judge proceeds to point out that Dallow not only was in the wrong at the time of the original incident, but that he is still wrong to maintain his innocence. The law is a dynamic entity, according to Dr. Berger, and just because it has changed doesn't mean that a previous injustice can be rectified. Everything is in a state of flux, and the amusing evening has merely demonstrated that it's a different year now; the river keeps flowing.

It turns out that the old student group has reconvened and performed their old tango number again. To be audacious, they invited the judge and the lawyer to the performance, and both claim jovially that they enjoyed the show immensely: "It showed us that we have made a little progress" (Ta 134), says Dallow's former lawyer—who, by the way, never appears in the story except in the company of the trial judge. When Dallow protests that he didn't know anything about it, Kiewer shows him the letter of invitation. It turns out that Dallow's name is missing among the signatures, which include those of his former fellow inmates. Dallow blows up and insists that this proves his innocence: he was only the tango player. And now he had not even been invited to the show. The lawyer explains that it would be senseless at this point in time to dredge up the old trial records in order to conduct a new hearing to clear his name. Dallow is enraged and the lawyer leaves, disgusted at Dallow's drunkenness.

Dallow proceeds to look up the leader of the student group, Ulrich Klufmann, now living in one of the many old, condemned buildings in the city of Leipzig. Klufmann is in good spirits, living with a young woman and earning his living as a writer of cabaret texts. Klufmann, of course, had simply forgotten to send Dallow any tickets; since he had just been a fill-in that evening, the ticket had probably gone to the regular piano player. The two characters present a contrast, especially in Dallow's mind, as he realizes that Klufmann has adjusted to his life and will not be brooding and wrestling with the problem at all. This is a bitter pill for Dallow to swallow, inasmuch as he views this circumstance as ironic and unfair: the guilty party living free and easy, enjoying the fulfillment of his sexual fantasies (an important value in Dallow's warped sense of priorities) and unconcerned about the past, while Dallow, innocent and unjustly imprisoned, continues to suffer and cannot get his life back into order. Events quickly begin to overtake Dallow, and the course of his life is accelerated by external circumstances. Schulze and Müller wake him up again and begin to insist that he find work. They explain his difficulty at finding a job as a truck driver quite logically by reasoning that those companies didn't want any trouble.

Hiring an overqualified PhD in history would reek with trouble for them. The factories had experience with such types: either they dump the job after a short period of time, or they want to lead discussions instead of working. And who needs this kind of trouble, they argue.

Schulze and Müller bring considerable pressure to bear on Dallow for his unwillingness to work in a "Worker's Country." Not only does everyone have the right to work, but each citizen has a duty to work as well. It's not really a private matter, they inform him. They have names for people like Dallow, people who violate moral codes and social standards. As Dallow himself answers, the names are *arbeitsscheu* ("shirkers") and *asozial* ("asocials"). The word *asozial* was often shorten to *asi* (pronounced "ah zee") and would have included a fairly substantial number of counter-culture types, such as Klufmann, as well as people who didn't want to work or to participate in society, be they social or political dropouts.

Schulze and Müller insist that historians are needed and that Dallow could be particularly useful because of his knowledge of Czech and Slovakian history. This he denies, claiming that he is only knowledgeable in the nineteenth century. "The present has never interested me" (Ta 151), he asserts—an additional, rather incriminating bit of unwitting self-irony in this case. At the same time, his self defense as "only the tango player" and his lack of interest in participating in discussions about Prague reveal the truth of his statement. It can also be understood as a commentary on the contradiction of the life led by someone who professes to be a historian but who has no perception of relevant historical or associative connections between the past and the present. The kind of historian Schulze and Müller say the country needs.

A few days later, Dallow again encounters the judge at the café bar. This time, he follows him home late at night and accosts him in a park. Dallow seems to be out of control; he insists on knowing why the judge condemned him "in the name of the people" (Ta 154) instead of in his own name, or in the name of the law, or in the name of the state. He finds his fingers squeezing tightly around Dr. Berger's throat. Confused by the judge's rising panic and fear, he lets Berger go. Surprisingly, he is not arrested for this incident (a little progress?), but it will have a significant impact on his future.

The next few weeks find him more or less mentally paralyzed. He finds it difficult to get out of bed. He rarely gets up before noon. He can't sleep or read, and he is unable to concentrate on any subject. He thinks he should let himself fall in love with Elke; perhaps that would be a way out, a sensible way out. The excess of free time is crippling him: "He was afraid that he would just one day dissolve. Finally he was driven out of his bed by a sudden fear of death which caused him to break into a cold sweat" (Ta 157).

106

Soon afterwards, he goes to a party with Elke, a party buzzing with animated discussions about Prague. It was the end of May, and Soviet military leaders had met with Dubcek, an event which led to intensified speculation about military intervention although such was denied heatedly in the Soviet press. One of the men asks Dallow his opinion about Dubcek's chances for political survival. "I haven't the least idea," responds Dallow, "and it doesn't interest me at all" (Ta 158). The people listening are dumbfounded by his answer. "If that is true, then you are the only human being in the entire country who is not pre-occupied by the events in Prague" (Ta 158–59). A girl says that he at least has to be interested as a historian. Dallow corrects her politely, stating that he is a pianist by profession, a tango player. But he has given this job up as well. Referring back to the sarcastic lie he had told earlier, he says that now he is writing a novel: "The hero is an idiot. And he gets what he deserves in the end. That's about it" (Ta 161). The self-fulfilling prophecy of these words, lost on Dallow, will become evident to the reader at the end of the story. Dallow seems to be attempting to fictionalize his life, to avoid reality, to withdraw from any accountability, to become a character in a book dependent only upon the whims of the author instead of taking some action to determine his own fate. However, Elke is not amused with Dallow's way of impetuously trivializing serious or important issues and asks him to not come by again until he has gotten over his personal problems.

The next day, Dallow meets with Roessler in the history department, and Roessler informs him that they were thinking about reinstating him. Dallow retorts that he is unwilling to forgive and forget and therefore has no interest in returning. Roessler admonishes him to forget the past "idiocies" which led to his arrest and to accept an advanced assistant professor position, one which could lead to a promotion in four or five years. Dallow isn't interested, but Roessler gives him until 15 June to answer anyway.

"Life has given me another chance and I want to take advantage of it" (Ta 165). With this statement Dallow again appears to be ready to take some concrete action, to intervene himself in his own fate, to determine his own future after all. Roessler mentions that the offer wasn't actually his idea, and Dallow surmises that the idea came from Müller and Schulze. However, Roessler says that Dr. Berger had called him with the suggestion.

Dallow discovers a letter from Dr. Berger in his mailbox, in which Berger requests his presence for a meeting in his office. Juxtaposed between the letter and the meeting is a reference to Dallow's reading the newspaper, which is dominated by reports on Prague. The newspaper reports accuse the Western press of inciting war fever by claiming that the Warsaw Pact countries were planning an invasion of Czechoslovakia. This contention was an evil invention equated with "gangster methods and the propaganda of a Josef Goebbels" (Ta 171). Dallow has a cup of coffee and listens to a program on a Western radio station which also included commentary about the crisis in Czechoslovakia and the threat of invasion. Dallow is bored with it all and changes channels until he can find some music.

The judge delivers Dallow an ultimatum: he is to call in within three days to report his place of work. He is left to believe that failure to do so will result in serious consequences. In a key moment in the novel, Dallow does not stand up to the judge. He says the incident in the park was a misunderstanding. His tone is apologetic, self-degrading, helpless. Somewhat desperate, Dallow stumbles around from place to place. His neighbor advises him to return to the university, but Dallow believes, prophetically, that this would "be tantamount to underwriting his condemnation" (Ta 177). Elke is not home, but Harry promises to see what he can do. The next day, he calls to tell Dallow he has arranged a job for him as a seasonal waiter on the resort island of Hiddensee, a popular summer vacation spot for East Germans in the Baltic Sea. Dallow is so pleased that he opens the piano cover and is barely able to suppress the urge to play. Elke, always the voice of social morality, regards this choice as a copout, another refuge to hide in, and repeats that she doesn't want to see him again until he clears up his problems.

The Future

Hiddensee is a narrow strip of an island, covered with bluish-hued heather, sandy beaches and a handful of houses and bungalows. Automobiles are not permitted, and the only way to get around is by bicycle or on foot. The atmosphere can have a liberating effect; time seems to stand still and, consequently, there is time for someone like Dallow to be introspective and to figure out what to do. However, Dallow's first actions consist of his taking the steps necessary to establish a comfortable and innocuous routine for himself. With the scarce housing and difficulty in obtaining quarters on the island, many day visitors try to find overnight accommodations before the last ferry returns to the mainland, about 8:00 p.m. Dallow exploits this situation to his advantage after allowing a young female student to stay in his room. Soon, he has a female in his room almost every night and, on one occasion, even two of them. Sometimes girls visiting the island look him up, having been told they could sleep there. Once again, he retreats into a cycle of daily banality and sexual gratification without love.

Dallow is still working on the resort island Hiddensee toward the end of August, when the Warsaw Pact troops invade Czechoslovakia, triggering impassioned discussions even on the island. He is together with a young, somewhat plump female student when the reports came in over the radio in the morning. She listens to the reports, stunned. A reporter reads a release from TASS, and Dallow turns off the radio. The girl asks him to turn it back on, and again she listens in horror. Dallow tries to caress her and is surprised to notice that her eyes are filled with tears. At first, Dallow is amused at the girl's crying about the radio reports, which are GDR reports, not Western radio reports. Dallow becomes aroused by observing the girl's emotional reaction to the news and picks her up and takes her to the bed. She makes no effort to resist and just lies there. On the bed, "he made love to her while the radio announcer read a second, heroic-sounding communiqué" (Ta 199). This episode creates an association between the girl and Czechoslovakia as victims of statutory rape, a familiar topos in Hein's works.

The girl asks him to say something about the reports, but he just shrugs his shoulders and asks her what she wants for breakfast. She is incredulous that such an event could leave him so cold. But Dallow says he is just a waiter. She objects: "You are a living human being, you are . . ." (Ta 199), but he interrupts to joke that he also used to be a tango player but that was a long time ago. Dallow accompanies her to the ferry. She is anxious to get back to friends in Berlin, and he, for his part, wistfully rues not having another opportunity to sleep with her, just when she was becoming interesting to him.

By 1968, the socialist movement in the Soviet Bloc countries had gone through a building period of over twenty years. Indeed, it had "made a little progress" over that period of time. That little progress came crashing down abruptly in August in Prague, and Dallow's stolid insensitivity to those monumental events left East German readers, good socialists and dissidents alike, recoiling incredulously at his behavior. No passage in *The Tango Player* could have been more disturbing to East Germans who still remembered the Prague Spring than this one about Dallow's insensitive and perverse sexual arousal during the major historical event which signaled the last hope for a socialist alternative form of society. To put this notion in perspective, imagine a story relating an American behaving as Dallow did on Hiddensee during the reports of John F. Kennedy's assassination.

The "unheard of event" in this story, however, takes place about ten days later, on 3 September, when the department secretary calls to hint about some changes and Sylvia takes the phone to ask him to find her quarters for the next day, a bed where she can sleep, not in Dallow's room. Sylvia arrives and asks him if he would be prepared to return to the department with a promotion to *Dozent.* It would be best if he could begin the very next day in Leipzig.

It seems that Roessler had experienced a bit of misfortune. He had a class at 7:00 a.m. on the day of the invasion of Prague. The students were stirred up and deluged him with questions about the events of the night. Unsuspecting, Roessler asked them what the source of their reports was. Since they all said that their information came from Western radio reports, Roessler stated that "the reports about an invasion of Prague were nothing more than a renewed provocation from the West, categorically rejected the notion of military intervention in allied Czechoslovakia and referred to earlier newspaper reports and commentary by government and party officials" (Ta 202). These were the reports which had accused the West of Goebbels-style propaganda. Moreover, Roessler adamantly rejected reports that GDR troops could have been involved as well—a particularly distasteful and outrageous thought, since German soldiers could never take part in an invasion of Prague for reasons of historical and political culpability. After class, a student brought him a daily newspaper which contained a TASS report verifying the opposite. Six hours later, Roessler was suspended from his duties.

Dallow learns that Roessler has been demoted to assistant (the job he had offered to Dallow) and will not be allowed to teach classes (he is not imprisoned; a little progress has been made). He tells Sylvia he wants to think it over, but he already knows what his decision will be. The next morning he quits his job and drives back to Leipzig. Home, Dallow takes a bath, turns on the TV, leaving the sound off, and sits down at the piano with a bottle of vodka. As he plays the Chopin pieces he knows, he watches the silent pictures in his TV, a GDR program showing soldiers being hailed by the people. Women with small children throw flowers to the soldiers sitting on their tanks. Other shots show Prague citizens in friendly conversation with soldiers. Dallow drinks the whole bottle and, before going to bed, sets the alarm so he will arrive punctually at the institute the next morning.

Thus ends the story of Dallow. He never was capable of any degree of self-realization. In the end, he accepts the offer, the same offer made by the *Stasi* and by the judge, sealing his fate forever. The ironical implication of Hein's story consists in the tacit exposure of the subtle and sophisticated educational system designed to keep citizens in a state of tutelage (*unmündig*) in the GDR, a system so advanced that GDR citizens like Dallow would choose this type of subjugation freely. Dallow was and is extremely uncomfortable when left to his own devises. Indeed, the tracks of his life have been pre-ordained, just as if he were a little toy train. His last chance to declare himself independent never gets off the ground. Briefly awakened from the darkness of the anesthesia which supplemented his tutelage, Dallow fights it off, and the only independent action he ever takes is to regain the security of his condition of tutelage. With that, he makes the transition from the compulsory tutelage of a model pupil to the self-imposed tutelage of an adult living in the "real-existing" socialism of the GDR. He is safe and sound back in a cell.

Notes

1. See Karin Hirdina, "Das Normale der Provinz—*Der Tangospieler*," *Chronist ohne Botschaft. Christoph Hein. Ein Arbeitsbuch. Materialien, Auskünfte, Bibliographie,* ed. Klaus Hammer (Berlin: Aufbau, 1992) 147.

2. Neva Slibar and Rosanda Volk, "'Das Spiegelkabinett unseres Kopfes.' Schreibverfahren und Bilderwelt bei Christoph Hein," *Text + Kritik* 111, ed. Heinz Ludwig Arnold (Munich: Text + Kritik, 1991) 59.

3. Hirdina 150.

4. The film was reviewed in *Der Spiegel* 9 (1991): 264. It was praised for its accurate insight into GDR society and criticized for generating nostalgia.

5. Hein was familiar with Max Frisch's works. Hein's "Achtung, Abgründe!"— presented 13 December 1989 in Düsseldorf in honor of Frisch as the recipient of the Heinrich Heine literary prize—was published in *Als Kind habe ich Stalin gesehen.*

6. Barbara Sichtermann, "Weder Außenseiter noch Pechvogel," *Christoph Hein. Texte, Daten, Bilder,* ed. Lothar Baier (Frankfurt a.M.: Luchterhand, 1990) 165.

7. Stefan Heym, *Nachruf* (Munich: Bertelmann, 1988) 671. Heym uses indirect speech to summarize a lecture of Havemann's during the winter semester 1963 at the Humboldt University in Berlin.

8. Biographical notes on Havemann are taken from Dietrich Staritz, *Geschichte der DDR 1949–1985* (Frankfurt a.M.: Surhrkamp, 1985) 180–81.

9. See *Das gespaltene Land. Leben in Deutschland 1945 bis 1990,* ed. Christoph Kleßmann and Georg Wagner (Munich: Beck, 1993) 500–501.

10. Staritz 178.

11. See Staritz (178), who attributes the term "as if" to Günter Gaus. The external form of "Nischengesellschaften" was manifest in the state's provision for citizens to build their own summer cottages and the corresponding (but much more elaborate) villa settlement in Wandlitz, north of Berlin, where party officials of rank resided. Hence, everyone had a little, private niche where they could putter about undisturbed.

12. See Hermann Weber, *Geschichte der DDR* (Munich: DTV, 1986) 389.

13. Weber 386.

14. See also Hirdina, "Das Normale der Provinz—*Der Tangospieler*." It is difficult to understand why Hirdina claims that *Horns Ende* is not a book about the 1950s and that *The Tango Player* is likewise not a book about the 1960s (149). For her, *The Tango*

Player is a book about normalcy, banality, and boredom (149–151). Normalcy and banality triumph over Dallow, as Hirdina correctly points out, but this very circumstance constitutes what Hein is trying to say about the 1960s in the GDR.

15. Perhaps the inability to cope with freedom was even more disquieting after unification, inasmuch as many GDR citizens felt helpless in the face of the pressures and stress of a capitalist system in which no kindly dictator looked after them in exchange for loyalty or, at least, neutrality. Although *The Tango Player* was published before the Wall was opened, the impact of the "Dallow personality" is still widely felt in the eastern parts of Germany today.

16. Friedrich Dieckmann, "Christoph Hein, Thomas Mann und der Tangospieler," *Chronist ohne Botschaft* 155.

17. Dieckmann 157.

CHAPTER FIVE

The Absence of Malice: *Das Napoleon-Spiel*

Das Napoleon-Spiel, 1993 (The Napoleon Game), Hein's most recent novel, appeared as a series in the *Frankfurter Allgemeine Zeitung* in the spring of 1993 before the book was released. While he was writing the novel, Hein's attention was diverted by the events of 1989 and especially by his own participation on the committee established to investigate police brutality in the GDR during the demonstrations of 7 and 9 October 1989. The following year, his work on *Das Napoleon-Spiel* was interrupted by two life-threatening brain operations and the ensuing long rehabilitation period, during which he was able to work only an hour or so each day. He had collapsed on stage during a cultural event as a result of hemorrhaging caused by a blood clot and probably owes his life to the fact that a neurosurgeon happened to be present in the audience and knew what to do while rushing him to the hospital.

In the broadest sense of the term, *Das Napoleon-Spiel* is an epistolary novel. It consists, however, of only two letters—each written by Friedel Wörle to his lawyer, Mr. Fiarthes. The first letter is written from his prison cell where he awaits his trial for the murder of one Bernhard Bagnall during a ride in the West Berlin subway through the East Berlin sector. The murder weapon is a billiard cue, and Wörle had carefully selected as his victim the most innocuous, neutral individual he could find. The second letter is written shortly after the trial and challenges Fiarthes to a new "game."

Parts of Wörle's biography bear a loose relationship to Hein's. At war's end, Wörle's parents fled from the Eastern sectors of Germany which had been made a part of Poland. Due to his father's occupation, he was not permitted to study in East Germany, and he went to West Berlin in order to do so. Wörle, unlike Hein however, remains in the West, becomes a successful lawyer and politician, and indulges himself in games of power. Wörle's ultimate game, which he compares to Napoleon's decision to invade Moscow, is his cold-blooded murder of Bagnall and his successful defense of this murder as a blameless instance of manslaughter.

The rapid political changes, the radical changes in day-to-day living, the illness, and the long haggling over which publisher Hein was to work with after unification (Hein himself remained with Aufbau) all failed to take any of the specific edge off *Das Napoleon-Spiel.* Hein works with his main character from a greater distance than usual, albeit still employing first-person narrative. This is a somewhat perplexing book. Much more difficult to interpret than Hein's earlier prose, *Das Napoleon-Spiel* leaves the reader with the suspicion that he or she has read an allegorical novel or a parable or a book with undeciphered keys to real-life individuals. It is not likely that Hein had a specific individual in mind, but his experiences with the crassness, the cold, manipulative attitude, and the outright denial of moral responsibility by the once-powerful men interviewed by the committee investigating police brutality undoubtedly influenced his portrayal of Friedel Wörle. The epitome of a man without morals or compassion, Wörle is the most cynical of all characters Hein has ever created, and Hein is a master at portraying cynical characters. Most of his other figures, like Claudia or Kruschkatz, are somehow trapped by their cynicism—a bitterness that seems to have social and political causes—and they are as much the victims of the circumstances which led to their cynical behavior as they are perpetrators of inhumane deeds against the people around them and, even more, against themselves.

The Rules of the Game

Wörle does not suffer from his cynicism. On the contrary, he thrives on it. It is the essence of his life, and he succeeds at everything he tries to accomplish. He is able to accomplish anything he wishes precisely because he has no moral qualms and because he defines his actions and his life as a game of billiards or pocket billiards, a hustle in which winning is vastly less important than the elements of the game itself—elements that include, above all, the cold, rational calculation of all the possible angles, variations, and reactions effected by other men's normal attitudes when they too are playing the game, men who may have almost as few scruples as Wörle himself. Napoleon would have been an equal, worthy opponent and is the game-master par excellence after which Wörle imagines himself to be molded.

Wörle is driven only by fear of boredom. Winning by itself, for the player, is a closure that can be fatal; it is the continuation of the game itself which keeps him alive, and the stakes and the difficulty of the lie and the stroke must constantly be increased. This boredom, the need to have a game without a predictable outcome, drives Wörle to kill a stranger whom he has determined to be an absolute neutral and then to defend himself by arguing that it was not murder or homicide but "compulsory homicide." The German words are *unerläßliche*

Tötung. *Tötung* is also used in the sense of "manslaughter" in German legal terminology, and the term *unerläßliche Tötung* ("compulsory homicide") itself is a play on the phrases *rechtmässige Tötung* ("justifiable homicide") and *fahrlässige Tötung* ("involuntary manslaughter"). This compulsory homicide, or obligatory manslaughter, is justified by Wörle in his exhaustive letter to his attorney, Mr. Fiarthes, which he writes in his cell while awaiting trial—a long, rambling, and numbing letter which takes up some 200 pages.

Language as Power

The very text itself is the most inaccessible of Hein's prose because Wörle is himself a lawyer, and the language he writes is an incredible mixture of a cynical panorama and an egocentric outlook on life, replete with legalese, bureaucratic formulations, and intentionally misleading statements, including long passages in parentheses. The language is often comparable to the euphemistic formulations which emit from official, military, and public life to circumscribe reality or to avoid the impact which more poignant and common descriptions of reality might have on ordinary people. Wörle uses language in the same way he practices billiards: the spin of each word, sentence, and phrase he uses is calculated to impact his colleague Fiarthes in a certain, predictable manner. Likewise, the spin placed on the language by Hein has an impact on the reader as well, a calculated impact which causes his or her disbelief to grow with the increasing realization of the potential for human atrocities contained in this man Wörle. He always calls his shots: he knows he is insulting Fiarthes's sense of decency and makes it apparent that this amuses him, as does his ready admission of the arrogance he takes from the knowledge that Fiarthes, as his attorney, cannot take action to expose his guilt or character on the basis of this letter but is sworn to defend him to the best of his ability and to the letter of the law.

Fiarthes becomes an inextricable part of the game and has no choice but to carom off of the edges with the spin given by Wörle. He is a passive figure in the novel. We never read a letter of his; we never see his actual reaction other than when Wörle himself refers to an expected reaction caused by the words in his letter. Wörle will run the billiard table before Fiarthes ever gets a chance, before anyone else will get a chance, and he will do it with the ball in an impossible lie.

Because of the language, the text is often tedious for the reader—even boring to the critic Volker Hage, for whom Hein's "hero speaks as if he were obligated to fill out an expense account report."[1] Fritz Rudolf Fries, on the other hand, himself a prominent writer in the former GDR and considerably better informed than Hage, finds the language to function like "flypaper, once you have touched it, you don't get loose so quickly."[2] The reader becomes part of the game, part of the parable being constructed by Hein.

Wörle opens his letter by expressing doubt that the truth will help his case. Society wants him to be convicted, but there has to be a proper defense as well, not so much a successful defense as one which satisfies both the law and the public. Wörle indicates that he had suggested that the defense be based on his legal inculpability due to his inability to recognize his deed as a criminal act or to acknowledge guilt. In his mind, the fact that this defense was rejected as absurd and cynical only served to confirm that he would "not be able to win the case with the truth" (NS 7).

Wörle is convinced that the behavior of the accused, including important non-verbal communication, will play the most prominent role. It had always been his experience as a lawyer that a common thief who provoked the judges with rude behavior had less of a chance of getting off with a light sentence than a charming and accommodating axe murderer: "In the bottom of his heart . . . the judge would rather free the courteous murderer and let the thief rot in jail" (NS 9). The accused is the main actor, and he has to take care not to be a ham. He cannot attempt to portray his situation as tragic; he must cause his audience to follow him against its will, just as Hein causes his readers, trapped on the flypaper, to reluctantly, and sometimes exasperatedly, follow Wörle's argument. Moreover, the public reaction to the case should not play a role since the judges cannot permit public opinion, itself driven by subjective feelings of revenge and pity, to influence their decisions, which must be—and appear to be—completely objective. Guilt and innocence are therefore subjugated to a legal game, to the manipulation of language according to established court procedures that themselves become more decisive than the facts. Hein calls merit into question. Image, show, and especially the mastery of timely manipulation with prudently loaded language render merit, real character, and truth into a secondary status.

Bernhard Bagnall, a clerk in a department store, lost his life on 21 June 1989 as a result of Wörle. But it is difficult to describe the motive, Wörle writes, choosing his formulation carefully: "it was neither murder nor homicide, but a killing, more precisely, a compulsory homicide" (NS 13)—something altogether different from murder. Bagnall died because Wörle had to protect himself from the experience of loathing and complacency. Implied is his right to "protect" himself and to always defend his self-interest, a principle which Western society holds sacred. Wörle is very much aware of this unspoken principle, and consequently, this really is the most correct answer he can give. He claims that he simply allowed himself to follow through with what most people probably feel like doing at one time or another anyway.

Early Games

Wörle begins to mix the story of his life into his defense letter, including many details, as he explains, which may appear irrelevant on the surface but which are important in understanding why he killed Bagnall, whom he had never met. Wörle was born in August of 1932 in Stettin, and his father was the owner of a candy factory, Frieder Wörle and Co., which had eighteen employees, almost all female—a situation due in part, perhaps, to the war. His mother was a society lady, and he was raised by a nanny. Wörle soon learned that he could control his nanny by virtue of the fact that his mother did not wish to be disturbed by children's prattle. He quickly discovered that tantrums or other disturbances which found their way to his mother's attention caused the nanny, not him, to be reprimanded, and hence he was able to use this as a leverage to coerce his nanny to follow his will.

Around the age of twelve, he began to hang around his father's place of business. He imagined he would grow up and take over the business—something that would please his father—and would eventually have a comfortable life selling packages of *Schoko-Wör* candies wrapped in foil. Although at twelve, he was old enough to no longer be teased and called "angel hair" by the women who processed the candies. He took advantage of the situation to go and sit on their laps, pressing his head against their breasts and breathing in their smell. The important point for him was that he knew that they knew he thought he was getting away with something and that he could continue his erotic play of beginning puberty anyway, letting them tease him in the manner they would a younger child in exchange for the not-so-clandestine liberties he took by wiggling around in their laps while they worked on the assembly line. From the very beginning, the objects of the games he plays are not very admirable.

Hein establishes the familiar pattern of a deleterious relationship with women on the part of characters he wishes to implicitly degrade in the reader's mind. This is a further point lost on Volker Hage, who claims that Hein imagines Wörle to possess everything that a successful man in the West could want, one item being "every kind of success with women."[3] Wörle's later "success" with women, which might resemble the sexual adventures of Dallow, is only hinted at, never includes real love, and does not conform to Hein's concept of healthy relationships between human beings. Wörle never marries. The only woman he names in his own narrative, Katja, is a "player" of equal or superior ability, and he beats a hasty retreat, fearing that she will defeat him soundly at his own game. Wörle is threatened by a female who is an equal. This certainly precludes any notion of "success" with women in the sense of successful relationships. Perhaps Hage means "conquests" of women, which has nothing to do with success in any sincere meaning of the word.

Within a year of Wörle's play with the women in his father's chocolate factory, the family flees Stettin, giving up all their possessions except for the few items they could carry. They move in with his father's cousin in Tiefenort, a small town. Evidently the relatives have a strained relationship because his father had disappeared with the bride of his cousin for a couple of hours during the wedding celebration. In spite of his obviously not being welcome, the elder Wörle moves into two rooms upstairs in his cousin's house. The exact meaning of this symbolic exploitation by the elder Wörle remains unclear. Structurally it provides a case of authoritative domination of a morally superior individual with a weaker constitution (the cousin), weaker due to the influence of moral values on his actions (his cousin Wörle is homeless and unfortunate due to the advancing Russians). Wörle's mother, however, is distraught by the new situation and confines herself to her room. A few months later, she dies, and the cause of death, according to Wörle's cynical but accurate view is the loss of the salon and music room where she has entertained society in Stettin—even though this diagnosis would hardly be legally permissible in a coroner's examination. It is nevertheless an analogy that Wörle plants like a seed in the mind of his lawyer, a subtle linguistic distinction to create a distraction.

His father obtains employment as a procurer in a wood-cutting company the day after they arrive. After a year, his father moves in with a widow whose husband has fallen in the war, and he takes over the postage stamp mail-order business she had inherited. She has a son named Johannes, two years younger than Wörle but a head taller. Wörle constantly refers to this stepbrother as "the bastard." Johannes attacks Wörle and then calls his mother before Wörle can retaliate. Wörle realizes that he has to develop a refined tactic in order to triumph over the "bastard." A game.

It is the games which keep us alive, he maintains: "Hunger, the quest for fame, and our sexual drive are supposed to keep us alive" (NS 36–37). He has experienced these and found them to be weak motivators: "What was left for me, the thing which keeps me going, is the thrill of the game. It relieves boredom, you know. When the game is over we are dead" (NS 37). Fair play is not possible with his brother: he is not a player and therefore not a real opponent; his brother just wants to win. Wörle will have to lead him into a trap.

Three of Wörle's father's neckties are cut up and strewn about in the garden, an offense carried out in such a manner as to make it look like Wörle is guilty. The problem is that such a conclusion is too obvious, and therefore his father thinks that the stepbrother has done it. Wörle is aware how difficult it is for his father to punish the stepbrother in the mother's presence. His father has made an effort to form a good relationship with the "bastard" for the sake of the widow. But now the stepbrother is whipped in front of his mother by the elder Wörle—a stark contrast to the pedagogical methods of Thomas's father in *Horns Ende*. Johannes, the "bastard," is caught totally by surprise, and, seeing Wörle's feigned sympathy, he begins to scream that Wörle was the guilty party, not he. This only makes the situation worse, inasmuch as it appears that Johannes is not "man enough" to take the blame for his act and is shamelessly trying to pin the blame on someone else, his half brother—only adding to his guilt. At this juncture, his own mother reaches over the table to slap him as well. For his part, Wörle shows his indignation at being falsely accused, although he holds this in check in order to demonstrate to his father and the widow some (feigned) brotherly solidarity with his punished stepbrother. Instead of being vengeful and happy that his stepbrother is being punished for denouncing him, he shows that he is aghast and appalled. The "bastard" is broken. He has been conquered. He will not be able to undertake anything without appearing vindictive. He has also lost his privilege as the widow's son, from now on Wörle's father can punish him whenever the occasion presents itself. Wörle can exploit the situation at will; he can make his brother the object or the medium of his games, whichever he chooses.

Three years later, the mail-order business is nationalized, and Wörle's father is named director of the business. His authority is restricted by the new accountant named by the state (a party official was assigned to each factory or business). Wörle continues his little business on the side, which he supports by taking "surplus" stamps out of his father's offices, selling them privately to schoolmates. He takes his stepbrother into the enterprise, a wise move to preempt any possibility of being exposed. They sell their stamps at a discount, and the mail-order business suffers a small loss of business. They continue after the business is de-privatized. At that time, the inventory of the firm shows too many stamps which might hamper the "antifascist and democratic education" (NS 45) of their customers and not enough progressive stamps commemorating socialist countries and the Soviet Union.

Wörle has observed that his side business tends to lose customers when they reach puberty, and as he nears the end of his own school years and applies to study law at the university, he turns over the entire "black market" enterprise to the "bastard." He finds that his status as son of a former capitalist prevents his acceptance at the university and determines to move to Berlin and study law in West Berlin. Meanwhile, the mail-order business experiences new troubles and is not showing a profit. His stepbrother's side business is discovered. Had the juvenile court judge not been a philatelist himself, Johannes would surely have been jailed, inasmuch as the damaged business now belongs to the state and constitutes a federal offense. The "bastard" contributes to the irreparable break with his own family by claiming that Wörle had started the business in the first place. But Johannes has no credibility because of the earlier incident with the ties, and his claim angers the family further, leaving him thoroughly victimized. Again, Wörle has an appropriate analogy: it is not so much malice—indeed, Wörle always insists that a player never acts out of malice—as it is simply an example of the fact that at some point in a bullfight, the bull is pierced by the bullfighter. It is not a case of bloodthirstiness or revenge, just a part of the rules of the game.

Two years later, his father becomes the director of another state-owned concern and joins the party so that the adopted son, Johannes, is able to matriculate at the university in Leipzig, where he studies history—a subject of consequence in Hein's works. Shortly thereafter, Wörle visits his father and the widow in Tiefenort, but he is placed under house arrest for having fled the GDR earlier. His identification papers are confiscated. However, these events place his half brother in a much more difficult situation than the one in which Wörle finds himself. As was standard procedure in the GDR, Johannes is required to break off relations with home in order to avoid contact with Wörle: contact with any Westerners would result in his expulsion from the university. The widow somehow seems to have a vague idea of what had happened: "She had lost her son and instinctively she turned on me, not able to know, however, that I really was the cause of the separation between her and her son" (NS 53). The Wall still has not been built, and Wörle is able to escape back to the West and finish his studies with high honors. He turns down an offer to continue his studies and pursue an academic career. He has studied law in order to learn the rules of the game, and now he wants to play, not fiddle around with improving the rules.

He moves to Boppard, a small town in the Rheinland and obtains employment with the law firm Wieser and Wieser (one of the brothers is deceased). By this time, Wörle's father and the widow have fled the GDR and also settled in Boppard, where his father took advantage of reparations paid by the FRG to those who had lost possessions in the East—he still has documentary proof of his ownership of the candy factory—in order to start up a mail-order business for embroidery. The "bastard" is left with a no-win situation. If he goes to the West, he will be ostracized from the family. If he stays in the East, his career will be severely limited because his entire family has fled the Republic. He remains behind, eventually finding employment as a high-school history teacher. History, although Hein does not make it the object of discourse in this novel, is relegated to a degraded status in the GDR, a harmless place of little influence to which less worthy individuals are assigned. The bastard sibling of society.

The Aura of Wealth and Beauty

Wörle remains in Boppard only a few years before it is time for him to move on to bigger and better things. One case he takes in Boppard, however, is highly instructive for him. He gets the case due to an illness of Wieser's, a case involving the owner and chief executive officer of a large producer of building materials, a third-generation owner who is highly respected in the community. Wörle is struck by his mannerisms and polished reserve; giving the impression of being tired but very alert, he behaves as a man who is unconcerned but not bored. In the smallest movement of his hand, he embodies the third generation of his firm and looks more like a high-church dignitary than a businessman and defendant. Hein's description, never quoting or naming the defendant, indicates that the latter is a man capable of very powerful non-verbal communication.

Wörle reflects that he has always been fascinated with beautiful women and rich men. They have an aura, the perfume of beauty and the aroma of money: "It is something other than what is commonly known as the odor of money, the gently penetrating smell of power and influence, which stinks slightly of greed, avarice, self-enrichment and envy" (NS 64). Beauty and wealth has another scent which attracts us: "A man of culture we can say and we mean this scent, this beauty" (NS 64) which inspires admiration and respect in us. The prosecuting attorney is also taken in by the "man of culture" and is only too happy to lose his case and to congratulate the executive. To Wörle it is clearly evident that his own extremely well-prepared presentation of the case has by no means been the deciding factor. The executive's behavior in court, his straightforward answers, the fact that he has appeared in person on behalf of his firm, all these elements have won the case for him. He is well aware of this fact and feels that he owes nothing to the firm of Wieser and Wieser other than the appropriate legal fees. The young judge is caught in a no-win situation. Whatever he decides, part of the media would have strongly critical opinions to express. A harsh judgement would only manifest that he has overreacted because of his own personal aversion to such wealth and power. Wörle takes mental notes of the judge's predicament and the player's (the defendant's) exploitation of the situation.

Wörle decides to move to Berlin and practice law on his own. He opens his office in October of 1960 with a part-time secretary. On 7 February 1967, he learns from his accountant that he has accumulated his first unencumbered million. Vanity is not the reason for him to report this fact; it has, he claims, a causal relationship to the death of Bernhard Bagnall. The precision of dates used by Hein throughout the story lends a documentary quality to the narrative, a ploy designed to create and enhance Wörle's credibility.

The Sophisticated Player

The player, Wörle states, "wants to place his bets and, of course, to win" (NS 73). But winning itself has only the purpose of allowing him to bet again. The task is to play; the stakes and the winnings are secondary. "Some games consist of matches that last for years, matches in which fortunes and the lives of people can be wagered. Players plan their strategies like field generals with full authority" (NS 73). Napoleon, he surmises, must have viewed the money and armies of his nation with a certain objective distance. It wasn't his own money or his own army which was at his disposal but the country's, and hence he did not need to be considerate of them as he threw them onto the game board Europe. He could play unreservedly, majestically, and successfully: "A player is one who bets. Perhaps this is the whole truth" (NS 73). He bets his money, his reputation, his reason, his life, but always without worry or fear of loss, and this distinguishes him from common gamblers, careerists, idealists, business executives, and normal people who risk something in order to attain something else, something greater, more beautiful—wealth, power, influence.

"The player just bets, nothing more. Winnings and losings are outside his field of vision" (NS 74). Unfortunately, people who behave exactly the opposite are usually referred to as the players, he states, because they attempt to enrich themselves in a banal manner. This applies to the little swindler on the street as well as to state-licensed lotteries, according to Wörle's analysis. This so-called gambling consists of nothing more than legal contracts with extremely poor business conditions covered over by marketing glamour. A player wants to wager in order to play. The winnings are already boring for him: "A game in which the player cannot intercede and act . . . is nothing more than an order placed for an unspecified capital return" (NS 74).

As Wörle's wealth amasses, he grows more and more bored. The thought that the game and therefore his life is at an end begins to depress him. The idea of continuing anyway makes him physically ill, and he broods long hours in his office, his firm having taken on other partners by then. He realizes that the game is much more than just a passion for him; it is the center of his life, his life itself. Without this passion, he thinks he might as well shoot himself (Russian roulette, of course). Hein seems to describe the process of addiction. As a gambler and a player, Wörle requires increasing challenges to satisfy his addiction.

Wörle relates his passion for billiards to Fiarthes. He compares it somewhat to the shabby passion of one of his last clients in Boppard, a businessman who has revealed his secret collection of women's panties in confidence to Wörle. Like the businessman, who then was too embarassed to retain Wörle's services, Wörle thinks that everyone has some little thing to hide, and this is the reason he keeps his billiard table in his house in Kampen, on the island of Sylt. He has another house in Northern Italy as well, in the Toscana, but the house in Kampen is off limits to women guests and other friends. He goes there to be by himself and to play billiards and to solve his problems.

All of Wörle's decisions are made at the billiard table, including how, when, and who (Bagnall) will die. The rest, which Fiarthes views as the actual deed, "is nothing more than the burdensome execution of the plan, the implementation and test run of the game" (NS 94). To Wörle's way of thinking, billiards includes not only the calculation of all the endless variations, the possibilities of striking the ball directly or indirectly, all the spins and possible runs of the ball. Even if you could program a computer with this information, you would be missing the element which is not subject to scientific calculation: the execution of the stroke of the queue on the ball. It is not like chess, where the move itself is only mechanical, he reasons. Not only do you have to plot out the variables and the reaction of your opponent; you must strike the ball correctly, and you can and should do this in such a way as to mislead and deceive your opponent. Wörle asks Fiarthes if he is bored by all this. Wörle is not, as Fiarthes probably thinks, "speaking about billiards, he just wanted to say something about the scene of the crime" (NS 102). As a concept appearing in a novel about the power of language to manipulate reactions, divert attention from the truth, and gain a distinct advantage, the "stroke" on the ball consists of the words chosen carefully to maneuver those who hear them or read them (Fiarthes and Hein's readers) into a position of reluctant collusion.

Not too long after the accumulation of his first million, in March 1967, Wörle decides to change his course. He reduces his activity as a lawyer to a few cases and enters local politics: "A player has no principles and his morals are dependent only on the roll of the balls" (NS 104). These thematic words appear in parentheses to soften their impact discreetly, and they are spoken to introduce Wörle's description of his political career. The subtext carries an implication about the workings of politics in general—i.e., Wörle is a politician, and politicians are often like Wörle.

His entry into politics is characterized by his apparent (real, as defined by his self-proclaimed status as a real player) unselfishness, a character trait often regarded with suspicion in political circles, and his independence—he did not join a political party. He has succeeded in gaining a foothold in non-partisan politics after a year and, by the end of four years, has made himself indispensable in the overall political scene. Winnings and power, as always, do not interest him. He is attracted by politics because its nature requires him to react to constantly changing conditions and relationships. He will spend twenty years in politics, up to about 1988, before he begins to play the game which leads to Bagnall's death.

It is tempting at this point in the novel to begin to look for political allegories. In spite of Wörle's personal biography, the dates of the murder and the trial seem to make it expedient to think of Wörle as somehow representative of the West, as the West German reviewer Volker Hage indeed has done, rejecting at the same time that Hein has captured any truth about life and attitudes in the West.[4] Although this is ironically reminiscent of East German disclaimers that Hein's earlier works are an accurate representation of life in the GDR, it nevertheless seems that Hein is trying to get at something broader here, at some element which exists in human nature that can take over when human existence is devoid of compassion, principles, morals, and ideals. If this applies to certain aspects of Western society, especially in the economic sector which ascribes to such notions as the maximization of profits for the good of the shareholders, then it applies to other aspects of society as well and in other parts of the world as well. The East German experience of unification, after all, was comprised of disillusionment and of the unfortunate realization that citizens would be exploited as much as possible by legally supported institutions. The *Treuhandgesellschaften*[5] often returned property to Western owners' descendents after these forty-five years of separation between East and West Germany. Sometimes they delayed use of the property for years until the matter could be resolved, and in some cases they intentionally stalled promised investments to allow East German-operated concerns to go under, enabling Western companies to move in and buy or invest cheaply. Most unkindly, West Germans came to regard their compatriots in the East as second-class citizens. From the perspective of East

Germany—an area in 1993 still struggling with astronomical unemployment figures and lacking the technical education to succeed as well as lacking investment capital—former GDR citizens might really feel as though they are being confronted with people like Wörle, even if he appears in an exaggerated form, almost as a caricature of the problem. Fritz Rudolf Fries conveys some of these notions in his review: "The confessions of this intellectual carpetbagger contain a bottomlessness" into which we all stumble. The case goes much deeper than the opportunism of Wörle; the depth of the abyss is temporarily held up by a story which "documents the ice cold climate of our times."[6]

Feelings and "The Game"

Feelings, according to Wörle, ruin everything: "Whoever enters a game with emotions is lost before he takes the queue in his hand" (NS 114). It is an irreparable handicap to allow emotions and feelings into the game, and whoever does so can never wipe out the damage caused by his attempting to eliminate feelings for the next shot or move. The mistake has already been made, and it will impact the rest of the game for him. It is certainly laudatory to have feelings. And the people with feelings "are quite possibly good persons," better persons, "but they just aren't real players" (NS 115).

Wörle meets up with only two or three real players during his time in politics. The rest are "idiots, fools, scoundrels and good family men" (NS 116). They want power, money, and fame. But after a while, they must surely realize that they are simply cogs in a well-structured and smooth-functioning bureaucracy and that they are only important and needed when they accurately fulfill the tasks given them. It makes no difference whether they are a small wheel or a big wheel. They have power, to be sure, but only when they perform what is required of them. They have a little power, but only insofar as they remain dependent and not free. This dependency makes them into slaves of the bureaucratic machinery, driven by fear of failure and the need for security. Wörle uses them as training for his games. It would be annoying to simply win such matches. In fact, he loses as often as not as a result of his experimentation with moves and spinoffs. Wörle becomes known in political circles as a "maker of kings," or, in other quarters, as a Rasputin.[7]

"Whoever plays is always alone" (NS 124), maintains Wörle. If this bothers you, you shouldn't play. You can never win anything with love, but with love it is easy to lose everything. Jealousy, meanness, envy, and even hate can be helpful in some circumstances, as long as you are in control or are occupied with manipulating these traits in others. After all, as Wörle points out to justify his argument, no one would claim that Napoleon was well-loved. His enemies hated him, and his soldiers feared him. To his officers he gave overblown titles. Wörle insists that he has found good years in his life. He has found a game which enables him to live on, but at the same time, he realizes that something is coming to an end and that he is approaching his Moscow. Bagnall's death was unavoidable; he would have fatally endangered himself had he not killed him. Wörle realizes in Kampen at the billiard table that his crime was a question of self-defense and that it is time for Fiarthes to accept this fact.

The Principle of Self-Interest

Wörle has to overcome his own disgust at the idea of killing someone. This is not so much because he values human life. He has a certain interest in his own life, as long as it is not boring, and the truth is he would be more upset by the loss of two small wooded areas in Berlin where he likes to go for walks than he would be at the report of the violent death of one of his neighbors. This is not a question of morality but of human nature, he maintains. Sure, he would regret the death of other people, but if he were faced with the choice between his house in the Toscana and the life of some thousand unknown people, he wouldn't have to think about it for a second. He would be sorry for the deaths of so many people, but his house cost him a lot of time and money, and its loss would be horrible, a catastrophe. Wörle is a bit sorry that this is the way he thinks, that he is not more noble and humane, but he questions whether thinking otherwise would really be normal for human beings: "It is human to not be all too unselfish" (NS 134). The monstrosity is not the self-serving person but rather the do-good natural healer and the charitable nurse who get on our nerves with their good deeds. Even though we admire them, they are strange and puzzling to us: "We would all get along better if we would accept ourselves as what we really are" (NS 134) is Wörle's logical and frighteningly callous maxim. One interpretation of the parable in this story presents itself as the reduction of Adam Smith's time-honored principle of self-interest—already the key to survival in the seventeenth-century philosophies of Thomas Hobbes and John Locke, and the fundamental idea behind capitalism—to its basic essence, devoid of all sentimentality: no one can expect Wörle to take any action which runs counter to his self-interest or to fail to take action which supports it.

The killing was unavoidable, and Wörle had to struggle with himself many months before he could bring himself to do it. What would have happened to

Napoleon if he had not gone to Moscow, he argues, or even if he had triumphed at Moscow? He would have had to run the administration of the conquered lands, to spend his time keeping them under control, and this task would have bored him; it would have killed him. It was a game of kings for Wörle. He had to structure the match so that it was in balance with the finiteness of his own life.

Wörle complains that he is being given unfair treatment in jail. For his fellow inmates, he contends, being put in prison is like being moved from a hole into a dog's hole. For the homeless man, it is actually an improvement. The conditions of Wörle's own confinement, compared to the standard of living to which he is accustomed, constitute a much more drastic reduction in the quality of his life than they do for the others. The equality fanaticism of the early nineteenth century is long out of date, and he maintains that he really ought to be placed in an apartment leased out to poor families by government agencies. He would pay for it, of course, and not only would the correct proportion of punishment during the time he awaits his trial be restored, but the government would be acting in a financially prudent manner, following its own self-interests. The conditions Wörle has dealt himself to continue the game from within the cell are beginning to disturb him, he informs Fiarthes, and he's not sure if he can really stand the confinement. This comment may well be the deception Wörle uses to elicit the response he desires from Fiarthes. The reader notices an involuntary, momentary lapse into sympathy for Wörle at this point. He seems to be suffering a little bit after all.

Freedom

Another digression of Wörle's is a treatise on freedom, in some respects an excellent commentary on Dallow of *The Tango Player.* The masses don't want freedom; they are born vassals, and to give them freedom would make them permanently unhappy. Under the yoke, they may have been thoughtlessly dissatisfied, but a little freedom makes them nervous and they hasten to find ways to use up their free time, usually by contracting someone else—the leisure time industry, for example—to fill it up for them: "The masses don't want freedom, they want only paradise" (NS 149). That paradise is the place of the lord, the place where all the other vassals are, happy vassals. Who would want to begrudge these vassals getting what they want (attaining the object of their self-interest): security, unshaken values, clear directions on how to behave, and a moral structure with the possibility for reward and punishment and the power to reward and punish. The vassal is subjugated to an external will, year in and year out. He takes directions and fulfills his duties. The task given him from the outside will becomes his happiness, whether in the machine shop or the editor's room, the office of a large company or a local agency. After death he won't have to fool around with travel agencies and the like anymore, and he will still have a heavenly paradise as a member of a society under an outside will, under a judging and commanding Lord. This digression is also an integral part of the letter, according to Wörle. It serves as a contrast to his own concept of freedom, unencumbered by sentimentality, by the need for security (that would be fatal to his personality) or by the need to win. He then proceeds to describe how he made his decision to proceed with the killing.

As Wörle describes it, he left Kampen on 12 May 1988 and set out for his Moscow, hoping to avoid Napoleon's St. Helena, for Napoleon's confinement there eventually killed him. A little over a year later, on 21 June 1989, Wörle killed Bernhard Bagnall. He argues that he is not a murderer or a homicidal maniac—these are terrible people. Napoleon sacrificed over 400,000 men in Russia, and no one ever accused him of being a murderer. It would be a mockery of logic to equate a compulsory killing with murder. People die frequently before their biological clock has run its course, sometimes in a war, sometimes because a stone falls off a building and strikes them in the head. None of these unavoidable killings activate the legal system. The destruction of an army or a city neutralizes the law by virtue of the large scope of the act. Yet in the case of smaller numbers, we are immediately inclined to look for motives and to look for criminal behavior. This is why the person Wörle chose for his killing had to be a completely neutral entity: he had to be representative of the average of the masses. It took him almost a year to find his man, and he often despaired, since everyone he investigated had some minor flaw. Bernhard Bagnall was the perfect ball waiting to be struck by Wörle's queue. The killing took place in public, but he was surprised to see "that Bagnall's sudden disappearance was noticed so quickly" (NS 170). Bagnall's status was irrefutably and absolutely neutral, which made it a "virgin game" (NS 168) unworthy of being degraded by "awkward and ridiculous" (NS 169) references to morality. It seems that in Wörle's mind, Bagnall's "disappearance" should have been more matter-of-fact.

The Ultimate Game

Every player, according to Wörle, eventually is confronted with a game in which he not only stands there with queue in hand, but in which he is also the ball. He is simultaneously the ball and the player. This "makes his risk incalculable and the chances of victory virtually impossible" (NS 176). His only hope is to create conditions which seduce his opponent into a certain plan of action. When the ball lies motionless on the table, he must make the effort to "leave the contact point which would create the desired spin advantageous to himself when [the ball is] struck by his opponent" (NS 177). There is almost no chance of this strategy's being successful, but if it were to be, what an incredible game: the player as the ball which plays with his opponent. What a thrill to dare to play such a game. And now, Wörle says to his lawyer, he is himself lying on the table (helplessly in prison) and awaiting just such a stroke. Everything has been prepared as best as it could, and now it is all up to Mr. Fiarthes, in whom he places his hope and trust. In order to win, however, the opponent must be an equal, capable of recognizing the strategy and striking the ball on a different point than had been predetermined by the player. Napoleon ran into an equal player and lost. But this fact shouldn't stop either Wörle or Mr. Fiarthes—who, Wörle implies, is not the equal of Napoleon, even though Wörle is audaciously calling Fiarthes's shot for him and challenging him to play it differently.

Wörle finally recounts the killing to his defense attorney. He entered the subway where Bagnall always got on. He had made an extra trip to Kempen and selected a queue stick held together in the middle with a metal screw. The subway car entered the Eastern sector of Berlin and had to slow down for the stations there; it was not allowed to stop or take on or discharge passengers. Wörle took out his queue and seemed to be playing with it. Just as the car began to move out of the last East Berlin station, Wörle placed the half of the queue with the metal screw up on the railing and delivered a precise blow to Bagnall's temple. He died instantly, without a sound. Wörle immediately began to look after him, aware that the witnesses would also report on his fervent, circumspect, and self-sacrificing care of the dead man. He asked them to make room to lay him on the bench and to get something to bind the wound. He also had to prevent one of the passengers from pulling the emergency brake cord in order to avoid being arrested by East German police, which could have ruined his game. When the subway arrived in the first West Berlin station, Kochstraße (the old location of Checkpoint Charlie), he took Bagnall in his arms and asked everyone to get out with him and to wait for the police as witnesses at the station. Seven of the approximately twenty passengers got out with him, although three of these went ahead and left the station.

Wörle ends his letter to his lawyer here and wishes him good luck with his next shot, which, as the reader sees, is to be played immediately after Wörle's detailed confession, his last preparation of the lay of the ball. It was self-defense, for if he had not been able to play this game, he would not have been able to resolve the excusable and understandable crisis threatening his own life: the irrepressible need to escape boredom, to play a more challenging game. As his lawyer is sworn to confidentiality, Fiarthes, of course, cannot make the contents of the letter known.

Infinity

The novel has a surprise ending. The killer has, incredibly, gone free, and his own lawyer, as Wörle surmises, is anguishing over the success of his defense of Wörle. In his second, and last, letter to Fiarthes, Wörle tells the defense attorney that the man who has just delivered the missive is waiting for it to be returned. He has been instructed to take it by force, if necessary, although Wörle does not think such will be the case. The prior evening, he had retrieved from his lawyer his first—long and self-incriminating—letter to prevent Fiarthes from copying it after reading this new letter. Moreover, in the second letter, he informs Fiarthes that he will not destroy the long letter, that he intends to publish it. Of course, he will remove incriminating evidence about himself as well as anything that might harm Fiarthes. This will simply be another ball played in the game. He plans to give the manuscript to an author who will publish it in his own name and receive the royalties. He suspects it will not be difficult to find a willing author among the starving writers—and one who can keep quiet, as well. Besides, this writer will not have anything "except a story in which neither your [Fiarthes's] name nor mine occurs and in which one can decipher the story of my case only with a great deal of fantasy" (NS 197). This statement could be an intentionally misleading device on Hein's part, or it could hint at the many former GDR officials who quickly put together a book—usually ghostwritten—in order to capitalize on the political atmosphere after the Wall came down and make a quick profit. It is not Hein's normal practice to write a roman à clef, however, even though Wörle states to Fiarthes that precisely this will be done. His characters possess universality and a quality of representativeness of real types. The statement functions to "prepare" the lie of the ball for the reader's response.

The man in the waiting room is none other than Wörle's stepbrother, the "bastard." The previous November, after the fall of the Wall, his brother had come to West Berlin and looked him up, visiting Wörle in the jail cell. After he explained who he was and that his first journey through the opened Wall had led him to Wörle, the latter welcomed him with opened arms: "Welcome to freedom" (NS 199). These words are spoken to deceive his brother, who naively

130

believes that the West means freedom when, in fact, freedom is the illusion of the masses described earlier by Wörle. Wörle recognizes that his brother, looking for paradise, also needs to subjugate himself to the will of a "lord," or boss. His stepbrother, of course, is willing to do everything he asks. He had been able to work as a teacher at the university for a while, but when the Warsaw forces marched into Prague, he had expressed his disapproval in front of students. He was dismissed, had to remain unemployed two years, then worked in a chemical factory, and finally was allowed to teach history in a high school, but only on the condition that he take over an undesirable party function in the local union.

The brother has been prepared for his encounter with Fiarthes and is not going to believe anything Fiarthes has to say which might contradict what Wörle has told him. Moreover, he doesn't know anything about the match between Wörle and Fiarthes. Wörle had chosen Fiarthes as his lawyer because he knew of an indiscretion committed by the latter some ten years earlier, a leverage he was able to use to ensure that Fiarthes did not drop the case and thus endanger his game. Of course that's all forgotten now, and Wörle is enjoying continued success in his law offices; numerous clients are seeking him out to represent them after reading the reports of his spectacular trial.

Wörle has a new game for Fiarthes, or perhaps it is the continuation of the previous one. This time no one will be killed, at least not in the literal sense of the word. He is planning to ruin a well-respected citizen, one with impeccable integrity, an educated and enlightened man, very likeable and honored publicly. It will be extremely difficult to ruin him, especially since there is no sign that even the smallest, most insignificant impropriety has ever been committed by the man. This is the very reason Wörle has chosen him to be his next game ball. In order to up the stakes to the maximum difficulty, Wörle now wants Fiarthes to enter the game as the protector of the man to be ruined. His stepbrother has a note which contains the man's name and will read this name to Fiarthes in exchange for the letter Fiarthes is reading at the very moment. Wörle hopes that Fiarthes is convinced to enter the new game as his opponent by warning the man chosen as the victim and doing what he can to prevent Wörle from ruining him. Thus ends the novel.

und diese verdammte Ohnmacht

Immediately after the opening of the Berlin Wall, Hein had agreed not only to participate in the hearings of the investigating committee which attempted to identify the guilty parties during the police brutality on 7 and 8 October 1989, during the fortieth-year celebration of the GDR, but he additionally agreed to help compile and edit the protocol for publication. This all took place during the writing of *Das Napoleon-Spiel*. The hearings themselves were characterized by denials on the part of the highest officials in charge at the time—including Egon Krenz, who had replaced Honecker for a short period of time; Günter Schabowski, a member of the Central Committee and the party chief in Berlin; the hated chief of the State Security Police (*Stasi*), Erich Mielke; and a number of other high-ranking officials such as the attorney general of Berlin, the interior minister, generals, police chiefs, military attorneys, and *Stasi* officials. The hearings dragged on for many months as the committee attempted to get to the bottom of things, continuing into the spring of 1990, when the first free elections in East Germany and the impending decision to reunite with West Germany rendered the committee's work largely moot. Follow-up work continued on into the fall of 1990, and the proceedings were published in 1991 with the title *und diese verdammte Ohnmacht* (And This Damned Helplessness).

Hein wrote in his introduction to the proceedings of the hearings that the public interest had been captured by the elections, the approaching end of the existence of the country, the creation of the new Federal States in the East, reunification, the implementation of the capitalist system, and above all, the introduction of West German marks on the basis of a two-for-one exchange. In November of 1989, the work of the committee had been a mind-boggling provocation and its members were aware that they could easily have spent many years in prison afterwards, but by the spring of 1990, time had rolled over it and obscured its importance. Hein's frustration with the failure of the committee to accomplish its goals is evident in an example he cites: "In the spring of 1990 the commission again recommended the indictment of a high officer of the State Security Police. A few weeks afterwards they learned that the officer indeed was in court, however not as a defendant but as the plaintiff, who requested the release of a confiscated sport motorboat of the Stasi, which he claimed as personal property" (Ohnmacht 11–12).

Members of the committee were never able to determine who gave the orders. If they were to believe the statements made at the hearings, the most powerful men of the country and its security forces, including those in the Politburo, had all secretly been resistance fighters, were not guilty, and were horrified at the events. The deployed *Stasi* officers could not be identified and located; no one knew who had ordered whom to do what, or even what had happened to the clubs used in the beatings. The state attorneys, sitting in the room next to where prisoners from the demonstrations were held, were unaware of the violence employed against those arrested, didn't hear their screams or see their injuries. The committee was left with the feeling of "damned helplessness," the precise situation in which Fiarthes finds himself. Further research may some day turn up connections between Wörle and one or more of the politicians or lawyers Hein encountered during his work on the committee. More important is the connection between the feelings of helplessness expressed in *Das Napoleon-Spiel* and in Hein's report. In such a context, the novel is a commentary on unscrupulous and arrogant behavior by men in power, presented as symptomatic of the time in which we live. Hein had always written about victims in the past and had usually done so with humor. This time, he turned his attention to a perpetrator, and his portrayal is totally devoid of humor.

It is not too difficult to understand the "bastard" as a fairly decent but clearly victimized individual representative of East Germany. Likewise, Fiarthes can be understood as a decent and responsible representative of West Germany, if the reader wishes. But who is the unscrupulous Wörle, a man capable of moving between East and West, a man of wealth and political influence who ruins everyone he chooses to ruin regardless of their place on the spectrum? He is an amoral force, living for the game, and the reader is left to wonder where he will strike next and whether something can be done about it. There is no redeeming social victimization in his biography: nothing happened in his life which caused him to become like he is; he seems more to be an abstract principle which can infiltrate the lives of individuals in society in an insidious manner.

Symbols of disconcerting abstractions appear throughout the text in fragmented form, presenting a temptation to risk badly misinterpreting the story. Hein complained about how distasteful it was for him to be so intricately involved in the political events after the fall of the Wall and how he longed to return to being a writer. It is almost possible to see him as Fiarthes, as someone who has been duped into defending a monster and who now cannot extricate himself. But Hein claims that he "never presents alien monsters"[8] and thus claims the right to be identified with Wörle as much as with Fiarthes.

Perhaps there is something to this, but a more helpful approach might be to consider Hein's intellectual activity during the writing of *Das Napoleon-Spiel* and his reaction to the neo-Nazi activity on both sides of the Elbe, his concerns that the outgrowth of the long-lasting *Historikerstreit* would overturn national guilt and awareness about the past.

Wörle, who always let the "bastard" take the blame, might symbolize the specter of fascism (always linked with capitalism in socialist ideology) raising its head again in Germany during and after unification, a ghost of the Nazi past who succeeds in duping the Germans (Fiarthes) into defending him and who is found not guilty (on legal technicalities) by the judges (historians), setting the monster free once again.

Hein had read numerous *Stasi* files and was appalled that cold-blooded murder was part of its repertoire as well as that of the secret police in other countries. Secret police are in a position to be self-justified, self-righteous— and should the self-righteous, wherever they are, be willing to "assert their justice, the ruin of all of us and the end of the already so endangered world will be advanced."[9] If history is rewritten, as the writer to whom Wörle gives his manuscript will do, to eliminate incriminating references, as Hein believes the *Historikerstreit* to promote, the stage will be set. In his essay "Die Zeit, die nicht vergehen kann" (Time Which Cannot Pass Away), he expressed his concern: "Certainly the interests of both the accused and the plaintiffs are in play during contemplation and evaluation of the past. One side points as vehemently to errors and crimes as does the other endeavor to push the uncontested accomplishments into the foreground, to banalize the unpardonable and to manipulate the unexplainable into an explainable context" (Als Kind 112). The consequences of a successful manipulation of history and people's knowledge of and attitudes towards history are embodied in the disturbing figure of Wörle and his justification of murder as a pardonable killing.

The affinity between this book and Choderlos de Laclos's *Les Liasons Dangereuses* (1782) can hardly be overlooked. Whereas the Marquise de Merteuil and the Vicomte de Valmont are vain, professional intriguers—making sexual exploitation the business of their ruthless game and being fully aware that any manifestations of feelings will ruin the play—Wörle is a dangerous 1990s version of the odious immorality of Merteuil and Valmont, equally intelligent, urbane and amusing, and equally disposed to reduce the logic of the heart to cold, cruel, and calculating reason, the unequivocal rationality of power unhampered by moral scruples. Attitudes embodied by Wörle expose human morality at the end of the twentieth century as a silly travesty, a mundane spectacle not worthy of great players' time.

Das Napoleon-Spiel was the first major work published by any of the important former GDR writers still living in the East after Germany was united. A general fear seemed to exist that these writers would have great difficulty succeeding under the new conditions, and critics seemed to expect continuing recriminations against the old GDR in works of fiction. This book certainly inspires fear that people like Wörle may walk among us, and it makes us hope that our society is not degenerating into nothing but a vicious game with high or low stakes, depending on one's point of view and capabilities. It does not fulfill the expectations of the German critics who, after bashing Christa Wolf and others, called for the "elevation" of literature to a purely aesthetic art form without any moral message or socially critical function.[10] If the broader interpretation of Wörle is considered, Hein has done his part to not relativize the Nazi past in such a way as to omit incriminating evidence. At the same time, he touches a nerve about how threatening unscrupulous power which exists beyond good and evil can be to us. Wörle is the principle of barbarianism before which the principle of hope gives ground. He now requests that we bear him no malice. But he will continue, even if we do.

Notes

1. Volker Hage, "Glückliche Knechte," *Der Spiegel* 12 April 1993, 239.
2. Fritz Rudolf Fries, "Das Feldherren-Syndrom, *Neue Deutsche Literatur* 41 (May 1993): 139.
3. Hage 239.
4. Hage 239.
5. Part of the unification agreement between East and West included the establishment of so-called *Treuhandgesellschaften,* trust unions created to mediate property issues. All the complaints mentioned here continue to be a common thread of what former GDR citizens regard as their ongoing disenfranchisement as citizens of the new Federal Republic of Germany, including their opportunities for financial success.
6. Fries 139.
7. Grigori Efimovich Rasputin (1871–1916), Russian mystic and advisor to Czarina Alexandria, was assassinated. Rasputin was noted for his cunning and duplicity.
8. Christoph Hein, letter to the author, 13 September 1993.
9. Hein, "Ansichtskarte einer deutschen Kleinstadt, leicht retuschiert," *Neue Deutsche Literatur* 40.4 (1992): 27.
10. See *Der deutsch-deutsche Literaturstreit oder "Freunde, es spricht sich schlecht mit gebundener Zunge,"* ed. Karl Deiritz and Hannes Krauss (Hamburg: Luchterhand, 1991).

CHAPTER SIX

No Message Intended: Dramatic Works

In the early 1970s, most of the GDR's great stage directors, actors, and dramatists had not yet joined the gradual exodus of talent to the West, and Hein's yearning to become involved in theater had led him at the age of nineteen to Benno Besson, the talented director from Switzerland. After his brief apprenticeship with Besson at the Deutsches Theater in the 1965–66 season, the years of struggle to gain admittance and to complete his education, the birth of his two sons, and his dependence upon Christiane's income to support the family, Hein finally landed the job as house author under Besson at the Volksbühne.

His first original plays—*Vom hungrigen Hennecke* (Hungry Hennecke), a short piece written in a variety of verse forms for children's theater directed by Thomas Valentin that ironically treats the heroization of the legendary GDR coal miner Adolf Hennecke, and *Schlötel oder Was solls,* 1981 (Schlötel or What's the Use), directed by Manfred Karge and Matthias Langhoff—both premiered on 25 September 1974 at the Volksbühne for what was only a one-night stand.

Schlötel: The Intellectual as Idealist

In the five acts of *Schlötel oder Was solls,* Schlötel—the young, idealistic intellectual—disrupts the lethargic stagnation of a GDR factory by taking the principles of socialism seriously and attempting both to exhort the workers to become activists on their own behalf and to act as their spokesman without consulting them. His relentless pursuit of his ideals costs him his family and his private life. The reforms he seeks are rejected by the workers. Having been fired and forbidden to set foot on the premises, he takes his own life. The reforms he had championed are then put into effect by the party. Hein calls the play a comedy, ascribing a sense of the ironic to the concept.

Hein wrote the first version of *Schlötel* around 1971, the year Honecker came into power. The play takes place in the realm of the factory and the worker, but it is not a traditional GDR "production play" of the socialist realism school in which positive solutions to social and economic contradictions are found by an energetic, forthright, and often heroic socialist worker who convinces his fellow workers to make some personal sacrifices and general changes for the good of the whole. The play also goes beyond the best of that genre, Müllers *Der Lohndrücker* (1957); *Der Bau* (1963–64), an adaptation of Erik Neutsch's *Die Spur der Steinen*; and Braun's *Die Kipper* (1965), whose heroes are stormy activists with ambitious initiatives for social reform and progress and who stumble against the resistance of the collective. The heroic individual perishes as a rule in those plays, but the battle is not in vain: the dialectical process of history is fulfilled when socialist progress within the collective is achieved in spite of the tragic inability of the engaged individual to cause the change.

Michael Töteberg distinguishes the new perspective in Hein's *Schlötel oder Was solls* from the earlier plays: "the engaged reformer takes his own life in the end, and the incentive system he propagated is introduced-by decree of the local government administration. A mischievous point: Schlötel's battle was superfluous, the workers were never asked anyway."[1] Hein's play also examines the role of the intellectual within the economic framework of socialism, specifically the conflict of interests between utopian intellectuality and the considerably less ambitious needs of the working class—a theme touched on briefly, but poignantly, in *The Tango Player* when Dallow tries to find work as a truck driver.

Hein incorporates Brechtian principles of epic theater in *Schlötel* and has already begun to use the fragmentation techniques which characterize his later plays and prose in order to stimulate independent and unpredictable audience reactions. Hein was dismayed by the Volksbühne's elimination of about one third of his text for political reasons. The original text portrays Schlötel as an enthusiastic late 1960s left-wing radical student who chooses to move to East Germany and expects to show the working class what is good for them. The published version (1981) changes Schlötel into a brilliant sociologist just graduated from the University of Leipzig. The new text places more emphasis on the changes brought about by the *Neues Ökonomisches System* (NÖS, or New Economic System), incorporated into official policy by the *Politburo* in 1966 to increase productivity. Greater worker incentives to meet or exceed their quotas, including bonuses, were incorporated into the centrally planned economy. One aspect of the NÖS program was to bring the universities into a close relationship with industrial plants. Cybernetics and sociology, for example, developed as key new academic disciplines which contributed significantly, but which, due to results of research into human motivation and values and into systems analyses, threatened to exceed the limits of party doctrine concerning the composition of the "new socialist man."

Schlötel sets out to convince the worker brigade to vote for a system of *Objektlohn,* which has been suggested by party leaders. *Objektlohn* consists of incentive pay for everyone at the completion of projects: the profits are to be divided into bonuses. If the goal is not reached, however, the losses are subtracted from wages. The issue for Schlötel—consuming his attention and causing him to sacrifice the possibility for happiness in his private life with his wife and newborn child—is for the workers to exercise self-determination instead of dutifully and uncritically accepting the party's mandate. After all, he argues, East Germany's government is supposedly the dictatorship of the working and farming class. However, the workers want neither incentive pay (it disrupts the leisurely pace at work) nor emancipation. They thus have him fired and banned from the premises as an unwanted activist. Schlötel ends his despair by drowning himself in the Baltic Sea. Shortly thereafter, the party decrees the implementation of the incentive pay system. "What's the use?" Whether citizens are engaged, apathetic, or opposed makes little difference: the party still makes the decisions. This fact leaves, as Antje Janssen-Zimmermann has noted, two existential possibilities from which to choose: either the kind of engagement of Schlötel's, with its unpredictable consequences, or "a life of apathy towards the ways of the world, withdrawal into a private sphere."[2] Moreover, the capitalist-style implementation of the performance principle (*Leistungsprinzip*) is problematical. The guarantee of work for everyone does not encourage high levels of performance, a fundamental contradiction of socialism which can never be resolved. Janssen-Zimmermann, writing after the fall of the Wall, sees *Schlötel* in retrospect as an *Endspiel,*[3] a play depicting the end of an era—in this case, the downfall of socialism defined as the triumph of capitalism, which is precisely how the Western media described it. This term was quickly applied to *Die Ritter der Tafelrunde,* but it may be questionable for *Schlötel.* On the other hand, Hein later claimed that many of his works could be understood as *Endspiele.*[4]

A capitalistic principle, based on reward for superior performance, functions to disrupt the ideology of a socialist utopian structure in the play. Moreover, the structure reveals additional shortcomings by its leaders' failure to gain the informed support of the working class and then by their disregard of the will of the working class. Hein clarifies his views on the failure of socialism in his essays as well, and he spoke freely in his acceptance speech for the Erich Fried literature award on 6 May 1990 in Vienna: "I think that the central cause for the collapse, the self destruction of the soviet system in the Soviet Union and in its allied countries was the missing performance principle."[5] This principle applies not only to economics. It is the basic principle of competition and is fundamental to democracy and public freedom, in Hein's view. The missing performance principle in the "countries of so-called real existing socialism destroyed them."[6] The administrative bureaucracy in Hungary, Poland, Czechoslovakia, and the GDR interrupted and destroyed each reform effort to experiment with reward based on performance. The Prague Spring was "the last attempt which still had a real chance of success."[7]

Hein refers to the working class as the ruling class on several occasions in *Schlötel,* echoing the language of the Communist party, a language often used to justify actions which were discriminatory to other factions of society. The de facto separation of the real working class from the real ruling class, and the resulting power structure which subsequently prevails, demonstrates how far the party swayed from the original theory of the power of the working class and its right to rule. In the early years of the GDR, the working class was privileged by decree and by action. By the time period of the play, the evolution of social relationships in the GDR which resulted from the restructuring of society had reached the point where the discrepancies portrayed in the play were recognized and commonly discussed, albeit not in the public forum. Party members, whatever their origins, continually exercised authoritarian control, and their actions came across as a hypocritical form of lip-service to the "ruling class" workers.

As a student of the eighteenth-century dramatist J. M. R. Lenz (Hein later wrote an adaptation of a lesser-known comedy by Lenz, *Der neue Menoza, oder die Geschichte des kumbanischen Prinzen Tandi*), Hein calls his *Schlötel oder Was solls* a comedy in the vein of Lenz's *Der Hofmeister* (The Tutor, 1774). The tragic end of the main character of both plays, although replete with humorous dialogue and comic situations, explicitly excludes the possibility of a happy ending for normal or well-meaning members of society, while at the same time allowing the ruling class, whoever they may be, to continue to do as they please.

The West German premiere of *Schlötel* and the first staging of the published text did not take place until 1986 in Kassel, West Germany, under the direction of Matthias Fontheim. Hein warned that the play came from "a far-away land" with respect to the socio-cultural aspects, the workplace and everyday routine elements which were odd to Western audiences. Indeed, many of the references to everyday life in the GDR and their political implications were omitted, so that Hein's text was distorted in the West as well. Fontheim's decision to portray Schlötel as a "Storm and Stress" figure undermined the sophisti-

139

cated intellectual cloak of superiority which had lent Hein's character the universal appeal of the idealistic, brooding, and enlightened outsider: "My life is too short and too important for me to just swallow everything. Practitioners, conformists, quiet treaders, careerists—I'll give them all something to think about" (Schlötel 63). The responsibility of each individual for social morality and the democratic function of society perishes in the sea with Schlötel, leaving only the "comic" figures of bureaucrats and lackeys to run things.

In 1989, after the end of censorship in the GDR, the play enjoyed an unusual production in Annaberg in a small, made-over movie theater—capacity, thirty-two seats—by a young experimental troupe under the direction of Hasko Weber. It had taken fifteen years before the play was performed a second time in East Germany. The figure of Schlötel was performed alternately by seven different actors in order to differentiate the character into variants which addressed a wide spectrum of the by-then democratic-thinking public.

The Rockefeller Revue

Hein's next actual stage production was his satirical revue for actors' ensembles, *John D. erobert die Welt* (John D. Conquers the World), which premiered with little fanfare 21 April 1979, in the provincial town of Neustrelitz. The *Drei-Dollar-Operetta* (Three-Dollar Operetta), as it was dubbed by theater critic Andreas Rossmann,[8] enjoyed generally favorable reviews in the West at the Berlin Vagantenbühne in 1983 and in the Theater im Depot in Recklinghausen in 1986 under the new title *Die Geschäfte des John D.* (The Deals of John D.). Doris Heiland directed the play with a variety of entertaining musical scores by Henry Krtschil and Wolfgang Florey, including a medley of American blues, country, and Dixieland. Burlesque, gags, skits, slapstick, and ragtime kept the ironic description lively and satirically reduced the Rockefeller character to trivial status. Hein had reworked a 1930 radio play by Friedrich Wolf into a satirical variety show about Rockefeller's unscrupulous monopolization of the oil industry during his climb from a small, cautious businessman in Cleveland to the pinnacle of American capitalism. At least one Western critic, Ulrich Schreiber, showed some irritation at the audacity of a "socialist author's" characterization of America, as embodied in Rockefeller, stating that Hein failed to develop an appropriate ambiguity in the myth of America, presenting murder but ignoring its stand on human rights.[9] Rockefeller's closing monologue, as reprinted in the Recklinghausen program, seems to include some of this ambiguity, even if only in the final scene:

I am America, I am the dollar
I have made this land arable and exterminated the Indians
I have built plantations and enslaved the negro
I am Abraham Lincoln and I am Wilkes Booth, who shot Lincoln
I am the Trust, the prosperity, Black Friday
I am progress, I am opportunity for everyone
I am McCarthy, I am peace between races and classes
I am the laughter of America and its ceaselessly bleeding wounds
I am Niagara and the nuclear rain over Chesapeake Bay
I, Sitting Bull, Uncle Tom, Joe Hill
I am the war in Korea, Guatemala, Vietnam, I
I, America, the dollar, John D. Rockefeller
Whatever is said and counted, decided and done, it will
Have to reckon with me
I am the unknown greatness, inevitable, constant
I am the gold and I am the blood
Your wealth and your ruin
I have to be reckoned with.[10]

Cromwell and the Failure of Revolution

The years at the Volksbühne were lean ones for Hein, but he wrote constantly, filling his desk drawers with manuscripts. He researched and wrote his first significant historical drama, *Cromwell,* in 1976–1977. By 1979, Besson was gone, and Hein was out of his regular job as well, committed to full-time writing, free-lance. Both sons were in school, and Christiane had a decent income working on documentary films for DEFA, the GDR television consortium. Finally, in July of 1978—Hein was thirty-four years old—his *Cromwell,* the first work of his to be published in the GDR, appeared in *Theater der Zeit* (Theater Times), the monthly theater journal issued by Henschel Publishers, who held the monopoly on all play manuscripts in the GDR and who printed one play each month in their journal for the limited readership of theater critics and professionals.

Cromwell is divided into fifteen diverse scenes with varying locations tracing the developments of the 1649 English revolution to the execution of King Charles I and the beginning of Cromwell's leadership of the Puritan republic as Lord Protector. The pre-Communist aspect of the revolution is ensconced by the association with the Levellers, who place Cromwell in a position of conflict between them and the bourgeoisie parliament which refuses to forego concepts of property rights. Cromwell's resort to violence and terrorism frames the failure of the revolution and identifies the fundamental problem of revolutionary movements with Cromwell's inability to extricate himself from the very radical solutions which undermine the realization of the ideals intended. Cromwell is prevented from providing the people with food when the property faction refuses to release supplies from the amply stocked warehouses. Having already compromised with the Levellers, with whom he tends to sympathize, Cromwell realizes tragically that the coalition of the bourgeoisie interests constitute the new class which emerges from the ruins of the revolution.

The historical Cromwell, originally a small landowner, was driven on the one hand by Puritan fundamentalism, which Hein incorporates in the figure of Cromwell's mother, and forced into a coalition with the Levellers, on the other hand, in order to prevent the revolution from failing. As a faction which formed in the army of the Long Parliament around 1647, the Levellers provide a key to the GDR reception of the play, inasmuch as they embodied pure Communistic ideals by advocating the levelling of all ranks and the establishment of a more democratic form of government. It was also their influence which pushed Cromwell to execute Charles I in 1649 and to have himself named Lord Protector of the Puritan republic.

Hein—whose mentors for this play are clearly Shakespeare, Brecht, and Müller, in addition to Büchner—allows the public to see itself within a panorama of history by means of two important innovations: the play is sprinkled with historical anachronisms taken from the periods of the French revolution and czarist Russia, with excerpts from "speeches by Stalin's star prosecutor Wyschinski,"[11] and with contemporary references to cigarettes, Mauser pistols, *Datschas* (weekend cottages popular with functionaries in the GDR), Red Brothers, and Companeros (from the 1974 Portuguese revolution), along with numerous colloquialisms from everyday GDR life. Hein described his use of anachronisms in *Cromwell* and other writings as partly an attempt to avoid changing his work into historical dramas. The story is not being related by a contemporary but by a voice from the second half of the twentieth century. Hein said that he "would not attempt to mix the two time periods, which he would regard as fatal."[12] Nevertheless, the use of such aesthetic means—more common to the dramatic techniques of Hein's period and especially prevalent in works by Heiner Müller—creates just such a possibility for the audience while at the same time keeping Hein's application of historicism intact.

The most stunning anachronism occurs after the defeat of the radical Levellers, who are loaded into train cars for the West coast. Ten miles from the Irish sea the train is stopped, the boxcar doors are thrown open, and the entire "counterrevolutionary" contingent of soldiers is liquidated by forty-three machine guns in four and a half minutes, according to the stage directions.

The other important innovation is the implementation of a Shakespearian court-jester figure, the puppeteer Ladybird, as an intermediary between the action on stage and the audience. Ladybird's loaded political commentary, stated in the cynical language of the ordinary GDR citizen, ultimately gives way to petty personal opportunism. As an "average" man on the street, Ladybird exhorts Cromwell—and, by implication, the GDR and other "revolutionary" leaders as well—that he must not forget the little people, that the swineherd who loses swine (such as GDR citizens fleeing to the West) is judged to be a poor swineherd. Cromwell replies cynically, "The people never know what they want. They can't comprehend what needs to be done. We're the ones whose task is to find out what the nation wishes, what is good for a nation" (Cr 55).

Cromwell's thinking is firmly entrenched in the virtues of dictatorship. The people are like children. To keep order on the streets, the government has the army: "You have to keep the people quiet if you want to rule them. . . . Of course hunger is unpleasant. But nations are like children and when there is no bread in the house beating the daylights out of them will put them to sleep. . . . We need to educate them. . . . Therefore a father mustn't be all too friendly. . . . You raise them to be men with the whip. . . . Our fatherly duty" (Cr 55). The underlying sarcasm expressed in such speeches on stage triggered a hefty response from GDR audiences and from the offices which blocked the premiere scheduled for Dresden the day before the play was to open. The fact that the historical Cromwell's Puritan fundamentalism led him to shut down the theaters in England as immoral institutions was not lost on Hein. Cromwell's mother regards Ladybird's "profession" as a showman and puppeteer with disdain, a "horrible profession" with "no morals" (Cr 19). Ladybird replies: "Much worse, your grace, it has no wages. If we play what the authorities permit, we can hang ourselves. If we permit ourselves to play something [we like], we will be hanged" (Cr 20).

The play was blocked no less than a dozen times before it finally premiered in the Theater der Stadt in Cottbus on 4 May 1980, directed by Peter Röll. Even though this play was also relegated to the provinces, it was cut extensively and the dramaturgical revisions incorporated associative references to Nazis in order to soften the impact of the anachronisms. But this was a weak and transparent attempt at redirecting attention along acceptable official party lines. While the West German premiere in Essen (24 October 1984) went to the opposite extreme by clothing Cromwell's soldiers in East German army uniforms and Cromwell's son in the blue shirt of the Communist Youth Pioneers, Hans Günther

143

Heyme's 1986 version in Dresden focused on the tension between Cromwell's Puritan background, the political impact of the Levellers and the business interests of Parliament. The 1984 East German productions in Gera by Klaus Krampe and in Eisenach by Michael Grosse succeeded in the portrayal of Cromwell's personal corruption, self-indulgence, and arbitrary exercise of justice to protect his power, probably the only performances which captured the spirit of what the author had in mind.

Hein's criticism of censorship consistently argued in favor of permitting the print media to discuss public issues so that writers could proceed with literature and drama unhampered by accusations of "dissident" writing or of the exploitation of political events and circumstances for their plots. Hein justifiably feared the replacement of sensational journalism with sensational literature. Censorship had caused literary consumers to look to fiction and the stage for information about the state of affairs in the society in which they lived—specifically, for revelations of hypocrisy or injustice. Hein had to struggle with his desire to write texts which provided an opportunity for critical interaction with social and political events of the day without himself falling to the temptation of lessening the literary quality of his work. As a chronicler, he was able to avoid editorializing, but his plays informed about the state of affairs as well. *Cromwell* was the first play he wrote in which he worked with the problems specifically inherent in revolutionary movements, problems which could and did prevent true revolutionary change from taking place. At the same time, many of these problems were evidently common to GDR society as well, and therefore, artistic renderings of them created serious barriers to getting the text onto the stage.

In the interview which accompanied the text in *Theater der Zeit,* Hein stated unequivocally: "Dramas which are written in the present are dramas of the present. Our interest in the English revolution is the interest in ourselves. Historical consciousness is egocentric: we want to know who our fathers were in order to experience ourselves."[13] Years before *Horns Ende,* Hein described the theme which is central to much of his work: "It's about history and historical consciousness, how past events touch and rub against the present."[14]

Not surprisingly, the reception of a play about what could be characterized as the first European bourgeoisie revolution would be subject to different criteria in West and East Germany. The latter invested the bulk of its ideological, pedagogical, and intellectual endeavor in the analytical contemplation, and the stylization, of historical revolutionary movements—all of which (Cromwell was no exception) reaffirm Danton's words in Georg Büchner's *Danton's Death*: "The revolution is like Saturn, it devours its own children."[15] Although the same maxim, often quoted, proved true for both the Communist party and, conversely,

144

for the GDR intellectuals who contributed to the downfall of the system in November 1989, any portrayal or intimation of the GDR *Politburo* as a privileged elite group was officially considered throughout most of the history of the GDR to be an intolerable act of defamation. *Cromwell* does not intimate the *Politburo* in the way that many people (incorrectly, according to Hein) equated the figures in *Die Ritter der Tafelrunde* with it. The play does bring discussions to light which were controversial and which called the polemical focus of the party into question, suggesting its energies would be best suited elsewhere. According to a comment by Heiner Müller, the "main production branch in Stalinist structures is the production of state enemies; this takes precedence . . . over heavy industry."[16]

Müller's comments were made in retrospect, but the figure Manchester's parroting of Cromwell's ideas provides an eclectic summary: "Progress, the sacred cow. Foreign competition is increasing. These are your words: The English revolution will not triumph on the battlefields, but in the factory; it doesn't measure the blood of its fallen but the sweat of all its working people, it defends itself against its foreign enemies not with the sword, but with the increased export of British products" (Cr 67). Cromwell responds that his words sound distorted coming from Manchester, even ironic, and he wonders if Manchester is parodying him. Manchester is not, but the parody of typical official proclamations surfaces ironically with Cromwell's remarks about his own words. In Hein's *Cromwell,* as Frank Hörnigk stated, the "historical episode is reduced to the anecdotal, it becomes the provocation leading to" reflections on "general questions about the dialectic of the means versus the ends, on the relationship between pretension and reality, the possibility and the necessity of actions within the historical process."[17]

For the East German stage, however, the lack of critical contemporary plays like *Cromwell* resulted in boredom, according to Hein, and tended to stimulate narrative-prose writing. The repertoire followed the same pattern year in and year out: "a drama from the so-called cultural inheritance, a little boulevard theater, a lot of boulevard theater and the obligatory Soviet play."[18] In this climate, Hein's play was risky, provocative, and highly progressive.

Revolution in the Salon

The conflict between the public and private spheres—public achievement leads to the dissolution of family and private values—carried out in *Schlötel* and in *Cromwell* became a central focal point for *Lasalle fragt Herrn Herbert nach Sonja. Die Szene ein Salon,* 1981 (LaSalle Asks Mr. Herbert about Sonja.

The Scene a Salon), which Hein described as both a critique and a continuation of *Cromwell*.[19] As a "salon play," it parodies the GDR's penchant for so-called boulevard plays. Equally important, the play recapitulates how politics function; it "designates the location where, beginning in the nineteenth century, current politics take place,"[20] in meeting rooms and salons.

In the case of *Lasalle,* based on the founder of the General German Workers Union, Ferdinand Lasalle (1825–1864), Hein creates a parallel between the historical figure and the present by placing the scene in a salon, which functions as the representation of a stagnating, superficial society. Lasalle, by his own admission, is unable to overcome his own petite bourgeoisie indulgences and his Jewish intellectual background to the point of developing some ability to identify with the workers whom he purports to represent and whom he attempts to inspire to undertake revolutionary action. His decadence is underscored by his womanizing, a common theme in Hein's writings. Tired and resigned, Lasalle says he cares about only one thing now: "I will no longer get worked up, engaged, or excited to sacrifice myself for any imaginary passions or duties to society. I want to screw a few women, very few, and when we have had enough of each other, then I won't want any more" (AhQ 63). This inclination ultimately becomes more important to Lasalle than his political program: he dies from a wound to the genitals received in a foolish duel over a woman to whom he had made advances. The woman is someone he pursued while waiting (in vain) for his advances to Sonja to be reciprocated.

The personal and public failure of Lasalle leaves his arrogant and authoritarian servant Herbert as his successor. One of his first acts is to dismiss the sincere and idealistic Marxist Vahlteich—an act which has been often repeated, not only in the history of German attempts at revolution but in the history of the GDR and other socialist states as well. The parallels are often unmistakable: Lasalle notes, before he dies, that the most capable citizens renounce the country and leave. Schweitzer, the romanticizer of socialist realism and party propaganda, admits cynically to the exploitation of art forms (literature) to manipulate the thinking of the masses. Vahlteich, the only true revolutionary, is excommunicated by the party.

This play sat for a number of years as well, and Hein decided to give the premier to a West German theater in Düsseldorf a few months after the debacle with *Cromwell*. It premiered on 9 November 1980, directed by Heinz Engels, the first work by Hein to appear in the West. Aside from antagonizing the West German left, the play was received with ambivalence by an audience largely unfamiliar with the implications inherent in it concerning the current GDR society—the equation of GDR politics and society with boulevard comedy.

Heinrich Vormweg found himself torn between what he saw as an intriguing but "irritating, even frustrating spectacle,"[21] attributable in part to Heinz Engels's overly direct conception, in part to the author's use of fragmentation, and in part due to weaknesses in playing with the aesthetic forms of nineteenth-century salon plays. While acknowledging the somewhat lukewarm audience reception, Andreas Rossmann recognized the combination of salon (private) and political engagement, however small the scale (Lasalle's worker's union had only eighteen members) as a "theatrically provocative mediation of current conflicts."[22] Lasalle's engagement for the hopes of others remains without echo, and this alienates him just as he alienates the people with his tragicomic and ridiculous involvements with women. He is more discouraged by the failure of Sonja to meet him than by the failures of his attempts to motivate the proletariat.

In his notes to the play, Hein described it as a piece of autobiography which used the nineteenth-century salon play form to characterize the end of an era and the beginning of another in German history. Again, the word "autobiography" should be understood as social autobiography, which Hein uses to designate the reflection of socio-political events in individual biography. Of primary importance to Hein's dramatic portrayals are the attitudes revealed, or "the transparency of the individual."[23] Society, according to Hein, "is now only experienced and received as the State; ideas which move our time require the form of law and the corset of regulations in order to be viable; the struggle between classes and vested interests is manifested in politicians" and "public affairs have become the affairs of specialists"[24] who work behind the scenes, in salons and the like, out of the public eye.

It took seven years and Hein's rapid ascent in international acclaim before the play was allowed in East Germany, opening in Erfurt on 2 February 1987, under the direction of Ekkehard Emig, to overwhelmingly positive reviews.

Armchair Revolutionaries: *Die wahre Geschichte des Ah Q*

In Hein's most successful play, *Die wahre Geschichte des Ah Q,* 1984 (The True Story of Ah Q), Ah Q is a harlequinesque, unemployed petite bourgeoisie dropout, and Wang is an armchair critic and intellectual. Both of them—self-styled anarchists whose roles are imbued with clever comic dialogue—are waiting à la Samuel Beckett's *Waiting for Godot* (which was not played in the GDR until 1987, in Dresden) for the revolution. Surprisingly, the revolution does, in fact, come, but Ah Q and Wang don't notice it until after it is all over.

147

Not much happens in the course of the play. The pragmatic Temple Guard keeps them locked in their room and irritates them with (some other authority's) ideas of work ethic (Ah Q and Wang are not interested in work) and stoic asceticism, and with official state exhortations about exercise and good health. A nun brings them milk soup every Thursday. Ah Q makes a pass at her and receives a whipping from the village policeman, Mask, on orders from above. Ah Q makes it out into the city and returns with cigars and other goods, which he refuses to sell to the Overlord (who never appears on stage). When the Temple Guard reports that the revolution is over, Ah Q and Wang don't think that it could have been genuine revolutionaries like themselves. Ah Q rapes the nun and is then executed for a burglary he did not commit.

The plot of *Die wahre Geschichte des Ah Q* is an adaptation of the Chinese writer Lu Xun's (1891–1936) short story of the same title written in 1921, a tale of the Boxer Revolution in China in 1911. Lu Xun presented this revolution as an event which ultimately changed nothing but the nomenclature. Hein incorporates dialogue from the story but changes the central character from a village beggar, which for Hein was analogous to the intelligentsia in middle Europe, to the self-centered bourgeois figure, dressed—under the direction of Alexander Lang at the Deutsches Theater in Berlin—as a "typical" GDR citizen.

The anachronisms, the dialogue, the gestures are all strongly associated with East German everyday life, and the temple in which Ah Q and Wang are "kept safe" in critical times—presented with no references to time and place—could be a locale during any revolution, or the GDR itself, or a room in any Western society where plaintive, passive intellectuality leads to estrangement and inaction during times which require socially responsible behavior. Above all, it is a room with a leaky roof which they, the intelligentsia and presumed representatives of the "new" man (unchanged from his old, lazy habits) were commissioned to repair. Impassive about this task, they instead hope the "revolution," when it comes, will cause the temple and all it stands for to be torn down, doing away with people like the Temple Guard and Mask, the brutal policeman for hire to all regimes, and with the Overlord who, however, quickly becomes the "revolutionary overlord" after the revolution, indicating that the status quo has just changed names after all.

Ah Q and Wang are housed in a dilapidated building designated in the text to be reminiscent of a grain-storage structure and described in the set directions as a grain elevator, an attic, or a dilapidated, forgotten church. They are supervised by the Temple Guard, a conformist and petty bureaucrat, one who follows orders and official policy unquestioningly, albeit always with an eye out for an opportunity to serve himself.

Hein rejects the equation of anarchy with terrorism, as it currently often is used. Anarchy, according to the German anarchist Gustav Landauer, "has no other task than to succeed in stopping the war of man against man in whatever ever form it may take."[25] The German anarchists rejected the patriarchal structure of society, were opposed to capitalist exploitation, and had a strong affinity with the pacifist movement around the time of the First World War. Ah Q's anarchistic act consists of throwing a bottle against the ceiling, breaking a new hole in it, as he yells to the Temple Guard, "We spit on you. On you and your roof" (AhQ 89).

Unfortunately, snow falls in through the new opening. Ah Q couldn't help himself. It was just a spontaneous idea, he maintains. Ah Q likes very much the way Wang uses the word "anarchy," the way it sounds. Wang explains its meaning: "It means that I am against everything. Against everything, understand? An anarchist is against everything" (AhQ 90). Ah Q wants to know if they are anarchists, and the reply is that they have no other choice. Ah Q experiments with saying the word out loud, finally yelling, "Long live Anarchy!" (AhQ 90). To him, the sound is beautiful: "It relieves me somehow." (AhQ 91). In an interview, Hein provided a definition for anarchy as an attitude which stands at the beginning of all philosophy and expresses doubt in everything: "The anarchistic moment, destruction in order to arrive at a tabula rasa, in order to come to a new beginning, to find a new hope, in order to expose illusions as illusions—this is the focal point around which the thoughts of both figures in the play circle."[26]

Ah Q and Wang are locked in (perhaps analogous to being confined to the GDR) in the hour of their destiny. They are beaten by the policeman Mask, himself forced to behave like a "dog"—Wang for stealing a book, and Ah Q for making his sexual advances to the nun. Ah Q gets away for a while, goes to town, becomes a businessman (dealing in stolen goods), and returns with cigars, hard currency, and a negligée for the nun, whom he eventually rapes and kills—evidently, without quite realizing what he is doing. Wang sleeps through it, though he is in the same room—a withdrawal which is a commentary in itself. The scene is enacted in the back of the set, with no overt violence, to ensure that the dramatic focus is not on the act itself. The poetic analogy to be drawn is the virtual, unwitting destruction of the one symbol of humanity, the one element containing some meaningful value (to Ah Q). Not that the simple nun is purely a symbol of piety; her dialogue contributes to the satiric atmosphere as well. Indeed, all the characters have been violated in some way by the conditions of their subservient existence, mentally and physically. Wang is beaten for "borrowing" a book but, in a broader sense, also for his attempts at intellectualism. Mask is disfigured by the overlord, whom he faithfully serves, with a blowtorch to the face. The Temple Guard is impotent. They all suffer additionally from terminal cases of self-induced tutelage.

As has been said, Ah Q does not intentionally kill the nun; it happens while he is out of control, raping her in a back corner of the stage (in Lang's production) so that the focus is on the symbolism rather than on the violence of the act. The inadvertent killing of the nun comes to symbolize drastically misplaced priorities when Ah Q is executed for stealing the overlord's belongings, which he didn't do, but as implicitly defined by the social structure, the goods are more important than the nun anyway.

On two occasions, Ah Q addresses the audience. In Lang's production, he goes into the sixth or seventh row of the audience as he attempts to formulate one single statement which expresses everything meaningful. Then he stops, returns to the stage, and declares: "I have no message to give" (AhQ 107). The audience will have to think of one on its own. In her review of the play, Ingrid Seyfarth questioned whether the audience should take this statement at face value, inasmuch as she suspected an underlying intended message.[27] In his review of the West German premiere in Kassel, Andreas Rossmann interpreted the message in the attitudes that were portrayed as a disclosure, an ideology critique, which points to "a great paralyzation, a great emptiness: Ideals are devoured, plans fade, messages become threadbare, life, our life, is a false, senseless preparation for death with no way out."[28] As accurate as Rossmann's view may be, it overlooks the comic aspects of the play, which are often arrived at with the use of laconic statements: "Sleep with me, nun" (AhQ 105); "Long live anarchy" (90); "He wanted to kill me," says Ah Q, to which Wang replies, "Don't take it personally" (105); "I'll give it to you with a steel whip" (117); "The revolution was here. A foreigner from the city [led the revolution]" (123).

The comic element lends an absurd quality to the ramblings of Ah Q and Wang, causing them to be understood more as helplessly ignorant dreamers trapped in the room by their own doing than as tragic figures. The other instance of direct audience address shows Wang and Ah Q claiming they are only performing scenes from the world of bureaucrats and professionals and that the members of the audience themselves are all nothing but bureaucrats—a statement that invites them (us) to identify with Ah Q and Wang, or with the Temple Guard and Mask, if they (we) choose.

Lang's stage direction was daring, and the play stirred a great deal of controversy. The senior editor at Henschel Verlag, Gregor Edelmann, attempted to soften the expected criticism with the public interview with Hein published in *Theater der Zeit* (and also printed in the program). But Hein chose not to publicly ascribe to any of the suggested interpretations, refusing to do so as a matter of principle, since he felt that authors should not play the role of commentators. Nor was he ever willing to tell readers and audiences what to think about his works. Having read of the text of *Ah Q,* some GDR party critics were especially displeased about the open-endedness and arbitrary multi-levels of potential meaning, the way Hein let his characters (and the audience) float in the wind, and his aesthetic contradictions of the socialist mission of realism. The failure to include a negative linkage to capitalism left the play unpalatable. Instead of providing such a link, Lang went to the other extreme by including GDR-associations with popular music from local and domestic rock bands like Pankow, Puhdys, City, and Keks, affirming the association with the GDR. As the younger portion of the audience responded with glee throughout the premiere performance, professional bureaucrats and official dignitaries got up and walked out in protest. Nevertheless, the play ran six years at the Kammerspiel (Chamber Stage) of the Deutsches Theater, a remarkable run for contemporary plays and strongly indicative of public support in the face of official disapproval. Hein and Lang had succeeded in breaking with the strict linguistic regulations which created obstacles for a theater of engagement, and had done it in Berlin.

The revolution was brought in by a "foreigner from the city" (AhQ 123)— i.e., there was never any revolution in the GDR as party dogma contended; it was introduced (forcefully) from elsewhere, from the Soviet Union. Ah Q and Wang live as isolated, locked in, daydreamers, but the revolution occurs outside in the streets, "drifting by like a ghost ship."[29] Wang steals away in the night, so as not to be held accountable for the nun's death. The execution of Ah Q was not as glamorous as executions in the past, according to the Temple Guard; there was no singing. Wang and Ah Q never reach the moment of anarchy, nor do they have any capacity to understand it. Ah Q did, however, yell out, "long live anarchy" at his execution, presenting such a moment to the audience to take it or leave it. For his part, Ah Q never understood what it meant.

Hein does not regard his dramas as "revolutionary dramas," a common genre on GDR stages which Hein views as contrary to the reality of the existence of the GDR: "There was no revolution here in 1945. The official historical writings . . . falsified this afterwards. . . . In 1945 one wanted all kinds of things, but definitely not socialism. The development here is a result of the Second World War and certainly not the result of a revolution. My plays have a lot to do with this, *Ah Q* as well as *Cromwell.*"[30]

Plays which portrayed alienation or the loss of definitive certainties in late twentieth-century human experience were virtually non-existent on the East

German stage when *Die wahre Geschichte des Ah Q* premiered. And it created a sensation—not in the provinces but in East Berlin, where it was performed at the Deutsches Theater with the best GDR actors—Christian Grashof, Roman Kaminsky, Dieter Montag—and with the most influential and creative director of the 1980s, Alexander Lang. The play, which had taken Hein ten years to complete, was ready the year after he finished *The Distant Lover* and was in fact, according to Hein, in some respects a free dramatization of *The Distant Lover*.[31]

Although the plots of the two works are totally unrelated, in common with the novella are the play's poetic analogies, which are left open to varying interpretations, the unsettling accuracy of the conditions depicted, and the Hein trademark that the reader/audience arrives at his or her own conclusion—all of which contributed to *Ah Q's* tremendous success on European stage in Strasbourg,[32] Paris, Bordeaux, Bern, Zürich, Vienna, Graz, London, Lisbon, Rio de Janeiro, Kassel (West German premiere), West Berlin, Düsseldorf, Hamburg, Tübingen, Paderborn, Nürnberg, Wiesbaden, and elsewhere, generating hundreds of reviews. If we can reflect back on *The Distant Lover* for a moment, it is worth mentioning that this novella achieves what Hein refers to as a precise inventory of his society, which itself functions as an explosive provocation for change. The story told in the first person by a female physician is unusual not only in that the work was written by a male but also in that it reflects an astonishing insight into female subjectivity. The story describes a successful professional who exercises complete denial to suppress her self-alienation and becomes a compassionless, empty person unable to recognize or to experience simple human feelings and attitudes, all the while proclaiming herself to "have it made." It turns out to be a life of insignificance and banality, like that of Lasalle—and that of Ah Q, only without the ironic, sarcastic humor. Formalistically, *Die wahre Geschichte des Ah Q* can been seen as a rendering of *The Distant Lover* into sarcasm.

Passage

Hein's return to the GDR from his USA trip in the spring of 1987 was marked by one of his most productive periods—with the publication of numerous essays; two more plays, *Passage,* 1988, and *Die Ritter der Tafelrunde,* 1989 (The Knights of the Round Table); and his novel *The Tango Player.*

The scene in *Passage* is the back room of a café in the south of France on the border with Spain in the year 1940. The title refers to the attempts by Jewish refugees to gain safe passage out of Europe. The word "passage" also associates the play with the last work of Walter Benjamin, *Das Passagenwerk* (Arcade Works), which bases its theories of modernity on the impact of European shops placed together in enclosed arcades, usually with skylights, which were the forerunners of shopping malls.

Hein's *Passage* presents the anxiety, hope, and despair of the refugees seeking to get across the border into Spain before the Gestapo closes in on them, through the Pyranees and eventually to a port where they hope to find passage on a ship taking Jewish refugees to America. When the Gestapo does find them, they are roused from the lethargy of waiting and hoping for the impossible. The catalyst for the existential choices is Frankfurther, who stuns the group by poisoning himself just as the Gestapo is inspecting their papers. The mayor, Paul Joly, who had been protecting them, decides to go to Paris to join the resistance. The others attempt to escape but are turned back to wait one more day until the Spanish border opens. Lenka decides to remain behind to sustain the small hope that her husband may escape from a concentration camp and join her.

The key figure of the play, however, is not the Benjamin-figure Hugo Frankfurther, but the seventy-five-year-old retired German officer Alfred Hirschburg, who is subjected to the scorn and ridicule of the group for his insistence on his identity as a German. His Jewish origin is of no consequence in his mind, and his current problems were merely attributable to a misunderstanding. At the same time, he breaches the fragile security of the village hideaway by inviting an old comrade-in-arms to join him. When his friend shows up leading a legendary group of fifteen old men in traditional caftan dress who had made a dream-like, miraculous trek from Zator, the old duchy of Auschwitz, Hirshburg's historical consciousness is jolted, and his adamant Germanness is transformed. To the awe of the others, Hirschburg leads the old men out of the village into the mountains by night. As Klaus Dieter Kirst, the director of the play at the Dresdner Staatsschauspiel viewed it, the image of the fifteen Jews setting out for the mountains with hopes contrary to all reason is a "staggering challenge to everyone to contemplate the limits of the possible."[33]

In *Passage,* Hein again uses the existential theme of waiting in a closed room, hoping to take a step into being, fearing to step into nothingness, with both alternatives dependent upon one's mustering the resolve to exercise a choice. All the while, the characters are frustrated and feel betrayed and helpless, dependent upon forces external to themselves to find a way out. The characters bear loose connections to historical figures. Hugo Frankfurther suggests Walter Benjamin, who committed suicide in Port Bou on 27 September 1940 after a failed attempt to flee following the capitulation by France to Hitler and Petain's agreement to the condition in Article 19 for retaining control of the South of France: "The French government is bound to turn over all Germans upon demand who are named by the German Government." Genier and Joly are reminiscent of French resistance fighters; Lenka, of the Prague Jewery and perhaps also of the Communist Jewish exile Anna Seghers; Lisa, of the Jewish group evacuated from the Alsace-Lorraine area; Studnitz and Kistner, of the German Red Cross Commission which was used as a Gestapo cover to ferret out Jews and resistance fighters; Hirschburg, of the non-practicing Jews who belonged to the Jewish division of the German army which lost 12,000 soldiers and officers in the First World War.

The story of emigration and exile functions as a confrontation with Jewish issues of the present—East Germany was notoriously lax in recognizing German responsibility for the Holocaust—but it also confronts readers and audiences with their own internal exile, not just that of East Germans. The dramatic escalation of the tension and danger of waiting forces the collage of anxiety-stricken people into the introspection of internal emigration; the perilous emigration across the mountains seems increasingly out of reach. As Erika Stephan has written, the "chain of motivation is dominated by the collision of the primeval need to take action and the paralyzing pressure of an intolerable, escalating compulsory situation which cannot be influenced."[34]

Toward the beginning of the play, Kurt and Frankfurther have a discussion about the conflict between conformity and self-expression. Kurt tells Frankfurther that he is *merkwürdig*—a difficult word to translate, meaning remarkable, but also odd, strange, curious, and in its literal sense, worthy of note. Frankfurther is glad to hear that Kurt thinks so, and he tells him why: "I have spent half a life attempting not to be remarkable, not to be conspicuous, to behave just like everyone else. For half a life I have sacrificed time and energy just so the others would consider me to be one of them. But that is foolishness. I am remarkable. And so are you. Otherwise you wouldn't be here. If you were not remarkable, you could live in Germany. Have the courage to be as remarkable as you are. You have a right to it, Kurt" (Pa 9). But Kurt replies that this is no time for Chinese philosophy. It might be useful to be remarkable, but they are better off to be inconspicuous since they are hiding from the police. Kurt is one of those still waiting in the stifling room after Frankfurther and Hirschburg are gone, waiting so that the audience can ask itself if he will be able to extricate himself from his internal emigration, from his inability to take action.

Hein refines the use of historicism in *Passage* to define the present. To forget the past would be to deprive ourselves of the kind of experience which provides cultural depth and continuity to life. As Hein had learned from Walter Benjamin, the consequences of history are more important than the facts, and in any case, historical consciousness defines the present. In *Horns Ende,* Hein causes his readers to grapple with distortions of historical facts and to define the present themselves. Hein's study of Benjamin's work on historical materialism was influential for his dramatic technique as well.[35] In *Passage,* he puts into practice the structural imperative of *Horns Ende:* remember. And the object of memory is the Third Reich's persecution of Jews; *Passage* can be understood as Hein's concrete dramatic answer to the attempts to relativize the Holocaust by conservative historians participating in the *Historikerstreit.*

The original plan for the premiere of *Passage* was to stage simultaneous opening nights in Dresden; at the Schauspielhaus in Zürich, Switzerland, directed by Urs Schaub; and at the Grillo-Theater in Essen, West Germany, directed by Hans Günther Heyme. Discrepancies in rehearsal times and organization, along with some foot-dragging by local censors in Dresden, caused the play to open on 25 October 1987 in Essen, on 15 November in Zürich, and on 28 November in Dresden.

Of the many stagings in both East and West Germany which followed, among the most interesting was at the Deutsches Nationaltheater in Weimar, directed by Christine Emig-Könning, one of the few female directors of stage. In this production, instead of the group's waiting in suspense for their moment to escape, they are tormented by a collective bad conscious, remaining at their places while only the mayor—who had resolved to join the resistance—shows any active solidarity with the mythical trek over the border by the old Jews. Operating in a small, eighty-seat theater, she could focus on the escalating, unbearable incapacity to act and its destructive effect on those forced to wait as their time to escape is being closed like a noose around their necks. Emig-Könning replaced the composure and solemnness of the staging in Dresden with fear, terror, and hysterics. The clash between the stifling pressure of the characters' inability to influence or determine their lives and their primeval need to take action was sharply defined.

Old Knights of the Round Table

Die Ritter der Tafelrunde, Hein's last play before the end of the GDR, is a work that in many ways virtually predicted the fall of the *Politburo,* depicting with audacity the petrified stagnation and senility of the older generation of rulers and their inability to cope with change. In a review in *Theater Heute* (Theater Today), Hartmut Krug called the play "The Knights of the Round Table, or: Honecker defends the Grail of the old Marxism against Glasnost and Perestroika."[36]

155

The plot consists of a "battle of opinions"[37] between the aging heroes about the value of the search for the grail and about the next generation's refusal to continue the search or uphold the ideal it represents. The tone is set in the beginning by the inability of Arthur and his knights to get a carpenter to fix a broken leg supporting the round table.

An anachronistic thread of generational conflict, social corruption, private resignation and disillusionment, glasnost, and women's and environmental issues weaves its way through the debates—all receiving a transparent cloak of cynicism, sarcasm, irony, and desperation as the old guard maintains that "history itself was mistaken" (R 26), rather than they who are the true believers, if the grail is not to be found. The knights are obliged by duty to procreate the belief in the "grail," the "incarnation of the promise of human happiness,"[38] even though they themselves have given up hope of ever finding it. Arthur—contrary to what is said in Krug's misleading review (written to be newsworthy)—bears no resemblance at all to Honecker; anti-authoritarian in his demeanor, he wishes in vain for a reconciliation and recognizes the need for a new approach.

Keie, dressed to look like Stalin in the GDR premiere, exhorts Arthur to kill his own son, Mordret, in order to preserve the old order, but Arthur answers, "If you murder Mordret and the young people then the grail will be lost to us for ever" (R 61). Lancelot, returning after having searched the world thoroughly, doubts the existence of the grail and reports that the people think of their leaders as nothing but a lot of "fools, idiots and criminals" (R 65). These words were spoken on stage in East Germany a few months before the Wall came down, creating an uproar of loud, spontaneous approval in the theater, which was packed by youthful patrons who had come to see their views incorporated in the brash Mordret's refusal to be intimidated or browbeaten by the stubborn, rigid old rulers. Spoken a few months earlier than that, Mordret's words could have landed the author and the actors in jail.

Mordret—whom Kunneware labels a *merkwürdiger* person (R 26), the same word Frankfurther uses to describe himself in *Passage*—regards all the knights as dinosaurs and says that he has no interest in assuming the throne, ruling a land, or becoming an entry in schoolbooks. Instead, if it were up to him, he would put the round table in a museum. The play ends with Arthur's saying to Mordret, "You are going to destroy a great deal, aren't you?" And Mordret responds, "Yes, father" (R 70). Unlike that of *Ah Q,* the end of *Die Ritter der Tafelrunde* does not change the nomenclature: things will be different; ideals, even if "Mordret cannot yet formulate them or articulate them,"[39] will change—among them, the quest for power as an end in itself.

As for the old, fading rulers, Keie himself remarks bitterly, "We have sacrificed our lives for a future which no one wants" (R 18). For Keie, the knights "created a paradise on earth for them [the next generation]," but Mordret replies that they "wanted to flog everybody into this paradise" (R 65). Keie and the alcoholic, cuckolded Orilus are alone in their hard-line views. Parzival has become a dissident publicist, even using the round table to correct galley proofs. Gawain has given up and retired to the "castle of the hundred women" (R 59) to till the earth and live like a farmer, and Ginevra, Kunneware, and Jeschute (who is still young) haggle, ridicule, and cheat on their men.

Die Ritter der Tafelrunde was completed four years prior to its premiere, and its intention was to describe any outdated regime or any erstwhile powerful consortium in control of political ideology, without denying the universal human quest for utopias; the grail is not necessarily socialism. The grail itself is defined enigmatically by Orilus:

> The reports are very contradictory. It was a gigantic jeweled stone, say some, from which a miraculous shining light emanates. Others say it was the sun table of the Ethiopians, which decked itself every night with new dishes of food. Even others say the grail is the place where the earthly paradise used to be. And even others call it a place of great sins, Mount Venus, where the people live in dancing and carnal desires. All agree only on one thing, that it is the highest and most secret thing in the whole world. This probably explains why some call the grail God, others the Mother Maria or, simply, the one you love. (R 42)

The play can be understood primarily as a critique of attempts to prevent the passage of power on to the next generation so that the new generation has a determining voice in how things will be and thus can assume control of its own destiny. The aged knights Keie and Orilus, by now devoid of all credibility, attempt to guarantee the preservation of the principles which had been valid for their lives. Except for Arthur—who recognizes the changeability of life and of human principles in general, and who attempts to understand this even though he does not understand Mordret—no one is able to conceive that the future lies beyond their control. Keie, in particular, wishes to forcefully keep future generations dependent upon the ideas and beliefs of the past. Anyone who doesn't agree should be wiped out.

Die Ritter der Tafelrunde is subtitled "A Comedy," and the scenes showing the round table in poor repair, the women sitting in the "siege perilous"—the famous seat which swallowed up unpure knights—making sarcastic comments about their husbands, along with the spirited insults tossed out by Mordret and Parzival, who plays the role of a disillusioned, dissident intellectual, all expose as a foolish supposition that the people themselves think the way their leaders insist they ought to. The people do not share any of the same goals. The play, which at some time in the future may regain relevance in another political-generational context is, however, very much a GDR-oriented play, and its bitter-comic posture mirrors and expresses the same public opinion which became so evident during the rejection by the public of its leaders in November 1989. Having written it in 1985, Hein did not intend for *Die Ritter der Tafelrunde* to toll the bell for the end of his country, but the intervention of history and the time during which it appeared on stage—at the historical end of the GDR—determined the reception of the play, making it, more so than all his other plays, a *Gegenwartsstück*—a "play of the present" that fueled the peaceful revolution in the fall of 1989. The future of this play will depend on a director's ability to convey the late twentieth-century theme of the loss of values.

The play was originally scheduled to premiere on 24 March 1989 in Dresden. As officials became aware of its nature, a controversy ensued about staging it. A "preview" or pre-premiere was staged on 24 March, and this was followed by five or six additional "previews," all sellouts. The official premiere finally took place on 12 April 1989, thus securing the rights for the GDR, but the play was performed only once more that season. After the opening of the Wall, however, the play appeared in theaters all over East Germany and, beginning with Kassel, in many theaters in West Germany as well, where it was widely misunderstood, perhaps due to the influence of Krug's review. Karla Kochta reported on a February 1990 theater visit by thirty-five students of Germanistik and Theater from the Freie Universität in West Berlin who were unable to understand why the play had had such a powerful effect on the GDR audiences: "They had come to see *the* 'Perestroika' play of GDR theater, expecting a comedian's cynical view of *past* GDR history." They wondered why Mordret did not smash the siege perilous, symbolizing that the "idea of socialism is perverted." But the seat remains on stage at the end, demonstrating the "necessity to debate a new direction."[40] That debate ended the following month with the elections and the decision to unify the two Germanies.

History over Art

Hein finished the libretto for *Don Quixote* in 1989, an opera planned for the Deutsche Oper in Berlin for 1991 or 1992, but circumstances after unification preclude the likelihood of this opera's getting onto stage in the foreseeable future. The figure of Don Quixote, the knight of the sad figure chasing wind-mills must have embodied a theme similar to that of *Die Ritter der Tafelrunde,* but history overtook the opera before it could be staged.

Notes

1. Michael Töteberg, "Der Anarchist und der Parteisekretär. Die DDR-Theaterkritik und ihre Schwierigkeiten mit Christoph Hein," *Text + Kritik* 111, ed. Heinz Ludwig Arnold (Munich: Text + Kritik, 1991) 36.
2. Antje Janssen-Zimmermann, *Gegenwürfe. Untersuchungen zu Dramen Christoph Heins* (Frankfurt a.M.: Lang, 1988) 33.
3. Janssen-Zimmermann, "Schlötel, Lasalle und König Artus. Aktuelle Anmerkungen zu Dramen von Christoph Hein," *Christoph Hein. Texte, Daten, Bilder,* ed. Lothar Baier (Frankfurt a.M.: Luchterhand, 1990) 181.
4. See chapter 1, note 8, above, where Hein states that he described the failure of socialism numerous times between 1974 and 1988, beginning with *Cromwell* and ending with *Die Ritter der Tafelrunde.*
5. Christoph Hein, "Unbelehrbar—Erich Fried," *Christoph Hein. Texte, Daten, Bilder* 27.
6. Hein, "Unbelehrbar—Erich Fried" 28.
7. Hein, "Unbelehrbar—Erich Fried" 29.
8. Andreas Rossmann, "Eine Drei-Dollar-Operette," *Deutschland Archiv* [Cologne] 16.9 (1983): 905. Numerous reprints.
9. See Ulrich Schreiber, "Amerika: kein Mythos. Christoph Heins Rockefeller-Revue in Recklinghausen," *Frankfurter Rundschau* 21 January 1986.
10. *Ruhrfestspiele Recklinghausen* (Recklinghausen: Werbeservice Schäperons, 1986) 20.
11. Christoph Hein, interview, "'Dialog ist das Gegenteil von Belehren.' Gespräch mit Christoph Hein," *Chronist ohne Botschaft. Christoph Hein. Ein Arbeitsbuch. Materialien. Auskünfte. Bibliographie,* ed. Klaus Hammer (Berlin: Aufbau, 1992) 19.
12. Hein, interview, "Dialog ist das Gegenteil von Belehren" 21.
13. Christoph Hein, interview, *Theater der Zeit* 33.7 (1978): 51. The interview was reprinted several times as an essay with the title *Hamlet und der Parteisekretär.*
14. Hein, interview, "Dialog ist das Gegenteil von Belehren" 51.
15. Georg Büchner, *Danton's Death,* Büchner, *Sämmtliche Werke,* ed. Hans Jürgen Meinerts (Gütersloh: Mohn, n.d.) 57.
16. Heiner Müller, *Zur Lage der Nation* (Berlin: Rotbuch, 1990) 14.
17. Frank Hörnigk, "Christoph Hein: Cromwell," *Weimarer Beiträge* 29.1 (1983): 38.
18. Hein, interview, *Theater der Zeit* 51.
19. See Hein, interview, "Dialog ist das Gegenteil von Belehren" 22–24.
20. Hein, interview, "Dialog ist das Gegenteil von belehren" 23.

21. Heinrich Vormweg, "Ein irritierendes Spektakel," *Süddeutsche Zeitung* 13 November 1980.

22. Andreas Rossmann, "Schau-Spiel im Salon," *Rheinische Post* 17 November 1980.

23. Christoph Hein, "Anmerkung zu *Lasalle fragt Herrn Herbert nach Sonja. Die Szene ein Salon*," *Die wahre Geschichte des Ah Q*. Stücke und Essays (Darmstadt: Luchterhand, 1984) 76.

24. Hein, "Anmerkung zu *Lasalle fragt Herrn Herbert nach Sonja. Die Szene ein Salon*" 76.

25. Gustav Landauer, cited in the program brochure of the Düsseldorf production of *Ah Q* (1985).

26. Christoph Hein, "Schreiben als Aufbegehren gegen die Sterblichkeit," *Christoph Hein. Texte, Daten, Bilder* 82.

27. Ingrid Seyfarth, "*Die wahre Geschichte des Ah Q*," *Sonntag* 15 January 1984.

28. Andreas Rossmann, "Keine wahre Geschichte," *Frankfurter Rundschau* 24 December 1984.

29. Töteberg, "Der Anarchist und der Parteisekretär" 40.

30. Hein, interview, "Dialog ist das Gegenteil von belehren" 24.

31. Christoph Hein, interview, Gregor Edelmann, "ansonsten würde man ja aufhören zu schreiben . . ." *Theater der Zeit* 38.10 (1983): 54–56.

32. The West German premiere in Kassel, directed by Valentin Jeker, was a month behind the French premiere, which took place at the Théatre National de Strasbourg in mid-November 1984 in cooperation with the Théatre de Geunevilliers in Paris. The French translation, *Entre chien et loup,* directed by Bernard Sobel, is generally considered to be one of the best productions. "Between Dog and Wolf" was Hein's own substitute title, used in the French version, and it reflects the dilemma of both Ah Q and Wang, who are caught between dogs and wolves and who seem to have no other choices but to become one or the other.

33. Cited in Lothar Ehrlich's review, "Herausforderung, über Grenzen des Möglichen nachzudenken," *Sächsische Zeitung* [Dresden] 1 December 1987.

34. Erika Stephan, "Das Kammerspiel *Passage* im Verständnis des Theaters," *Chronist ohne Botschaft* 215.

35. For a commentary on the connection between Walter Benjamin's thought and *Passage,* see Peter Reichel, "En passant," *Theater der Zeit* 42.5 (1987): 50–53.

36. Hartmut Krug, "Ritter von der traurigen Gestalt," *Theater heute* 7 (July 1989) 23.

37. Ingrid Seyfarth, "Palaver am Runden Tisch," *Sonntag* 14 May 1989. Also in *Christoph Hein. Texte, Daten, Bilder* 185.

38. Gerhard Ebert, "Parabel auf das Streben nach menschlicher Vervollkommnung," *Neues Deutschland* 3 May 1989.

39. Seyfarth, "Palaver am Runden Tisch," *Christoph Hein. Texte, Daten, Bilder* 185.

40. Karla Kochta, "Austreibung des Grals?" *Chronist ohne Botschaft* 225.

CHAPTER SEVEN

An Invitation to Reality without Moralization: Short Prose

Hein keeps a drawer of short literary sketches and prose at home and, from time to time, he publishes one of these. His early short stories brought him praise as a highly skilled craftsman of the German language, and it is a genre in which he himself feels that he does much of his best work. His method of writing consists of reducing language to its essentials, eliminating embellishing descriptions. To hone his storytelling skills, he studied Kafka, Kleist, and Johann Peter Hebel, all three of whom he regards as masters of economical expression and of objective chronicles. Although it was reprinted by several publishers, *Einladung zum Lever Bourgeois* (Invitation to the Lever Bourgeois) remained the only collection of Hein's stories until *Exekution eines Kalbes* (Execution of a Calf) appeared in 1994 with sixteen stories written between 1977 and 1990. *Einladung* was his first book-length publication, appearing in 1980. The short pieces he wrote since *Einladung* have appeared in many different literary journals and feullitons, sometimes in more than one.

Art and Patronage

The title and opening story, "Einladung zum Lever Bourgeois," is a narrative of Jean Racine (1639–1699) as the court historiographer for Louis XIV— an account of Racine's obligation to accept an invitation from the king and his struggle with a piece of history which the ruler, in the interests of national security, doesn't want made public. In his essay "Lorbeerwald und Kartoffelacker," 1984 (Laurel Forest and Potato Field), based on a guest lecture at the University of Jena he gave a year after publishing the short stories, Hein described the historical significance of the system of patronage—under which poets and writers were compelled to live exclusively during the centuries before it was possible to make an independent living from the sales of mass-reproduced copies of literary works—as a necessary stage in the educated middle class's efforts to gain access to power and to represent its own interests within the aristocrat-ruled system of feudalism. This access, and the accompanying potential for political and social influence, had to be acheived and maintained within the restrictions imposed by the scope of the educated bourgeoisie's administrative activities in the service of the nobility. The conflict between the necessity to act in a manner appropriate to the conditions of his employment and the need to maintain integrity and truth in his own behavior causes Racine to become seriously ill, and the advanced stage of his illness mirrors the mental torment and frustration he experiences from his increasing degrees of helplessness. In the slice of time covered by the story, towards the end of his life, he has, however, anonymously contributed to a political flyer exposing criminal acts of the king's soldiers. The public call to correct this injustice is tantamount to a treasonable act.

A Dutch peasant woman had been raped. She was found dead with her child in the stalls. The investigation was terminated in deference to higher interests; after all, such things happen during war. The farmer who had turned the guilty soldiers in committed suicide later on, as reported by the French commander in the village. The unusual thing about his suicide, as Racine is unfortunate enough to learn, is that he must have stabbed himself over twenty times with a pitchfork, tearing his body in half.

Racine anguishes over whether one should open the door to the barn where the peasant died. Experience and prudence, and the commander's uneasiness at seeing the court historian poking about, compel Racine to leave it alone. After all, anyone could open such barn doors: "Only idiots and children ask themselves questions about the world. The police and the army are always bestial, but this is not a topic for meditation" (ELB 12). Perhaps, Racine muses, the ability to keep quiet about crimes is a key condition of the human race for living in a society. The "national interest" may be bestial, but acceding to it may possibly be the prerequisite for the continued survival of the individual. Why open such a barn door—"in order to never be able to sleep at night, in order to feel horror and disgust?" (ELB 12). This would be contrary to reason; after all, as Racine realizes, more powerful people than he had closed their eyes and ears in order to see that the world was good. Later that day, back in his quarters, he vomits a green fluid. As Marianne Krumrey succinctly put it, "Racine is portrayed as the representative type of the accommodating citizen. Disease is a synonym for the violation [rape] of his own spirit."[1]

The flyer, "The Misery of the People," appears later, and Racine notices that its effect is satisfying, inasmuch as the police can't just ignore it and that the author has to be a courtier, an insider. Meanwhile, for a short period of time, other protest pamphlets appear in the city, until the police suppress them. Racine continues to grow extremely ill from what seems to be intestinal cancer, but as he contemplates his forthcoming invitation to the king's lever, he feels satisfied with his small roll in the agitation and giggles over the words "provincial asses, ass provinces" (ELB 24), which he repeats again and again. As Heinz-Peter Preußer has pointed out, there never was an oppositional pamphlet titled "The Misery of the People," which Racine toys with in his mind; this is all part of a legend which sprang up around him from his son's biography of him. These and other "discreet accentuation[s]" are "methodological." In Hein's fictional Racine, "we always feel ourselves to be close to the historical image of his person and of his century and we miss the target in decisive passages by just a little bit."[2] For Preußer, the combination of fictional literary historiography and non-fictional historical text causes meaning to be generated where lacunae occur. The two have a relationship like pre-text to text, where the pre-text provides a communicative link to the present and encourages an interpretation.[3]

Socialist Justice

"Der neuere (glücklichere) Kohlhaas" (The Newer [Happier] Kohlhaas) is a descriptive gem of GDR everyday existence written somewhat in the style of Heinrich von Kleist's famous story "Michael Kohlhaas," in which the horse trader Michael Kohlhaas behaves with extreme violence, sacrificing everything in order to right a wrong perpetrated on him by a young squire who has mistreated two of his horses. Michael Kohlhaas ultimately winds up leading a peasant revolution, sacking the town where Martin Luther lived along with several other towns, and sacrificing his wife and loyal servants in the process of finally gaining his vengeance and justice. The question always asked is "Was it worth it?"

Hein's humorous parody of German exactness takes place in a socialist context: Hubert K. is an accountant in a chair factory and discovers that his yearly bonus is forty marks short. It had been thus calculated due to absenteeism on his part, but these absences were taken within the legal auspices of sick leave and, hence, were justified. Hubert K. nevertheless receives several hundred marks, a sum which enables him and his wife to take a nice vacation.

Michael Kohlhaas is enraged by totally arbitrary injustices perpetrated by the ruling class, and his actions, if less excessive, could be wholly justifiable, supported by his argument that he is fighting for a principle, not for his own personal gain. But Hubert K. does not see himself as a champion of the rights of others as well as his own, as does Kohlhaas. Hubert is concerned about getting his share of the pot, however small and insignificant this might be, and has no interest in asserting himself as a defender of public rights. He is quite content

163

with the socialistic status quo; he is not a troublemaker; he wishes to fade back into anonymity. An engineer he meets during the vacation, possibly because he is attracted to Hubert's wife, Elvira, encourages Hubert to take some action.

Hubert's legal pursuit of the matter reveals a comical contradiction between the principle of cooperativeness to which socialist ideology claims to aspire and what is clearly not much more than Hubert's selfishness and unwillingness to see beyond the issue of "getting his share." The subtext elucidates and parodies how socialism functioned to keep order within the context of the routine life of its normal citizens. Hubert loses his case and must pay the court costs in addition (another 250 marks), and his wife moves out because the affair is making her "into a public spectacle" (ELB 88) as the object of town gossip. He also loses the respect of his colleagues and becomes bitter. When, however, he utters the words, "I no longer have any faith in socialist justice" (ELB 89), the state steps in, appearing in a pompous self-parody: a state limousine shows up, and the senior member of the supreme court steps out. He reverses the decision, orders the factory to pay the forty marks and to reimburse him for the earlier court costs, and, above all, orders his reputation to be restored. This action contrasts with that taken in Michael Kohlhaas's case, in which the horses are restored and returned and all other injustices are corrected. But then he is executed in the market place for his criminal excesses, a death sentence he willingly accepts under the circumstances. In Hubert's case, his faith in socialism is restored, and he is won over for socialist society as a good citizen. His wife then files for a divorce and, presumably, gets together with the engineer. The irony is evident in the apparent character of the type of citizen whom officials of GDR society chose to defend and win over to its cause. The trivial quality of the incident adds to the proportional absurdity: Hubert gets his forty marks and loses his wife.

Jochen Marquardt's excellent article on the ironic intertextuality in this short story concludes by describing it as a document of "de-illusion," a term that refers to social structures prevalent in the GDR in which everyday consciousness was entrapped. Hein presents a nearly complete picture of GDR reality as people lived through it; and, at the same time, the unresolved antagonisms of any given social organization in the manifest relationship between citizen and state are clearly discernible. Marquardt suggests that the forty-one-year existence of the GDR took its toll in the form of the "continual pressure to conform and adhere to convention which influenced social existence" in such ways as to leave open the question about the "ongoing effect" of these pressures, which then contributed to the downfall of the country and which may explain the "foundering in a new social organization of every day life"[4] which exists almost everywhere in the Eastern states of Germany. The humor and irony, however, has abated, as people are faced with serious existential problems, and, unlike in Hubert K.'s case, they will have to rely on themselves.

City Sights

A number of Hein's most poignantly written short sketches are grouped under the heading "Ein Album Berliner Stadtansichten" (An Album of City Sights in Berlin); they are the best example in Hein's writings of Walter Benjamin's theory of understanding history on the basis of glimpses at small, supposedly insignificant people and their lives. The first of these stories is about three generations of women—Friederike, Marthe, and Hilde. Friederike had married a thirty-seven-year-old Jewish haberdasher at the age of seventeen in order to get out of the two-room apartment in which she lived with her parents and seven siblings. Her husband is baptized, and they remain childless. After fifteen years, Friederike has an affair with a schoolboy, the son of a banker, and gives birth to Martha. Her husband is aware of this and is happy that she has a child. She, however, despises him for his impotency and creates scenes in front of Martha. When her husband dies, Friederika proves to be incompetent at running the business, which has to be liquidated after a few years. At the age of fifty-one, she marries a streetcar driver who falls in France seven years later. She dies in 1926.

Martha is unattractive but mild mannered. She is able to attend a business school and become a secretary. Since her mother is ashamed of their apartment and the poverty in which they live, Martha is not allowed to have any visitors and, consequently, leads the existence of an old maid. Her stepfather brings some visitors around, however, and Martha eventually marries a train conductor at the end of the First World War, a widower with a three-year-old daughter. The marriage goes well, and their child Hilde is born in 1921. They also have two more daughters and a son. There is a complication with the last birth, however, and Martha's husband becomes enraged that a male physician is treating her. He cannot tolerate a male, doctor or no, examining her and thus prevents the doctor from making his house call. Martha dies as a result of this neglect; her husband gets drunk at her funeral and marries his third wife four days later. Hilde moves in with her aunt and uncle.

Hilde's foster parents love her but punish her regularly because she is not a good student in school. She is required to address them as mom and dad. In 1932, her uncle joins the Nazi party, and Hilde is sent to a boarding school in

1935 to learn cooking, sewing, and national-socialist propaganda. Her day is highly organized and disciplined, an atmosphere in which she seems to thrive. Although she is an outstanding pupil, her stay is ended abruptly in 1938 when it is (incorrectly) discovered that she has a Jewish grandfather and is one-quarter Jewish. The uncle takes her in again, but he does not allow her to marry for racist reasons—Jewish women should not bear children.

The young man who loves Hilde falls on the East Front in 1942, and she suffers a nervous breakdown. In 1944, she marries a war invalid, and they have a retarded son, for which reason her husband leaves her. After the war, she becomes one of the *Trümmerfrauen*—women who salvaged the bricks from the ruins of bombed-out buildings for rebuilding—and eventually marries a man who had also fathered a retarded child. After the war, she runs into her real father but refuses to acknowledge him. She describes her life as average, nothing unusual, fairly satisfactory. This kind of storytelling is Hein's signature. No sympathy is given or asked for, and the reader is left somewhat in a state of shock. Each story in the *Berliner Stadtansichten* is told in a similar manner. The widow of a mason who is a victim of the Nazis, a Jewish actor who hides his family in a shallow vault in a Jewish cemetery, an act of violence by a youth group on a political outing in West Berlin prior to the construction of the Wall, the son of a Communist official who rebels and then conforms, a night trip by an East German driver paid to smuggle a family into the West, and the suicide of a young man pressured to excel in school: each tale a remarkable portrait in miniature of life in Berlin.

Columbus Turns Back

One of Hein's later stories—which appeared first in English in the *New York Times* on 25 June 1990 as "No Sea Route to India" ("Kein Seeweg nach Indien")—relates in ironic prose Columbus's journey as an allegory of socialism's failed attempt on German soil.[5] The crews, of course, are skeptical and inclined to mutiny from the beginning, and the journey is ridiculed by those at the farewell. In order to keep the spirit of the crews up, regular ceremonies and celebrations are held—including music, dance, alcohol, and marches—and the common goals and the togetherness of the crews are praised. Parades of armed sailors across the small decks testify to the power and unbroken battle-readiness of the heroic crews. Included in the propaganda are daily reports on the successful forward progress of the journey and the expected landing in India, all designed to demonstrate that the great captain is, indeed, steering the right course.

Mutinous acts, including the public expression of skepticism, are punished by death, and the slogan is "paradise or death."[6] Sometimes the crews would receive reports from the old country (i.e., West Germany), but these are discounted as enemy propaganda. However, the counter propaganda is so unbelievable that the captain soon loses credibility for his cause. The captain is captured and bound to the mast, and the new officers turn the ships around. Back in their home port, the crews stagger in wonderment at the great wealth and prosperity the old country has attained. They are placed under quarantine for a while, and their ships are taken into possession. Finally, they all agree to terms. Writers and chroniclers had been on the ships as well, but they now realize they have recorded nothing but the adventures of the ships of fools.

Notes

1. Marianne Krumrey, "Gegenwart im Spiegel der Geschichte. Christoph Hein, *Einladung zum Lever Bourgois*," *Temperamente* 6.4 (1981): 143.

2. Heinz-Peter Preußer, *Zivilisationskritik und literarische Öffentlichkeit. Strukturale und wertungstheoretische Untersuchung zu erzählenden Texten Christoph Heins* (Frankfurt a.M.: Lang, 1991) 33.

3. Preußer 35.

4. Jochen Marquardt, "Es war einmal ein Land, das hieß DDR oder Wie Kohlhaas zum Staatsburger ward. Zu Christoph Heins Kleist-Adaption," *Chronist ohne Botschaft. Christoph Hein. Ein Arbeitsbuch. Materialien, Auskünfte, Bibliographie,* ed. Klaus Hammer (Berlin: Aufbau, 1992) 66.

5. In her comparison of "No Sea Route to India" to Fritz Rudolf Fries's 1975 short story "The Sea Route to India," Frauke Meyer-Gosau describes Hein's parable as an oversimplification in its representation of the GDR as a country which floundered for forty years. However, as a genre, parables do oversimplify, and the transition from the utopian search for a better human being to wealth and comfort for all embodies the floundering of the GDR fairly accurately. See Meyer-Gosau, "Linksherum, nach Indien! Zu einigen Hinterlassenschaften der DDR-Literatur und den jüngsten Verteilungskämpfen der Intelligenz," *Literatur in der DDR. Rückblicke,* ed. Heinz Ludwig Arnold (Munich: Text + Kritik, 1991) 267–79.

6. Christoph Hein, "Kein Seeweg nach Indien" ("No Sea Route to India"), German first edition in *Christoph Hein. Texte, Daten, Bilder*, ed. Lothar Baier (Frankfurt a.M.: Luchterhand, 1990) 14.

CHAPTER EIGHT

Art, Courage, and Integrity: Critical Essays

The events of the peaceful revolution engulfed Hein along with other leading intellectuals. The tumultuous events of 1989 found Hein actively engaged in demonstrations with speeches and with countless interviews in both East and West. Having publicly denounced the GDR attorney general for his failure to act to prosecute the offenders, Hein then worked directly with the committee established to investigate police brutality during the national celebrations 7 and 8 October 1989, which had preceded the massive November demonstrations and the opening of the Wall. Hein's hopes for a democratic form of socialism were dashed with the unification of Germany, but he felt it would have been hypocritical of him to not have engaged himself concretely in the political activities which flurried immediately after the fall of the Wall. After all, Hein had been a leading intellectual spokesman for democratic reform and freedom of literary expression for many years and this was evident not only in his literary works but had been a frequent topic of his speeches and essays since the early 1980s.

The German tradition of literature is sprinkled with many writers who distinguished themselves with excellence in the form of literary, aesthetic, and political essays. Among recent German writers who thus took to the public forum, Günter Grass, Hans Magnus Enzensberger, and the late Heinrich Böll come to mind. The German media regularly provide and often encourage a forum for intellectual debate within the pages of the leading newspapers and weekly journals and on TV and radio programs. Whereas in American public life intellectuals and literary writers seldom can access the mainstream media, and are generally confined to university symposiums or specialty publications, for Germans, the concept of *Öffentlichkeit,* which means "pertaining to the public sphere," is a serious part of life and attracts widespread participation of readers and writers. The very language employed in the public media—aside from the commonplace *Bildzeitungen* (picture news papers)—is considerably elevated over the "common denominator" journalism practiced in most media publications in the US. Christoph Hein has a prolific record of essays, including a number that appeared in such prominent and widely read publications as *Die Zeit* and *Der Spiegel.*

Many of Hein's seventy-odd essays, dialogues, and speeches, including some which first appeared in volumes of his dramas in the West, have been collected into two editions: *Öffentlich arbeiten* (Working Publicly), which did not appear in East Germany until 1987, and *Als Kind habe ich Stalin gesehen* (I Saw Stalin Once When I Was a Child), which appeared simultaneously in the GDR in 1990 and in the FRG under the title *Die fünfte Grundrechenart* (The Fifth Math Function), in which three of the essays in the GDR edition are omitted. The title of the essay "Als Kind habe ich Stalin gesehen" was inspired by a 1981–82 painting by two obscure Soviet artists, Komar and Melamid, depicting Stalin looking out of the rear window as his car, which appears to be a Model A, as it is being driven away. Hein saw this painting at the Museum of Modern Art in New York during his visit to the U.S. in 1987 and was struck by the contrast between the warmth of the look which Stalin casts upon the children behind him and the violence not only of his acts, which ultimately destroyed so many of his own countrymen, but also, because of the dogmatic rigidity which came to be known as Stalinism, of the socialist movement itself.

A little fewer than half of Hein's essays appeared between 1989 and 1990. They are politically charged pieces, replete with the exposition of injustices perpetrated by the expiring regime, defenses of individuals and groups who had been victimized by these injustices, and warnings about false opportunism and a swiftly emerging mentality which fostered a stampede for Western money and goods, which, in the end, prevailed. The essay oeuvre could be categorized loosely into several groups: aesthetical writings and poetics, censorship and freedom of artistic expression, politics and social criticism, and laudatios for other authors and intellectuals, including Arno Schmidt, Thomas Mann, Friedrich Dieckmann, Benno Besson, Gustav Just, Max Frisch, Kurt Tucholsky, and Erich Fried. In addition, there is a small group of dialogues and notes to several of Hein's own works and an unusual, fascinating piece on the history of magic, which was published as an introduction to a GDR edition of an early eighteenth-century collection of herbal and magic cures.

Poetics

Early in his career, Hein sought to break the traditional—if artificial—roles generally assumed by writers and scholars. As he saw it, a work of literature is not meant to be delivered as an opportunity for literary critics to explore how that work fits in with the theories of deconstructionism, poststructuralism, or other critical approaches that are often used to distance readers from literature and to intellectually undermine the essence of literary forms of culture: "Literature and literary scholarship," Hein writes in "Lorbeerwald und Kartoffelacker" (Laurel Forest and Potato Field), are as different as

> the butterfly and the lepidopterist. The latter manifest in the large glass cases in which all the red admirals and night skippers, peacock butterflies and monarchs, as well as the simple cabbage moth, impaled on a needle, gather dust and arouse the illusion that they, the crucified, should be the lively red-blooded image of the once living. What sensitive soul does not feel, at the sight of the glass cases with their impaled and useless butterflies, or the drab, many-chambered buildings in which the scholars are at work, a quiet, painful needle prick through his heart? (öa 10–11)

Pervading all his poetic essays is the rejection of the classical element or of stagnation in literature. A literary work should not be like a piece of carved stone, a masterpiece completed by the sculptor as a monument to his own genius. Literature is an act of communication between the author and the reader, and only when the reader is stimulated to take the author's thoughts a step further, modified perhaps by his or her own individuality and experience, is the author successful. The standard of quality is the author himself.[1] For Hein, as he states in "Öffentlich arbeiten," literature is what he calls autobiography and, therefore, essentially valid only for the author himself. If the author reaches a satisfactory understanding with himself, the texts which result may be of interest to readers and then become social autobiography (earlier described in relationship to the discussion of his works), or the communication of experience and insight by individuals about other individuals in the world. Such communication contains meaning for society, interpreting social interaction and chronicling the behavior of human beings in varying conditions and historical contexts. Literature cannot exist in an aesthetic vacuum; the real world needs to be rendered into poetic concepts. It is a world which each writer appropriates as his or her own, according to his or her knowledge, ability, and disposition: "Without the real world," Hein states in "Waldbruder Lenz" (Forest Hermit Lenz), "nothing would remain of the work but maculature. The poetic image carries the metaphor within itself" (öa 72).

In an essay originally delivered at the Kentucky Foreign Language Conference in 1987, entitled "Leserpost oder ein Buch mit sieben Siegeln" (Readers' Mail, or a Book with Seven Seals), Hein takes issue with arguments favoring the elimination of content from literary interpretation, a step which does not solve the problems of interpretation. Message and moral will always manifest themselves in works of art, and the discovery of these elements reveals the ideology of the artists and their times, their political tendencies and artistic modes. More often than not, however, interpretation reveals our own ideologies and tendencies, as defined by how we are trapped in our own time. Hein recalls a visit to the theater to see *Hamlet* during a stay in Finland. He was incredulous to meet an engineer who had never read the play nor seen it on stage. Hein suddenly realized that he himself would attend the show with a "head full of commentary and interpretations of theater, literature, theory" (Als Kind 46). He would only see things that fit with his preconceived ideas. He would not go inside to really see *Hamlet*; he would see only his own interpretation of it. The engineer, on the other hand, would really see a work of art. He would experience something, and Hein would simply "expand the commentaries in his head by one more" (Als Kind 47).

In order for a work of art to be experienced, it has to be changed by our experiencing it: "The experience, the feeling of being overwhelmed by a work, presupposes that I engage in a relationship with it, that I bring the work into contact with myself. The work of art which I see is a different one than the one which the artist delivered from his hands. He spoke about himself, but I see myself. I have interpreted it, I have transferred the work into myself. Without this translation, the work remains intact, it couldn't touch me, I couldn't experience it" (Als Kind 51). The author, in order for this relationship to work, must avoid moralizing or writing prose specifically intended to enlighten the reader. Such a work ethic implies that the author somehow is superior to his or her reader and is in a position to dole out advice on how to live. This explains Hein's decision to write as a chronicler, as one who reports what he knows without telling readers how to understand or interpret the meaning of the chronicles. For Hein, activating a dialogue is the opposite of moralizing. As long as there is no moralizing, it remains possible for a meaningful dialogue between author and reader to occur.

The intentional creation of conceivable dialogue and the consistent adherence to the aesthetic form of chronicles, however, inevitably leads into the realm of social and political conflict. For Hein, this meant an ongoing conflict with rigid authoritarianism, censorship, and a conflict centered on the defense of truth and integrity as the foundation of his engaged poetic endeavor. GDR authors were acutely aware of a statement expressed in Ludwig Wittgenstein's seventh thesis from the *Tractatus logico-philosophicus*: "What one cannot speak about one must remain silent about."[2] Christa Wolf had formulated a modest but significantly progressive extension of this statement in 1976 in her famous novel, *Kindheitsmuster* (Childhood Patterns): "What one cannot speak about one must gradually stop remaining silent about."[3] In 1985, Hein wrote an essay entitled "Worüber man nicht reden kann, davon kann die Kunst ein Lied singen" (What One Cannot Speak About, Art Can Sing a Song About). In this essay, Hein questions the exaggerated effect which literature can have on the public—a theme which recurs in later essays. If literature has, in some small way, contributed to the progress of civilization, then it certainly must have contributed its share to acts of barbarity. As he had indicated in earlier essays, especially "Öffentlich arbeiten," Hein holds that government interference in the production of literature and art can only be counterproductive, achieving the opposite of its intention: censorship acts like a magnet to readers rather than preventing their access to a work.

"Literature has no real power, but it is not helpless. It has no force [*Gewalt*] with which to suppress and coerce" (Öa 49), he writes. The world itself often functions counter to the natural self-preservation drive of mankind: "Our world, our century has become unbearable to us" (Öa 50). But we are cognizant of this only insofar as our natural thick skins permit the information about hunger, suffering, and injustice to filter into our consciousness. If we were acutely aware of these things, we would be "unable to drink a cup of coffee in a leisurely manner" (Öa 50); we could not survive. The danger, however (see the earlier discussion of *The Distant Lover*), consists in the ability of this necessary, protective skin to actually bear that which is unbearable and therefore to imperil life in general. Literature is bound together with language, and language reveals the world to us and makes it accessible in human terminology. Language allows us to recognize things which we may never have seen, to conceptualize the unknown. When used to fantasize—to produce literature as an art form—it loses its congruence with reality but at the same time provides us with a key to the world, to enrichments which other forms of understanding, such as science, are incapable of providing. Where science and technology may supplant art and literature—after all, art turns everything over to science which can be proved—art retains for itself the realm of "unsolved riddles" (Öa 55).

Censorship and Political Criticism

In order for literature to function as Hein has conceived it, it must be free to describe and formulate focal points essential for understanding aspects of the world from the standpoint of the present time with which we are familiar. Hein's most famous essays, the ones attacking censorship and the arbitrary and malicious distortion of history, were published at great risk to his personal safety and ultimately had a significant impact on the events which speeded the GDR to its end. The first one was a speech given at a workshop of the Tenth Writers Union Conference in November 1987, entitled "Die Zensur ist überlebt, nutzlos, paradox, menschenfeindlich, volksfeindlich, ungesetzlich und strafbar" (Censorship is Outmoded, Useless, Paradoxical, Misanthropic, a Public Enemy, Illegal and Punishable). It generated a considerable uproar. The *Stasi,* by now suspicious that Hein would do something controversial, had attempted to obtain a copy of the speech in advance, but Hein repeatedly put them off by saying he had not yet written it down.

To put the speech in perspective, it should be noted that 1987 was the year in which Erich Honecker visited the town of his birth in West Germany, his first visit to the West—an event which was followed in East Berlin by an attack on people coming out of the Zion Church by a group of skinheads. The Zion Church was one of the several churches where intellectuals and reformists met. During the attack, the police stood by and observed without taking action, as Hein's son, Jakob, who was in the church, had reported (see discussion of *Horns Ende*). Since, as Ferdinand Kroh summarized, this was not the first instance of attacks by neo-Nazis, in response the Anti-Nazi League was founded by underground intellectuals. Their headquarters, the Environmental Library, was visited on 18 November 1987 by police looking for Anti-Nazi League flyers and, of course, for subversive underground publications, for which the Environmental Library was known. The existence of an "Anti-Nazi League on socialist territory was, of course, unthinkable and intolerable, implying that the regime had not, as it claimed, long since eradicated fascism.[4] The unnerving manifestation of neo-Nazi movements centered primarily in the former GDR portion of Germany suggests that an Anti-Nazi League was appropriate and should have been acknowledged and supported by the regime. On 24 November, however, the police raided the Environmental Library, confiscated its primitive presses, and arrested some thirty people, releasing all but two the next evening. Two months afterwards, the police forcefully put down a demonstration led by members of the Environmental Library on Rosa Luxemburg Day (17 January), carrying banners proclaiming Luxemburg's famous words, "Freedom is only the freedom of those who think differently."[5] Hein had visited the United States that spring and was still displeased about the censorship of *Horns Ende.* He had decided to take another courageous step. His speech took place on 25 November, the day after the raid on the Environmental Library.

Literature brings the inner conditions of society and its citizens to light in a unique manner, according to Hein. Literature creates a certain effect, but this effect reveals above all the "reader's existing state of mind" (Als Kind 78). This explains the special relationship which critical and even dissident authors living under regimes like that in the GDR have with their readers. Although the quality of literature suffers due to the political interpretations ascribed to it by these readers, it nonetheless mirrors currently evolving historical events and situations. The real literary quality of such works won't be known for decades, according to Hein, but something can and ought to be done to enable literature to function qualitatively and not merely as a public forum for current political issues.

The first problem is the lack of power on the publisher's part to carry out his profession, which consists of making judgements about the quality and the marketability of books to be published. Instead, this authority ultimately rests with those in charge of the state's approval procedure, which is known as the *Genehmigungsvervahren*. Hein discards this euphemism for the real word: censorship, which the GDR officially claimed not to exist within its borders.

Censorship is outmoded because the justification for it after 1945, deemed essential as part of the de-nazification of Germany, had fulfilled its purpose and was no longer necessary. Censorship is useless because it "cannot prevent the circulation of literature" (Als Kind 81). Everyone had learned that many censored books were finally authorized some years later, so everyone knew that such books would eventually be printed. Censorship is paradoxical "because it causes exactly the opposite of its intended effect" (Als Kind 82). Anything censored does not disappear; it gains greater importance and can no longer be overlooked. Censorship ultimately functions as a means to increase sales—or, basically, as free advertising.

Censorship is "misanthropic to author, publisher, reader and even to the censor himself" (Als Kind 82). During the decade between 1976 and 1986, the country had lost many excellent writers whose intellectual input into society was irreplaceable. Moreover, the phenomenon of self-censorship—widely practiced by many authors in the GDR in a guesswork effort to write books which could meet with approval and be published—constitutes a betrayal of the literary text. Censorship places the reader in a state of tutelage where he or she is no longer allowed to make judgements about the quality and readability of a book purchased or borrowed. Censorship destroys the publisher, his authority, and his credibility, prohibiting him from acting as a publisher. And censorship abuses the censor, forcing him to ignore the artistic sense of a book and to look for displeasing passages and causing him to come up with the most ridiculous interpretations and absurd misunderstandings imaginable. Censorship is a public enemy, a crime against the so-called wisdom of the common people. The idea that a bureaucrat can decide what the public can cope with or what might be unappetizing only reveals the arrogance of the bureaucratic offices. Censorship is illegal as specifically declared in the binding constitution of the GDR. Censorship is punishable because it does irreparable damage to the international reputation of the GDR.

Such language as summarized here was never before uttered publicly in the GDR. But this is only the beginning of Hein's bold speech. Hein called for the decentralization of publishing houses, most of which had been merged into a few state-controlled monopolies. He was especially concerned about the publishing house for theater, Henschel Verlag. Since this was the only publisher available, playwrights had no alternatives, nor did the publisher, who, as a matter of practice, printed both good and bad texts for distribution to the theaters. As previously mentioned, Henschel Verlag was one of several publishing houses whose employees worked very hard to get texts by controversial authors, including Hein, approved for staging. But a look at the many texts it distributed shows a lack of qualitative discrimination. Hein called for the elimination of monopolistic publishing. Such a measure would have far-reaching implications, inasmuch as almost the entire GDR economy was a state-monopolized enterprise.

Hein then went on sarcastically to give thanks to the press and other media of the GDR for causing the literature of the country to attain such an important status and a broad effectiveness in society. The GDR was recognized as a reading country, and this fact, according to Hein, was directly attributable to the dearth of news, information, discussion, and opinion available in the state-controlled media. The entire population was obliged to turn to literature to obtain information about what was really going on in the country. A one-sided press which "communicates only a desired reality . . . robs itself of its potential effect" (Als Kind 88) and destroys its own credibility. A good example of lost credibility is the fact that a book praised in a review by a GDR newspaper would automatically be condemned to a long shelf- life in the bookstores. The lack of a public forum to discuss the controversial issues of the times gave the literary sector more power than it had perhaps had in any other historical framework.

The sad part of this, it must be said, is that Hein was absolutely right, and after the fall of the Wall, GDR literature became virtually extinct, except for that produced by a very few authors, as the reading public rushed to buy the magazines, newspapers, and countless trivial publications heretofore only available in the West—leaving literature once again to a small minority, to the few with genuine interest in culture and intellectual activity. Hein deplored the failure of literary criticism to do its job as well. Hampered by the need for ideological conformity (and required party membership, for that matter), it seldom attempted to discuss aesthetic issues pertinent to literature and invariably subjected issues of content to a utopian standard which was largely irrelevant.

The application of censorship to the theater was much more inhibiting than for other forms of literary endeavor. Not only did each play have to make it through Henschel Verlag and then through the central state censorship apparatus, but it was subjected to additional scrutiny at the regional, county, and local city level in each location where plans existed to stage it. The director was, therefore, not in control of the choice of plays at his theater, and many plays were censored after the expense of considerable rehearsal had already taken place. Under these circumstances, the country could only hope for mediocre but somewhat blandly entertaining theater, but it could never hope for theater as a public forum. European and especially German theater is renowned for its public and political engagement, and the East German playwrights and directors were frustrated, according to Hein, in spite of isolated successes, with their inability to interact with their public in a stimulating and critically forthright manner.

A separate group of dramatists, including Heiner Müller, had earlier tried to organize to demand a centralized censorship institution in order to eliminate the local censorship bureaus, but not much ever came of the effort. On the other hand, Hein's speech was instrumental in bringing change to the publishing industry. It was printed in West Germany in *Die Zeit* on 4 December 1987, and this brought additional pressure to bear on the bureaucracy. It was then printed in the GDR as part of the proceedings of the Tenth Writers Conference in the late spring of 1988,[6] and by then, negotiations had actually taken place to assign more power to the publisher. One cynical aspect of the transfer of power was the fact that it let the individual government censors in the state Ministry of Culture off the hook. The arrangement was to allow the editors to make the decisions, and if they felt inhibited or unable to do so (or simply didn't have the courage), they would have the option to send the manuscript to the state as before. At any rate, a flood of new literature began to appear that had never made it through the censorship procedure before, including texts by younger, unestablished and often controversial authors, even though many publishers exercised enough caution to protect their own jobs. Hein's own texts, *The Tango Player* and *Die Ritter der Tafelrunde,* would not have made it through the censorship office prior to the restructuring of control over literary texts.

The Battle for Control of History

The second essay, a speech at a meeting of the Berlin Writers Union on 14 September 1989 and published in *Die Zeit* on 6 October 1989—the day before the police brutality during the fortieth-year celebration—is entitled "Die fünfte Grundrechenart" (The Fifth Math Function), dedicated to Gustav Just. Hein had attempted to publish the speech in East Berlin, but it was not allowed. This is one of the earliest and most powerful political writings in a series he continued throughout the fall of 1989 and the spring of 1990.

In the schools and universities of the GDR, Hein explains in the essay, one learns the fifth basic function of arithmetic in order to cope with the painful contradiction between theory and practice. It's actually the first basic function, since it supersedes all the others. It is based on the principle that "the conclusion is drawn first, writing in the required and desired result on the bottom" (Als Kind 145). Then one adds and subtracts, divides and multiplies; the formula is abstracted and negated, emphasized and de-emphasized, beautified as needed; the root is extracted and eradicated and lied about where applicable.

Applied to history, the method consists of "omissions, neglections and scholastic trickery" (Als Kind 146). Items are left unmentioned and glossed over in order for one to get through the labyrinth of history unsoiled and arrive as quickly as possible at that specific present which corresponds best to the desired truism. These principles apply to virtually every country's historians. But Hein—stirred by his countrymen's mass exodus, the tremendous upheaval in the GDR, the rejection of glasnost by his government, the threat of violent reprisals against the population, and the Stalinist abuse of socialism which characterized his country's history—directed his essay at GDR distortions of historical events. Specifically, the Russian media had begun to expose the terror of its earlier Stalinist regime, and the GDR media were trying to gloss over these reports with omissions in order not to "injure the totality of the truth," a statement which for Hein was "hypocrisy and demagogic scholasticism" (Als Kind 149).

Hein points out that the Stalinist show trials in his country had been punctuated by officials' informing the general prison population that their unseen (in isolation) fellow inmates, like Gustav Just, were really Nazi war criminals. These political prisoners, when released years later, were then told that the old history which had led to their imprisonment was long forgotten and forgiven, a tale not easily swallowed by the victims themselves. Hein takes it upon himself to state some of the omissions regarding events under Stalin's regime which were being ignored in his country: the Hitler-Stalin Pact was nothing more than an "imperialistic . . . deal to guarantee . . . annexation of foreign countries to each side" (Als Kind 151). The fact that the pact was broken and that Stalin broke Hitler's back in the war doesn't change the reality that somewhere between 5 and 18 million people were wiped out by Stalin. Stalin's dictatorship refused Ernst Thälmann's suggestion to let the Polish Communist Party decide the matters of Poland alone.

To mention the Thälmann incident in this manner is a distortion: it reveals only that Thälmann—a hero in the annals of East German history—showed some courage and that a discussion took place. Each reporting is simply a way of glossing over what had happened to Poland in all the years towards the end of the war and afterwards—events including the murder of several hundred Polish officers by Russians who laid the blame on Hitler's soldiers.

Hein enumerates:

Of 29 members and candidates of the Central Committee of the Communist Party of the Soviet Union, 14 were murdered. Out of 60 members of the Revolutionary Military Committee in Petrograd, 54 were murdered. Between 1935 and 1940 all the members of the first Soviet government except Stalin and two others were murdered. Of 1,986 delegates to the party congress in 1934, during which 300 voted against Stalin, 1,108 were dismissed. Of the 139 elected members and candidates of the Central Committee, 110 died in concentration camps and torture chambers. 40,000 officers of the Red Army were executed. (Als Kind 152–53)

This, according to Hein, was only the tip of the iceberg. Never before had anyone dared to make such statements about the eternal brothers in the Soviet Union. Glasnost had emphatically not been welcome in the GDR, and its public impact had not changed anything other than to cause threats of suppression and reprisal to emanate from government officials. Egon Krenz, who replaced Honecker after the fall of the Wall, had gone to China that summer to congratulate the regime there on their handling of the Tieneman Square massacre. Krenz's China trip, as well as his other activities as Honecker's handpicked protege, was unnoticed by the American press, which initially welcomed him as a new hope after the demise of Honecker. But the East Germans knew better. Hein clarified the issue publicly in an interview published in *Der Spiegel* on 29 October 1989 with the title "The GDR Is Not China."

Hein's bitterness and anger over the stubborn foundation of his own government in Stalinism is evident: "It makes me sick, it makes me physically and mentally sick to live in a country and in a city where citizens are uninterruptedly requesting emigration papers and are leaving" (Als Kind 154). He was especially sick about how the media attempted to reduce the impact by making it into only a small statistic when parents were being separated from children and friends from each other, all irreplaceable emotional and physical losses. Hein called for a dialogue between the government and the people, for the initiation of measures to end the conditions causing the mass exodus. It was not long in coming, but it turned out much differently than Hein and other intellectuals had hoped.

Most of Hein's essays from that time on were written or spoken to encourage the population to not sell out to West Germany, warning of the problems to come, in a voice drowned out, however, by euphoria and, understandably, by impatience—and, most of all, by the promise of hard cash. After the unification, Hein wrote essays and short prose pieces which lamented the exploitation and annexation by the West. He then turned his pen to an essay in which he decries the violent neo-Nazi anti-foreigner mentality which had taken over, especially in the Eastern sectors. In this piece, published in *Der Spiegel* and entitled "Eure Freiheit ist unser Auftrag. Ein Brief an (fast alle) Ausländer—wider das Gerede vom Fremdenhaß der Deutschen"[7] (Your Freedom Is Our Task. A Letter to (Almost All) Foreigners—against the Talk of the Germans' Hatred of Foreigners), he laments that Germans don't hate foreigners, just those who are poor (usually of darker skin) who seem to infringe on the Germans' right to enjoy their own prosperity without fear of losing any portion of it.

Historikerstreit

In the mid-1980s, a number of prominent West German historians were engaged in the so-called historian dispute (*Historikerstreit*) on the pages of newspapers and feuilletons, especially the *Frankfurter Allgemeine Zeitung* and *Die Zeit* in 1986, about the same time as the delayed appearance of *Horns Ende*. That dispute was caused by an essay published by the conservative historian Ernst Nolte, in which he suggested that it was time to subject the history of the Nazi period in Germany to some revisions in order to allow Germans to reestablish their individual subjective feelings about German history with a less encumbered national identity. Nolte questioned the singularity of the Nazi's extermination of millions of Jews, comparing these acts with those of Stalin's during the Gulag, those of Pol Pot in Cambodia, and, on a smaller scale, to those of the United States in Vietnam, the Soviet Union in Africa and Afghanistan, and of the fundamentalist Islamic priests during the Iranian revolution.

For Nolte, Auschwitz was not so much a result of anti-Semitism as it was a fear-driven copy of the Russian killings during and after the Russian revolution. The Third Reich cannot, therefore, be seen in isolation, according to Nolte, but is relativized by comparing it to other historical atrocities.[8] Jürgen Habermas expressed the general outrage of many Germans at Nolte's ideas by claiming that his revisionist history was intended to restore a conventional national identity which, however, would result in the loss of history and the forgetting of the burden of the German past.[9] Some moderate historians were in favor of a limited revision of history in order to free the younger generation from the burden of guilt their forefathers had conferred upon them. As sympathetic as such thinking might be—why should the children be punished for the sins of the parents?—it nevertheless left the door open for the negation of history, the relativization of history, and, for the Germans, a surging nationalism sprinkled with excesses from the radical right which became especially manifest in the violent acts toward foreigners during the period shortly before and after the fall of the Berlin Wall. Eventually the excesses led to the murder of a number of foreigners by the radical right, a national embarrassment to Germany, which had granted them political asylum.

In the spring following the attack on the Zion Church in Berlin by skinheads, Hein was in Essen for the summer semester as the first recipient of the *Lehrstuhl für Poetik* (endowed chair for poetics) at the Folkwang-Schule in Essen and gave a lecture in response to the *Historikerstreit* entitled "Die Zeit, die nicht vergehen kann oder Das Dilemma des Chronisten. Gedanken zum Historikerstreit anläßlich zweier deutscher vierzigster Jahrestage" (The Time Which Cannot Vanish, or The Dilemma of the Chronicler. Thoughts on the Historians' Dispute on the Occasion of Two German Fortieth-Year Anniversaries). Hein was particularly alarmed at several of Nolte's formulations regarding Jews, German guilt, and historical revisionism. Nolte's attempted comparison of "German guilt" with "Jewish guilt," which had been a principal argument of the Nazis, seemed to deny the fact the "Jewish guilt" was the product of intolerance and centuries old anti-Semitism. The mixing of terminology like "racial murder" and "class murder" obscured the truth: it was ludicrous to classify Jews murdered by Stalin as a component of the class murder. Again, Hein rejected the notion of any zero hour—for 1945, 1933, or any other period—and pointed out that ascribing the guilt to the person of Hitler, tacitly releasing Germany and Germans from guilt, is insensible and fatal. The historical consciousness of Germans cannot overlook the fact that Hitler was elected and supported by the Germans: "Hitler was and remained a brother of the Germans. Stalin and Pol Pot were not brothers of their populace but murderous tyrants to them" (Als Kind 125).

Hein argued for a normalization of historical consciousness that included awareness of German fascism and the recognition of the irreversible impact it had on German history: "historical heritage cannot be selected. Our past, personal as well as social history, can neither be declined nor is there anything else to choose from. We are heirs in prosperity and ruin" (Als Kind 132). The past cannot disappear. On the contrary, Hein fears that it threatens to return if it is not confronted and remembered: "The new Jews have already been identified and in my country they are the foreigners. The basis of a National-Socialist ideology still exists and none of us should be reassured by statistics. It ought to disturb us . . . that German pride has remained inexorable and German memory is on the verge of capitulating" (Als Kind 136).

Notes

1. "Ich bin das Maß, mit dem ich messe" (I am the standard by which I measure, öa 9) were the words Hein first used in the essay "Lorbeerwald und Kartoffelacker" in 1981 to describe his often-repeated insistence that he writes until he has satisfied himself. The finished work may or may not then wind up on a publisher's desk.

2. Ludwig Wittgenstein, *Tractatus logico-philosophicus,* cited in Fabrizio Cambi, "Jetztzeit und Vergangenheit. Ästhetische und ideologische Auseinandersetzung im Werk Christoph Heins," *Chronist ohne Botschaft. Christoph Hein. Ein Arbeitsbuch. Materialien, Auskünfte, Bibliographie,* ed. Klaus Hammer (Berlin: Aufbau, 1992) 111.

3. Christa Wolf, *Kindheitsmuster* (Berlin: Aufbau, 1976) 235. Therese Hörnigk recalls the connection between Wittgenstein and Wolf in her article "Eine Suche nach der verlorenen Zeit? Christa Wolf und ihre Erzählung *Was bleibt,*" *Der deutsch-deutsche Literaturstreit,* ed. Karl Deiritz and Hannes Krauss (Hamburg: Luchterhand, 1991) 95–101. Cambi ties Hein into the discussion in his article (see note 2, above).

4. See Ferdinand Kroh's expansive essay on dissident movements in the former GDR, "Havemanns Erben—1953 bis 1988," *"Freiheit ist immer Freiheit . . ." Die Andersdenkenden in der DDR* (Frankfurt a.M.: Ullstein, 1988) 10–58.

5. Rosa Luxemburg, "Zur russischen Revolution," *Gesammelte Werke,* vol. 4 (Berlin: Dietz, 1974) 351.

6. Christoph Hein, "Die Zensur ist überlebt, nutzlos, paradox, menschenfeindlich, volksfeindlich, ungesetzlich und strafbar," *X. Schriftstellerkongreß der DDR. Arbeitsgruppen,* ed. Schriftstellerverband der DDR, vol. 2 (Berlin: Aufbau, 1988) 224–47.

7. This essay has also been published in *Chronist ohne Botschaft* 51–55.

8. See *"Historikerstreit." Die Dokumentation der Kontroverse um die Einzigartigkeit der nationalsozialistischen Judenvernichtung* (Munich: Piper, 1987) 32.

9. See Jürgen Habermas, "Eine Art Schadensabwicklung," *Historikerstreit* 62–76.

Conclusion: The Conservation of Morality

Unified Germany remains more chaotic than not, and many citizens in the Eastern portion of Germany have been deprived of possessions, livelihood, and dignity. It will take considerable time to complete the unification, not four or five years as the politicians had indulgently promised in anticipation of forthcoming elections, but four or five decades. The complaints and prejudices of both sides, as Hein noted, won't have much effect on the length of this time, but they may affect the individuals who must live with their own history, the unfortunate consciousness of the Germans which is, in Hein's words, "above all . . . a ridiculous consciousness."[1] As the deliberations were carried on and the vote neared for German unification, Hein believed that there was no plan for unification at all; the plan was for annexation (*Einverleibung*). His analysis has proven to be accurate:

> The fall of the Wall and everything which followed caught the population completely unprepared. This was apparent even on 4 November 1989: there was tremendous enthusiasm for those people who were on the verge of overthrowing their government, and in the central offices of ARD [one of two West German nationwide TV networks] . . . there was even a discussion for a few minutes about whether or not they should broadcast this gigantic demonstration [500,000 people] on Alexander Square live. But then they came to the conclusion after all to continue with the Boris Becker match. And, I think, this was the right decision because this Germany, that is, the former Federal Republic, identified itself much more with Boris Becker—and still does—than with this remarkable country on the other side of the Elbe.[2]

The first years of unification found Hein concerned with the rise of neofascism in his new country. His essays in response to the *Historikerstreit,* and to the German prejudice towards foreigners of a darker skin-color, express his concerns. The euphoria over unification, expressed in the transition from "We are the people" (*Wir sind das Volk*) to "We are one people" (*Wir sind ein Volk*), gave cause for Hein and many other intellectuals to ponder the uncertainties of the fledgling new German nationalism: "Until now I regarded it as a great virtue of my country—I mean in contrast to West Germany—that it did not succeed in developing something like a national consciousness. I regarded it to be a virtue—although not actively aspired to—because a German national consciousness has always proven to be not only especially proud, but also aggressive; not just a common union for the rejection and exclusion of that which was different, but because it constantly required intolerance and arrogance towards that which was foreign [in order to thrive]."[3]

Dieter Schlenstedt, internationally one of the most respected former GDR Germanists, reflected that the conditions determined by the kind of socialism which existed in the GDR created a situation in which "the artists . . . were essentially the only ones who were able to speak widely in the public sphere" and to exercise an "individual responsibility" with respect to enunciating the state of society "which one hoped to attain." No one else was able to have a credible effect in the public sphere, a fact which "revalorized the authors incredibly."[4]

The willingness to take the responsibility, to function in the sense of the Enlightenment by relaying information and thoughtful dialogue to the public with sincerity may well have provided GDR literature with its charm and attractiveness. Frauke Meyer-Gosau makes the following distinction: GDR literature was "the living preservation—quite positively the conservation—of a morality, from which the [West German] Zeitgeist distanced itself with a jeering smirk at least ten years ago."[5] For Hein, enlightenment is no longer possible in the twentieth century in middle Europe. Everyone has access to virtually every form of information. No individuals, not writers or philosophers, have any privileged access to more information than anyone else: "Whenever enlightenment takes place today, as enlightenment of an enlightened public, it is pedagogy. . . . It is the tragedy of our century that we all have information. From the perspective of the Enlightenment the entire public would have to sit weeping in front of the TV news broadcasts every evening—but . . . they sit there and eat their french fries. For nothing is better than when somebody is slaughtered and if he has a familiar face besides, that is especially exciting. No sign of shaken emotion."[6] This doesn't leave much hope for an enlightenment, which most definitely has to do with information, and certainly that hope has disappeared with the end of the tiny GDR and its provincial morality as it is swept into the modern—or the postmodern—world. For Hein, "Enlightenment was the hope for the departure from self-inflicted tutelage; postmodernity is the chance to arrive at a self-inflicted tutelage, which one can make use of with no inhibitions.

183

It's quite warm and comfortable."[7] As Gustav Just wrote about Hein, Germany needs people like him more than ever, people "who always lay their finger on the open wound and think at least one day in advance."[8]

Near where Hein lives in the Weißensee area of Berlin is the venerable old Jewish Cemetery, a place that takes days to explore. Germans are fond of taking walks, and doing so in the peaceful atmosphere of cemeteries is a favorite; it is a meditative homage to the memories which hover around those who lie there. During Hein's visit to the United States, he wanted to know if there was a local cemetery where he could walk, where he could feel whether or not remembrance and commemoration here were similar to those customs as they are practiced in Berlin. The Jewish cemetery in Berlin remained in a state of disrepair during the forty-year history of the GDR—many graves inaccessible, the ground overgrown with vine-covered trees and shrubbery; headstones with faded and illegible inscriptions, many of the monuments still lying about where Nazi vandals had left them during the Hitler period. If you walk around long enough, you can find a large crypt with gravestones asunder, revealing a crawl space underneath, perhaps the crawl space where the Jewish actor in one of Hein's stories attempted to hide his family. In another section, an exception which is cared for meticulously, lie the bodies of the Jews from Berlin who fell in the First World War in the service of Germany, neatly in rows with white stone crosses. The officers' graves are surrounded by a wall with honorary inscriptions carved into it. One of the names I remember from the officers' section is Frankfurther. In the middle of this section is a monument commemorating their bravery and their sacrifice to the fatherland. Even as plans were underway to restore the cemetery—a measure which in itself would sadly cover over and obscure from memory the unique preservation of nature's own random and majestic commemoration of historical neglect, capturing in its uncultivated growth much of the past spirit of this cemetery—vandals from the new, unified Germany entered another, small cemetery next to the Bertolt Brecht house in the Friedrichstraße and desecrated his grave with the word *Saujud,* which means "Jewish Swine."

Hein once said that if he were to move to the West, it would take him years before he could write again. At about fifty years of age, he still has time on his side. But now the West has come to him. He nevertheless found himself able to work within a relatively short period of time after the unification of the two Germanies, but the first long and fruitful period of intellectual productivity in his life, from 1978 to 1990, has clearly defined historical landmarks which provided both the resistance to his material and the inspiration for the content of his literary efforts—efforts which have gained him recognition as an important contemporary German writer, dramatist, and intellectual with an international following. "The past is the stage to which we are called for our unique appearance in the present,"[9] he wrote. As we learn from Horn, to extinguish memory is to extinguish humanity.

Notes

1. Christoph Hein, "Ansichtskarte einer deutschen Kleinstadt, leicht retuschiert," *Neue Deutsche Literatur* 40.4 (1992): 23.

2. Hein, "Ansichtskarte einer deutschen Kleinstadt, leicht retuschiert" 19.

3. Christoph Hein, "Die Zeit, die nicht vergehen kann oder Das Dilemma des Chronisten," *Kopfbahnhof. Das falsche Dasein*, ed. Andreas Tretner (Leipzig: Reclam, 1990) 267–68.

4. Dieter Schlenstedt, "Integration—Loyalität—Anpassung. Über die Schwierigkeiten bei der Aufkündigung eines komplizierten Verhältnisses. Ein Gespräch mit Frauke Meyer-Gosau," *Literatur der DDR. Rückblicke*, ed. Heinz Ludwig Arnold and Frauke Meyer-Gosau (Munich: Text + Kritik) 175.

5. Frauke Meyer-Gosau, "Christoph Hein, Politiker," *Chronist ohne Botschaft. Christoph Hein. Ein Arbeitsbuch. Materialien, Auskünfte, Bibliographie*, ed. Klaus Hammer (Berlin: Aufbau, 1992) 176.

6. Christoph Hein, "Ich bin der Leser, für den ich schreibe. Ein Gespräch mit Frauke Meyer-Gosau," *Text + Kritik* 111, ed. Heinz Ludwig Arnold (Munich: Text + Kritik, 1991) 87.

7. Hein, "Ich bin der Leser, für den ich schreibe" 87.

8. Gustav Just, "Er speiste nie an der Tafel der Mächtigen," *Christoph Hein. Texte, Daten, Bilder*, ed. Lothar Baier (Frankfurt a.M.: Luchterhand, 1990) 191.

9. Hein, "Die Zeit, die nicht vergehen kann" 250.

Bibliography

Works by Christoph Hein

Books

Einladung zum Lever Bourgeois. Prosa. [Invitation to the Lever Bourgeois. Prose.] Berlin: Aufbau, 1980. Licensed as *Nachtfahrt und früher Morgen.* [Night Journey and Early Morning.] Hamburg: Hoffmann und Campe, 1982.

Cromwell und andere Stücke. [Cromwell and Other Plays.] Berlin: Aufbau, 1981. Includes *Lasalle, Schlötel,* and *Der Neue Menoza.*

Der fremde Freund. Novelle. Berlin: Aufbau, 1982. Licensed as *Drachenblut.* [Dragon's Blood.] Darmstadt: Luchterhand, 1983. *The Distant Lover. Novella.* Trans. Krishna Winston. New York: Pantheon, 1989.

Das Wildpferd unterm Kachelofen. Ein schönes dickes Buch von Jakob Borg und seinen Freunden. [The Wild Pony under the Tiled Stove. A Lovely Thick Book about Jakob Borg and his Friends.] Berlin: Altberliner Verlag, 1984. Licensed as *Das Wildpferd unterm Kachelofen.* Weinheim: Beltz, 1984.

Die wahre Geschichte des Ah Q. Stücke und Essays. [The True Story of Ah Q. Plays and Essays.] Darmstadt: Luchterhand, 1984. Includes *Lasalle,* "Waldbruder Lenz" [Forest Hermit Lenz], "Öffentlich arbeiten" [Working Publicly], and "Lorbeerwald und Kartoffelacker" [Laurel Forest and Potato Field].

Horns Ende. Roman. [Horn's End. Novel.] Berlin: Aufbau, 1985. Darmstadt: Luchterhand, 1985.

Schlötel oder Was solls. Stücke und Essays. [Schlötel or What's the Use. Plays and Essays.] Darmstadt: Luchterhand, 1986. Includes *Cromwell,* "Worüber man nicht reden kann, davon kann die Kunst ein Lied singen" [That Which One Can't Speak About Art Can Sing a Song About], "Hamlet und der Parteisekretär" [Hamlet and the Party Official], and "Linker Kolonialismus oder Der Wille zum Feuilleton" [Left Colonialism or the Will to the Feuilleton].

Öffentlich arbeiten. Essais und Gespräche. [Working Publicly. Essays and Conversations.] Berlin: Aufbau, 1987.

Die wahre Geschichte des Ah Q. Passage. Berlin: Henschel, 1988.

Passage. Darmstadt: Luchterhand, 1988.

Der Tangospieler. Roman. Berlin: Aufbau, 1989. Frankfurt a.M.: Luchterhand, 1989. *The Tango-Player. Novel.* Trans. Philip Boehm. New York: Farrar, Straus & Giroux, 1992.

Die Ritter der Tafelrunde. Komödie. [The Knights of the Round Table. Comedy.] Frankfurt a.m.: Luchterhand, 1989.
Als Kind habe ich Stalin gesehen. Essais und Reden. [As a Child I Saw Stalin. Essays and Speeches.] Berlin: Aufbau, 1990. With some changes, as *Die fünfte Grundrechenart. Aufsätze und Reden.* [The Fifth Math Function. Essays and Speeches.] Frankfurt a.M.: Luchterhand, 1990.
Bridge freezes before Roadway. Berlin: Berliner Handpresse, 1990.
Die Ritter der Tafelrunde und andere Stücke. [The Knights of the Round Table and Other Plays.] Berlin: Aufbau, 1990. Also includes *Die wahre Geschichte des Ah Q, Passage,* and *Brittanicus.*
Das Napoleon-Spiel. [The Napoleon Game.] Berlin: Aufbau, 1993.
Exekution eines Kalbes. [Execution of a Calf.] Berlin: Aufbau, 1993.

Play Productions (Premieres)

Vom hungrigen Hennecke. [Hungry Hennecke.] Volksbühne, Berlin. 25 September 1974.
Schlötel oder Was solls. [Schlötel or What's the Use.] Volksbühne, Berlin. 25 September 1974.
Die Geschäfte des Herrn John D. [The Deals of Mr. John D.] Stadttheater, Neustrelitz. 21 April 1979.
Cromwell. Theater der Stadt Cottbus, Cottbus. 5 April 1980.
Lasalle fragt Herrn Herbert nach Sonja. Die Szene ein Salon. [Lasalle Asks Mr. Herbert about Sonja. The Scene a Salon.] Schauspielhaus, Düsseldorf. 9 November 1980.
Der Neue Menoza oder Geschichte des kumbanischen Prinzen Tandi. Komödie nach Jakob Michael Reinhold Lenz. [The New Menoza or History of the Kumban Prinz Tandi. A comedy adapted from the play by Jakob Michael Reinhold Lenz.] Staatliche Bühnen, Schwerin. 30 May 1982.
Die wahre Geschichte des Ah Q. [The True Story of Ah Q.] Deutsches Theater, Berlin. 22 December 1983.
Passage. Triple premiere: Grillo-Theater, Essen. 25 October 1987. Schauspielhaus, Zürich. 15 November 1987. Staatsschauspiel, Dresden. 28 November 1987.
Die Ritter der Tafelrunde. [The Knights of the Round Table.] Staatschauspiel, Dresden. 24 March 1989.

Selected Articles

For a complete list of all periodical publications, including interviews and several articles not listed here, see Klaus Hammer, ed. *Chronist ohne Botschaft. Christoph Hein. Ein Arbeitsbuch. Materialien, Auskünfte, Bibliographie.* Berlin: Aufbau, 1992.

"Laudatio auf den Heinrich-Mann Preisträger Friedrich Dieckmann." [Laudatio for the Heinrich-Mann Award Winner Friedrich Dieckmann.] *Neue Deutsche Literatur* 31.7 (1983): 159–61.

"Massa Sloterdijk und der linke Kolonialismus." [Massa Sloterdijk and the Left Wing Colonialism.] *Konkret Literatur.* Herbst 1983: 36–41.

"Damit Lessing nicht resigniert. Rede." [So Lessing Won't Resign.] *Frankfurter Rundschau* 8 October 1983.

Interview. "Interview mit Christoph Hein." By Janice Murray and Mary-Elizabeth O'Brien. *New German Review* 3 (1987): 53–56.

"Das Verschwinden des künstlerischen Produzenten im Zeitalter der Reproduzierbarkeit." [The Disappearance of the Artistic Producer in the Age of Reproductibility.] *Freibeuter* 31 (1987): 63–71 and 32 (1987): 11–19.

"Von der Magie und den Magiern." [Of Magic and the Magicians.] *Windvogelviereck. Schriftsteller über Wissenschaften und Wissenschaftler.* [Delta Wing: Writers on Science and Scientists.] Ed. John Erpenbeck. Berlin: Buchverlag Der Morgen, 1987. 11–34.

"Literatur und Publikum. Ein Briefwechsel mit Elmar Faber." [Literature and Public.] *Sinn und Form* 3 (1988): 672–78.

"Die Zensur ist überlebt, nutzlos, paradox, menschen-und volksfeindlich, ungesetzlich und strafbar. Rede auf dem X. Schriftstellerkongreß der DDR." [Censorship is outmoded, useless, paradoxical, misanthropic, illegal and punishable.] *Die Zeit* 4 December 1987. Also in *X. Schriftstellerkongreß der DDR. Arbeitsgruppen.* Ed. Schriftstellerverband der DDR. Berlin: Aufbau, 1988. 224–47.

"Die fünfte Grundrechenart. Rede zur Geschichte im Ostberliner Schriftstellerverband am 14. September." [The Fifth Math Function. A Speech on History at the East Berlin Writers Union Sept. 14.] *Die Zeit* 6 October 1989.

"Leserpost oder Ein Buch mit sieben Siegeln." [Readers' Mail or A Book with Seven Seals.] *Christa Wolf. Ein Arbeitsbuch.* Ed. Angela Drescher. Berlin: Aufbau, 1989. 398–413.

"Rede am Berliner Alexanderplatz." [Speech at the Alexander Square.] *Der Weg zur Demonstration auf dem Alexanderplatz in Berlin.* [The Path to the Demonstration at the Alexander Square.] Ed. Initiativgruppe 4.11.89. Köln: Kölnische Verlagsdruckerei, 1990. 55–57.

"Die Aufklärung wird zunehmend behindert. Erklärung des Schriftstellers Christoph Hein. National Verteidigungsrat sagt nicht aus." [The Enlightenment is Being Increasingly Impeded. Comments of the Writer Christoph Hein. The Attorney General Stonewalls.] *National-Zeitung* [Berlin] 1 December 1989.

"Die Vergewaltigung. Erzählung." [The Rape. A Story.] *Neues Deutschland* 23 December 1989.

"Nachdenken über Deutschland." [Reflections on Germany.] *Die Weltbühne* 6 March 1990. 295–98.

"Unbelehrbar—Erich Fried. Rede zur Verleihung des Erich-Fried-Preises am 6. Mai 1990 in Wien." [Stubbornly Unenlightenable—Erich Fried. Acceptance Speech for the Erich Fried Award 6 May 1990 in Vienna.] *Freibeuter* 44 (1990): 24–33.

"No Sea Route to India." *Time* 25 June 1990. 68. In German as "Kein Seeweg nach Indien." *Freitag* 49 (30 November 1990), and *Christoph Hein. Texte, Daten, Bilder.* Ed. Lothar Baier. Frankfurt a.M.: Luchterhand, 1990. 13–19.

"Die Zeit, die nicht vergehen kann oder Das Dilemma des Chronisten." [The Time Which Cannot Fade Away or The Dilemma of the Chronicler.] Final revision in *Kopfbahnhof. Das falsche Dasein.* Ed. Andreas Tretner. Leipzig: Reclam, 1990.

"Kein Krieg ist heilig, kein Krieg ist gerecht." [No War Is Holy, No War Is Just.] *Berliner Zeitung* 13 February 1991.

"Ansichtskarte einer deutschen Kleinstadt, leicht retuschiert." [Sightseeing Map of a German Small Town, Slightly Touched Up.] *Neue Deutsche Literatur* 40.4 (1992): 9–30.

Other

Wallbergen, Johann. *Sammlung natürlicher Zauberkünste oder aufrichtige Entdeckung vieler bewährter, lustiger und nützlicher Geheimnisse.* [Anthology of Natural Magic Arts or Genuine Discovery of Many Tried, Tested, Amusing and Useful Secrets.] Ed. Christoph Hein. Leipzig: Kiepenheuer, 1988.

Just, Gustav. *Zeuge in eigener Sache.* [Witness in His Own Case.] Forward by Christoph Hein. Berlin: Buchverlag Der Morgen, 1990.

und diese verdammte Ohnmacht. Report der Untersuchungskommission zu den Ereignissen vom 7. und 8. Oktober 1989 in Berlin. [And This Damned Helplessness. Report of the Investigating Commission on the Events of 7 and 8 October 1989 in Berlin.] Ed. Daniela Dahn and Fritz-Jochen Kopka. Berlin: BasisDruck, 1991. Includes "Erinnerung an eine Zeit" [Remembrance of an Era] by Hein.

Selected Critical Works

For bibliographies, see the entries below for Arnold, Baier, Hammer, and especially Behn. For a thorough and complete list of all important articles up to 1992 written on Hein, categorized by works treated, see Hammer's *Chronist ohne Botschaft,* listed below.

Arnold, Heinz Ludwig, ed. *Christoph Hein.* Vol. 3. Munich: Edition Text + Kritik, 1991. This collection includes three essays by Hein (*A World Turning Point, Vorwort zum Bericht der Untersuchungskommission* [Forward to the Report of the Investigating Commission], and *Ich bin der Leser für den ich schreibe* [I Am the Reader for Whom I Write]) as well as several critical essays on prose and dramatic works and on Hein's theoretical orientation. Contains an extensive selected bibliography by Heinz-Peter Preußer and Klaus Hammer as well.

Arnold, Heinz Ludwig, and Frauke Meyer-Gosau, eds. *Literatur in der DDR. Rückblicke.* Munich: Edition Text + Kritik, Sonderband, 1991. A collection of twenty-six essays reflecting on GDR literature, including Meyer-Gosau's article "Linksherum, nach Indien" [To the Left, Towards India] on Hein's short parody of GDR history, "Kein Seeweg nach Indien." Also includes an overview of the history of GDR literature. The articles are by the best-known GDR specialists from the East and the West, and in their entirety constitute the best reflective analysis to date.

Baier, Lothar, ed. *Christoph Hein. Texte, Daten, Bilder.* Frankfurt a.M.: Luchterhand, 1990. Contains a concise biographical sketch with photographs, critical essays on prose and dramatic works, and several laudatios for Hein. Also includes a number of conversations with Hein which appeared in various feuillitons, important for the insightful commentary by Hein regarding his writing and his political position. His acceptance speech for the Erich Fried Award and the German text to *No Sea Route to India* are included. The bibliography is selective.

Behn, Manfred. "Christoph Hein." *Kritisches Lexikon zur deutschsprachigen Gegenwartsliteratur.* Vol. 3. Ed. Heinz Ludwig Arnold. Munich: Edition Text + Kritik. Continuous, updated every five years. Standard bibliography of living German authors, in loose-leaf form for easy updating.

Fischer, Bernd. *Christoph Hein. Drama und Prosa im letzten Jahrzehnt der DDR.* Heidelberg: Carl Winter, 1990. Critical monograph with a good theoretical foundation for the interpretation of Hein.

Hammer, Klaus, ed. *Chronist ohne Botschaft. Christoph Hein. Ein Arbeitsbuch. Materialien, Auskünfte, Bibliographie.* Berlin: Aufbau, 1992. By far the most thorough reference work on Hein. In addition to an excellent biographical sketch it contains a complete guide to Hein's play performances and their reception, including excerpts from the most important reviews. All printings of his books up to 1992 are listed, with information on first printings, excerpts of reviews, and listings of contents. Also listed are all essays and short stories, as well as all the many published conversations with Hein, including a new one with Hammer, which is thorough. Translations of Hein's works into all other languages are listed. Reviews, monographs, and critical articles are listed together with each of Hein's works for easy reference. Also contains reprints of many important critical essays on Hein's prose, dramatic works, and political activities. Hein's essay criticizing the German attacks on foreigners ("Eure Freiheit is unser Auftrag. Ein Brief an (fast alle) Ausländer— wider das Gerede vom Fremdenhaß der Deutschen" [Your Freedom Is Our Task. A Letter to (Almost All) Foreigners—Against the Talk about the Germans' Hatred of Foreigners]) is included as well. Indispensable for studies of Hein.

Janssen-Zimmermann, Antje. *Gegenwürfe. Untersuchungen zu Dramen Christoph Heins.* Frankfurt a.M.: Lang, 1988. Analyses of the plays from *Schlötel* to *Passage.*

Lücke, Bärbel. *Christoph Hein. Drachenblut. Interpretation.* Munich: Oldenbourg, 1989. Pedagogical orientation with ideas for teaching *The Distant Lover.* Contextualizes the book in GDR life, the death motif, stylistics, and the self-centered perspective of Claudia.

Preußer, Heinz-Peter. *Zivilisationskritik und literarische Öffentlichkeit. Strukturale und wertungstheoretische Untersuchung zu erzählenden Texten Christoph Heins.* Frankfurt a.M.: Lang, 1991. Preußer worked with both Arnold and Hammer in compiling the bibliographical entries to the books they edited and his monograph contains solid bibliographical work along with the only lengthy interpretive treatment of Hein's short stories. Essays on *The Distant Lover* and *Horns Ende* focus on social criticism and narrative concepts. Appendix compares the *Tango-Player* to the film based on it. Solid theoretical-historical approach.

Index